Joint Insolvency Examinations Board

Administrations, CVAs and Receiverships

Study Manual

For the November 2009 examination

JIEB Administrations, CVAs and Receiverships Study Manual

ISBN: 9780 7517 6564 9 (previous edition 9780 7517 5488 9)

Second edition January 2009
First edition 2008

British Library Cataloguing-in-Publication Data
A catalogue record for this book has been applied for from the British Library

We are grateful to the Joint Insolvency Examinations Board for permission to
reproduce the syllabus and past examination questions and answers.

Printed in Great Britain by

Ashford Colour Press
Unit 600 Fareham Reach
Fareham Road
Gosport
PO13 0FW

Your learning materials, published by BPP Learning Media, are printed on
paper sourced from sustainable, managed forests.

Contents

		Page
▶	Introduction	v
▶	JIEB syllabus	vi
▶	The JIEB exam	xii
▶	How to use this study manual	xiii
▶	Chapter summary	xiv

Introduction

This is the second edition of BPP Learning Media's ground-breaking new study manual for the Administrations, CVAs and Receiverships paper of the Joint Insolvency Examinations Board. It has been published specifically for the November 2009 JIEB exam.

Features include:

- Full syllabus coverage
- Fully up-to-date at 31 December 2008
- A user friendly style for easy navigation
- Chapter introductions to put the topic into context and explain its significance in the exam
- Section overviews and chapter summaries
- Self test questions and answers
- Suggested practice on past exam questions.

Other JIEB papers and products

BPP Learning Media publishes a range of learning materials for the three JIEB examinations, including Question Banks, Passcards, Audio CDs and Home Study programmes.

For further information, or to order, call 0845 0751 100 (within the UK) or +44 (0)20 8740 2211 (from overseas) or order online at www.bpp.com/learningmedia

Feedback

We at BPP Learning Media always appreciate feedback about our products. If you have any comments about this book or any other products in the BPP Learning Media JIEB range, please contact Pippa Riley, Publishing Projects Director by e-mail at pippariley@bpp.com.

JIEB Administrations, CVAs and Receiverships syllabus

The syllabus

Candidates must be able to demonstrate a thorough working knowledge of Insolvency Practice, including relevant law and guidance as described in this syllabus, sufficient to enable them to carry out the functions of an authorised insolvency practitioner. Insolvency Practice includes both non-formal and formal practice. Non-formal practice is defined as the provision of analysis and advice to stakeholders concerning an entity in financial difficulties. Formal practice is defined as acting as office holder, from appointment through all the stages of the relevant insolvency procedures to release from the office. The jurisdictions for the purposes of this syllabus are England and Wales; and Scotland. The offices and procedures described in this syllabus relate to both jurisdictions except to the extent that legislation applies differently between them. The relevant offices for the purposes of this syllabus are as follows: those described in the Insolvency Act 1986 and the Bankruptcy (Scotland) Act 1985; receiverships under the Law of Property Act 1925, the Agricultural Credits Act 1928 the Agricultural Credits (Scotland) Act 1929: court appointments; and offices held by virtue of EU Insolvency Regulation 1346/2000.

Relevant law and guidance comprises the legislation referred to above, the Company Directors' Disqualification Act 1986, the Insolvency Rules 1986, the Insolvency (Scotland) Rules 1986, all as from time to time amended, and any other primary legislation, secondary legislation, case law or other guidance that is directly relevant to the performance of an office holder's duties. Examination questions will be based on the relevant law and guidance in force on 30th April for the year of the examination. Questions will not require more recent case law, but demonstrating knowledge of any that is relevant may attract additional marks.

Candidates will also need to demonstrate knowledge of cross-border insolvency issues (including foreign entities located in the respective jurisdictions) but not of the insolvency legislation in foreign regimes. Candidates will need to be aware of industry licensing, environmental and other regulatory requirements, agency and other issues, and the civil and criminal risks arising from them, but will not need in-depth knowledge of industry-specific legislation.

Candidates will be assessed by means of three separate papers, all of which may include questions relating both to non-formal practice and to formal practice although the emphasis will be on the latter. The three papers are distinguished by the different types of entity and the different formal insolvency procedures to which they relate.

The Personal Insolvency paper may include questions relating to any of the following types of entity: individuals, partnerships (except Limited Liability Partnerships) and the estates of deceased individuals. Questions on formal practice will focus on the following procedures: Bankruptcy and Individual Voluntary Arrangements; Voluntary Trust Deeds and Sequestrations. However, questions may also test knowledge of Administrations, Liquidations and Receiverships as they relate to individuals (e.g., individuals in partnerships or individuals subject to Receivership).

The Liquidations paper may include questions relating to any of the following types of entity: all forms of registered and unregistered companies (whether or not in a group structure), including Limited Liability Partnerships (but excluding other partnerships). Questions on formal practice will be limited to the following procedures: Members' Voluntary Liquidations (including Section 110 schemes); Creditors' Voluntary Liquidations; Compulsory Liquidations; and the appointment of Provisional Liquidators or Special Managers. Candidates will be expected to recognise that the following types of entity require special treatment, but they will not be required to deal with these entities in detail: Industrial Societies, Provident Societies, Friendly Societies, Commonhold Associations and Community Interest Companies.

The Administrations, Company Voluntary Arrangements and Receiverships paper may include questions on any of the same types of entity as for the Liquidations paper. Questions on formal practice will be limited to the following procedures: Company Voluntary Arrangements; Partnership Voluntary Arrangements; Administrations, Administrative Receiverships, Receiverships (Scotland), Court Appointed Receiverships and Receiverships under the Law of Property Act 1925.

Non-formal Insolvency Practice

This section of the syllabus refers to engagements for the provision of analysis and advice about matters relating to entities that might already be, or that are at risk of becoming, insolvent. The potential clients for this advice include the entities, their representatives, their creditors, and any other stakeholders.

Engagement

The following learning outcomes refer to the process of engagement for non-formal Insolvency Practice. They do not refer to the process of appointment to an office in a formal insolvency procedure, which is addressed later in the syllabus.

1   Candidates should be able to identify legal, regulatory and ethical considerations affecting the engagement, and also practical considerations (eg staffing levels, relevant experience, and qualifications) to determine whether the engagement can be accepted.

2   Candidates should be able to set out and confirm the adviser's and the client's duties, responsibilities and obligations in connection with the engagement.

Analysis and Advice

The following learning outcomes refer to analyses of the entity's financial affairs, and to the provision of advice with regard to those affairs.

The analyses will be necessary to provide the basis for the advice, which is why the learning outcomes dealing with analyses are in this part of the syllabus. Similar analyses will be required for formal Insolvency Practice, which is addressed in the next section of the syllabus.

3   Candidates should be able to assess an entity's overall financial state and solvency by

- ▶   ascertaining the value of assets and the amount of liabilities, including contingent and prospective liabilities

- ▶   considering the achievability of profit and loss, and cash flow forecasts.

4   Candidates should be able to establish whether an entity that appears to be insolvent should be made subject to a formal insolvency procedure or whether a non-formal insolvency procedure such as a turnaround or a debt management scheme might be appropriate . However, candidates are not required to be able to advise on the detailed techniques that may be used in any such non-formal insolvency procedures.

5   Candidates should be able to identify the most appropriate formal insolvency procedure and estimate the financial outcome of an entity's insolvency by

- ▶   ascertaining the values of assets and the amounts of liabilities that would arise in the formal insolvency

- ▶   comparing and contrasting the estimated outcomes from the available procedures, and from alternative strategies within the available procedures.

6   Candidates should be able to provide advice to the entity or its representatives with regard to

- ▶   their duties, responsibilities and potential liabilities

- ▶   any need to seek additional legal or other guidance

- ▶   how best to proceed.

7   Candidates should be able to provide advice to others who are affected by the financial state of the entity with regard to protecting their interests.

8   Candidates should be able to adapt their advice to take account of new information and changing circumstances.

Formal Insolvency Practice

This section of the syllabus refers to appointments as office holder.

The different subsections refer in turn to case management, case strategy, and the operational requirements to make realisations, to deal with any misconduct, and to agree and pay claims.

Questions on formal Insolvency Practice may also include requirements to carry out the same sorts of analyses as are described above in the previous section of the syllabus on non-formal Insolvency Practice.

Case Management

The following learning outcomes refer to any appointment as an office holder under relevant legislation.

9   Candidates should be able to identify legal, regulatory and ethical considerations affecting the appointment as office holder, and also practical considerations (eg staffing levels, relevant experience, and qualifications) to determine whether the appointment can be accepted.

10   Candidates should be able to manage the statutory, regulatory and contractual procedures required to institute, progress and close the relevant insolvency procedure, including

- establishing and maintaining files, including Insolvency Practitioner Records

- appointment to the office

- obtaining bonding and insurance

- calling and holding statutory meetings of relevant participants as required, including initial, general and final meetings

- banking, managing and disbursing funds

- obtaining sanction for specific actions, as required from creditors (or the relevant committee/s), the court, or the Official Receiver

- ceasing to act and release from office.

11   Candidates should be able to prepare and file the relevant notices, reports and returns required by the office, including to

- the insolvent entity

- creditors

- members

- HM Revenue and Customs

- the Secretary of State for the Department of Business Enterprise and Regulatory Reform

- Companies House

- the London Gazette

- the relevant court

- the Serious Organised Crime Agency

- the office holder's authorising body

- the Pension Protection Fund, the Pensions Regulator, and the trustees or managers of the pension scheme.

Case Strategy

The following learning outcomes refer to the overall strategies, which will guide the office holder's actions to optimise the result.

12   Candidates should be able to identify whether the optimum result is more likely to be achieved by

- a formal procedure that involves disposals of assets

and/or

▶ a formal procedure not involving disposals but which may include, for example, voluntary contributions, debt rescheduling and/or debt restructuring.

13 Where appropriate, candidates should be able to identify the overall strategy that is likely to optimise realisations by means of disposals, which strategy may include

▶ continued trading

and/or

▶ the sale of assets (either as a whole or piecemeal).

14 When determining the most appropriate strategy, candidates should be able to take into account

▶ the taxation implications of the different possible strategies

▶ the possible effects of interactions between concurrent and/or consecutive procedures.

15 Candidates should be able to identify steps that might properly be taken to mitigate liabilities (including any liabilities arising from the strategy itself).

16 Candidates should be able to adapt their strategies to take account of new information and changing circumstances.

Realisations

The following learning outcomes provide a general list of the activities which candidates should be able to carry out to achieve realisations by disposals of the entity's assets and by other means as appropriate.

17 Candidates should be able to identify, seek out, establish ownership, take control of and protect the entity's assets and records, including by means of

▶ investigation

▶ physical and practical controls

▶ legal proceedings

▶ insurance

▶ banking arrangements and investment of funds.

18 Candidates should be able to manage the continuation and/or cessation of an entity's business having proper regard to the rights of all affected parties, including dealing with

▶ finances, using cash flow forecasts and trading budgets

▶ employees, taking account of their rights (including Transfer of Undertakings and pension rights) and of the office holder's duties

▶ management of operations

▶ tax including VAT compliance

▶ compliance with industry licensing, environmental and other regulatory requirements, including for personnel and premises

▶ business assets, including

    – freehold and leasehold premises

    – fixtures and fittings

    – plant and equipment

    – motor vehicles

    – stock and work in progress

    – contracts

    – intellectual property, including goodwill.

19   Candidates should be able to realise value from the entity by executing

▶   sales of the business as a going concern, either as a whole or in part/s, making use of hive-down companies if appropriate

and/or

▶   sales of assets, either as a whole or piecemeal, including, where relevant and appropriate, dealing with assets that are subject to

–   security

–   execution, attachment or distress

–   lien

–   reservation of title

–   special legal requirements

–   onerous provisions.

20   Candidates should also be able to achieve realisations from sources other than asset disposals, including from

▶   actions that may only be available to the office holder, including those in respect of misconduct, or voidable transactions

▶   amounts that may be recoverable by the entity in its own name

▶   contributions from net income

▶   contributions from third parties.

21   Candidates should be able to identify circumstances that give rise to potential recovery actions, the creditors who might benefit from pursuing them, how such actions might be funded, and whether they should be pursued.

Dealing with Misconduct

The following learning outcomes refer to the duties of the office holder to assess and report on conduct.

22   Candidates should be able to identify and, where appropriate, investigate misconduct relating to the insolvency, including such matters as are identified in the Insolvency Act 1986 and in the Company Directors' Disqualification Act 1986.

23   Candidates should be able to prepare and submit reports as required in cases of misconduct, including to the

▶   Official Receiver

▶   Secretary of State for the Department of Business Enterprise and Regulatory Reform

▶   Serious Organised Crime Agency.

Agreeing and Paying Claims

The following learning outcomes provide a general list of the activities by which candidates should be able to agree and pay claims in an insolvency procedure. Not all of them will apply in every case.

24   Candidates should be able to determine the validity of charges and the charge holders' rights, and to compute the amounts payable.

25   Candidates should be able to determine the validity and quantum of preferential claims and compute the amounts payable.

26   Candidates should be able to evaluate and resolve claims in special categories, including

▶   retention of title
▶   lien
▶   hire purchase and leasing
▶   execution and distress.

27   Candidates should be able to determine the validity and quantum of unsecured claims and compute the amounts payable.

28   Candidates should be able to rank all of the valid claims, and duly pay them in the statutory order having taken into account, as appropriate, interest, set off, the Prescribed Part, subrogation and marshalling.

29   Where there is a surplus after the payment of relevant creditors, candidates should be able to determine the amounts and entitlements to the surplus and the procedures for passing it across.

The JIEB exam

The exam paper

(a)   The JIEB exam consists of three papers each of three hours, with an additional 30 minutes reading time per session. (In 2009 the examination will be held on 2, 3 and 4 November).

(b)   Exam questions are set on the basis of European and UK legislation on insolvency and statements of insolvency practice in force on the 30th day of April for the year of examination. Knowledge of case law after 30 April will not be specifically examined, however demonstration of knowledge of recent case law may attract additional marks.

(c)   The subject of the three papers is:

> ▶ Liquidations
> ▶ Administrations, Company Voluntary Arrangements and Receiverships
> ▶ Personal Insolvency

(d)   Each paper consists of four compulsory questions, with two questions attracting 20% of the marks and two questions attracting 30% of the marks.

(e)   The examination is essentially practical and relevant experience, whilst not essential, is an advantage. The examination aims to assess whether candidates have sufficient knowledge of insolvency law and practice to enable them to carry out the functions of an authorised insolvency practitioner. Candidates are expected to have a basic knowledge of taxation, accountancy and business law, directly relevant to the performance of an office holder's duties in the practice of insolvency.

(f)   Marks are awarded in the exam for the ability to communicate effectively.

(g)   The exam is open book and candidates are provided, in the exam hall, with the latest edition of the Butterworths Insolvency Law Handbook.

How to use this study manual

This is the second edition of the BPP Learning Media study manual for the Administrations, CVAs and Receiverships paper of the Joint Insolvency Examinations Board. It has been written to cover the JIEB syllabus.

To pass the examination you need a thorough understanding in all areas covered by the syllabus.

Recommended approach

(a)   To pass you need to be able to answer questions on **everything** specified by the syllabus. Read the text very carefully and do not skip any of it.

(b)   Learning is an **active** process. Do **all** the activities as you work through the manual so you can be sure you really understand what you have read.

(c)   After you have covered the material in the Study Manual, work through the questions suggested in the Exam Practice section.

(d)   Before you take the exam, check that you still remember the material using the following quick revision plan.

     (i)   Read through the chapter learning objectives. Are there any gaps in your knowledge? If so, study the section again.

     (ii)   Read and learn the defined terms.

     (iii)   Read and learn the diagrammatic summary of each chapter.

     (iv)   Do the self test questions again. If you know what you're doing, they shouldn't take long.

This approach is only a suggestion. You or your college may well adapt it to suit your needs.

Remember this is a **practical** course. Try to relate the material to your experience in the workplace or any other work experience you may have had.

Chapter summary

Chapter 1 – Legislation

This chapter introduces the main legislation governing insolvency law and the Insolvency Code of Ethics and provides important background information. The principles of the Insolvency Code of Ethics are a very examinable topic in the JIEB exam.

Chapter 2 – Statements of Insolvency Practice

This chapter introduces Statements of Insolvency Practice (SIPs), what they are, who produces them and lists what SIPs are currently in use. A good knowledge of the content of the SIPs is required in order to pass the JIEB exam. Insolvency Guidance Papers are also introduced here.

Chapter 3 – Introduction to administration

Administrations are introduced in this chapter: the purpose of administration, routes into administration and the status, powers and duties of the administrator. Routes into administration is a popular topic in the JIEB exam.

Chapter 4 – Conduct of administration

Practical aspects of administration are covered in this chapter including the moratorium and its effects, how to deal with creditors seeking leave to enforce their security, statutory returns and dividend payments to creditors. These topics are not regularly tested in the JIEB exam however it is still important to understand the effects of administration and what statutory returns have to be made by the administrator.

Chapter 5 – Ending administrations

The procedures for ending administration are covered in this chapter and how the administrator vacates office and his duties on doing so. These topics are regularly tested in the JIEB exam so this chapter should be learnt thoroughly.

Chapter 6 – Charges

Fixed and floating charges are covered in this chapter, their main identifying features and the priority of charges. The topics covered in this chapter give basic background information which is essential for the JIEB exam.

Chapter 7 – Introduction to receiverships

The different types of receiver, and their duties and powers, are introduced in this chapter. This chapter provides basic background information.

Chapter 8 – Administrative receivership

Administrative receivership is dealt with in this chapter, especially how to ensure that an administrative receiver has been validly appointed, his powers, duties and agency and the requirements of SIP 1 and SIP 14. Administrative receivership remains a popular topic in the JIEB exam.

Chapter 9 – Closure of administrative receivership

How administrative receivership is affected by the liquidation of the company, the circumstances in which an administrative receiver may vacate office and his duties upon doing so are covered in this chapter. The effect of liquidation on administrative receivership has been regularly tested in the JIEB exam.

Chapter 10 – Trading on and selling the business

The matters dealt with in this chapter and the following two chapters are relevant to both administration and administrative receivership. It is a very practical chapter covering both the decision to continue trading, practical matters to be considered whilst trading and steps to take to sell the business. These topics are regularly tested in the JIEB exam.

Chapter 11 – Practical matters – administration and administrative receivership

This chapter deals with the completion of director's disqualification returns, IP Records and creditors' committees. It also provides a closure checklist which may be relevant to any insolvency appointment. These topics could be tested under any of the three JIEB exam papers so are important topics to learn.

Chapter 12 – Numbers questions

This is a very practical chapter detailing how to prepare financial statements such as:

- Statement of Affairs
- Deficiency account
- Estimated outcome statement
- Receipts and payments account
- Bank reconciliation

At least one numbers question has appeared in every JIEB exam to date.

Chapter 13 – Company voluntary arrangements

This chapter introduces company voluntary arrangements (CVA), the procedure to enter into a CVA, the contents of a CVA proposal and the effect of entering into a CVA. It also compares CVA with a s425 Scheme of arrangement. CVA's appear regularly as a JIEB exam topic. Partnership voluntary arrangements are also covered in this chapter. Whilst partnership voluntary arrangements appear on the syllabus for the Administrations, CVAs and Receiverships paper, partnership insolvency options are more usually tested in the Personal Insolvency paper.

Chapter 14 – Options

This chapter discusses the options available to the directors of a company which is, or is about to become, insolvent and lists the options available to a charge holder seeking to enforce their security. These are very examinable topics in the JIEB exam. Antecedent transactions are also covered in this chapter.

Legislation

➤ ➤ ➤ ➤ ➤ ➤ ➤ ➤ ➤ ➤ ➤ ➤ ➤ ➤ ➤

Contents

Introduction

Examination context

Topic List

Summary and Self-test

Answers to Self-test

Answers to interactive question

Introduction

Learning objectives

▶ Understand the main legislation governing insolvency law ☐

▶ Identify the fundamental principles and apply the Insolvency Code of Ethics in practice in relation to appointments as supervisor of a voluntary arrangement, administrator or administrative or other receiver ☐

▶ Understand implications of money laundering regulations for an office holder ☐

▶ Understand the implications of the EC Regulations for office holders ☐

Working context

All aspects of insolvency work are governed by legislation, it is therefore important to understand the requirements of the legislation in your daily working lives.

Stop and think

Why should the area of insolvency require regulating? Why shouldn't an administrator act as an auditor of a company? What are the fundamental principles? Why are they important?

BPP LEARNING MEDIA

Examination context

Ethics is a very examinable topic appearing regularly in any of the three JIEB exam papers. It is important to learn not just the fundamental principles but also to be able to apply the requirements of the Code of Ethics in practice.

The EC Regulations are unlikely to be tested in their own right, however an understanding of the Regulations is required.

Money Laundering Regulations came into force in 2003 and therefore in terms of the exam this is relatively new material for the examiner. It appeared in the 2005 exam (Sec A Question 1a)) and you should therefore be aware of the issues for office holders in respect of money laundering.

Past exam questions to look at include:

2005	Question	1(a)
2001	Question	2(a)
1996	Question	1(a)

1 The Insolvency Act 1986

Section overview

▸ The Insolvency Act 1986 ("the Act") consolidated the Insolvency Act 1985 (never brought fully into force) and those provisions of the Companies Act 1985 relating to receiverships and corporate insolvencies.

▸ The Act came into force on the 29 December 1986 (effect of s443 of the Act, s236(2) of the Insolvency Act 1985 and the Insolvency Act 1985 (commencement No 5) Order 1986).

1.1 The Act and corporate recovery procedures

The Act introduced two new procedures which it was hoped would aid in the rescuing of financially troubled but viable businesses.

▸ The Company Voluntary Arrangement (Part I, ss.1-7 of the Act) and

▸ The Administration Order (Part II, ss.8-27 of the Act)

In addition the Act introduced the concept of the 'administrative receiver' a statutory modification of existing and familiar 'receiver and manager' appointments.

The Insolvency Act 1994 amended the provisions of the Act in relation to the liability of administrative receivers on adopted employment contracts.

1.2 Impact of the Insolvency Act 2000 and Enterprise Act 2002 on the Insolvency Act 1986

The Insolvency Act 2000 received Royal Assent on 20 December 2000. The provisions relating to administrations and disqualifications were brought into force on 2 April 2001 (Insolvency Act 2000 (Commencement No. 1 and Transitional Provisions) Order 2001) and provisions relating to CVAs and IVAs were not brought into force until 1 January 2003 (Insolvency Act 2000 (Commencement No.3 and Transitional Provisions) Order 2002).

The Enterprise Act received the Royal Assent on 7 November 2002. Much of the Act relates to competition law and is not directly related to insolvency. The main insolvency reforms introduced by the Enterprise Act 2002 are contained in Part X (s248 – 272). The corporate provisions were brought into force on 15 September 2003 and the personal insolvency provisions on 1 April 2004 (Enterprise Act 2002 (Commencement No.4 and Transitional Provisions and Savings) Order 2003).

Neither the Insolvency Act 2000 nor the Enterprise Act 2002 constitute "stand alone" items of insolvency legislation. In both cases their function is to amend or make additions to the Insolvency Act 1986.

It follows that it is not necessary either in the Joint Insolvency Exam nor generally in practice to refer to the 2000 and 2002 Acts.

In these notes 'the Act' refers, therefore, to the 1986 Act and all references unless otherwise stated are to that Act.

1.3 The Insolvency (Amendment) (No.2) Rules 2002

These rules came into force on 1 January 2003 and made amendments to the Insolvency Rules 1986 consequential on the changes made by the Insolvency Act 2000. It follows that the main changes were to parts 1 (CVAs) and 5 (IVAs) of those rules.

In particular a new chapter 9 in Part 1 of the 1986 Rules (R1.35 – 1.54) applies where Directors have filed for a 'small company' moratorium.

In some cases the old rules (i.e. without the 2002 amendment rules changes) will continue to apply. These are where

▶   Written notice of a proposal for an IVA or CVA was endorsed before 1 January 2003

▶   Or where in the case of a CVA a liquidator or administrator summonsed a meeting of creditors before that date.

2   The Companies Act 2006

Section overview

▶   The Companies Act 2006 (CA 06) was given Royal Assent in November 2006. Its aim was to modernise existing company law to provide a simple, efficient and cost effective framework for British businesses in the 21st century.

2.1   Implementation

The CA 85 was changed in order to meet four key objectives:

(i)   To enhance shareholder engagement and a long term investment culture.
(ii)   To ensure better regulation and a 'Think Small First' approach.
(iii) To make it easier to set up and run a company.
(iv)   To provide flexibility for the future.

The overall arrangement of the CA 06 is as follows:

PART	SUMMARY
1 to 7	The fundamentals of what a company is, how it can be formed and what it can be called.
8 to 12	The members (shareholders) and officers (management) of a company
13 and 14	How companies may take decisions.
15 and 16	The safeguards for ensuring that the officers of a company are accountable to its members.
17 to 25	Raising share capital, capital maintenance, annual returns and company charges.
26 to 28	Company reconstruction, mergers and takeovers.
29 to 39	The regulatory framework, application to companies not formed under the CA and other company law provisions.
40 to 42	Overseas disqualification of directors, business names and statutory auditors.
43	Transparency obligations.
44 to 47	Miscellaneous and general.

The company law provisions of the 2006 Act (Parts 1 to 39) restate almost all of the provisions of the 1985 CA, together with the company law provisions of the CA 1989 and the Companies (Audit, Investigations and Community Enterprise) Act 2004.

The 2006 CA will not be fully implemented until October 2009. The provisions of the Act have been implemented in stages in April 2007, April 2008 and October 2008 with the final implementation in October 2009. Where provisions of the 2006 Act have not yet been implemented, the provisions of the 1985 Act still apply. You will note that the study manual refers to both the 1985 and the 2006 Companies Acts.

3 The Insolvency Code of Ethics

Section overview

▸ The Code of Ethics governs the conduct of practitioners. All practitioners should be guided by the fundamental principles contained in the Code of Ethics. It sets out to assist the Insolvency Practitioner (IP) in the application of legislation and also in matters not covered by legislation. Failure to observe the code may not, of itself, constitute professional misconduct, but will be taken into account in assessing the conduct of an IP. An IP should not engage in any business, occupation or activity that impairs or might impair integrity, objectivity or the good reputation of the profession and as a result would be incompatible with the fundamental principles.

3.1 Fundamental principles

The Code identifies five fundamental principles with which the IP is required to comply:

1   Integrity – an IP should be straightforward and honest in all professional and business relationships.

2   Objectivity – an IP should not allow bias, conflict of interest or undue influence of others to override professional or business judgements.

3   Professional competence and due care – an IP has a continuing duty to maintain professional knowledge and skill at the level required to ensure that a client or employer receives competent professional service based on current developments in practice, legislation and techniques.

4   Confidentiality – an IP should respect the confidentiality of information acquired as a result of professional and business relationships.

5   Professional behaviour – an IP should comply with relevant laws and regulations and should avoid any action that discredits the profession.

3.2 Threats

The Code requires the IP to identify, evaluate and address threats to the fundamental principles. Many threats fall into five categories:

1   Self interest threats - these may occur as a result of the financial or other interests of a practice or an IP or of an immediate or close family member of an individual within the practice.

2   Self review threats – these may occur when a previous judgement made by an individual within the practice needs to be re-evaluated by the IP.

3   Advocacy threats – these may occur when an individual within the practice promotes a position or opinion to the point that subsequent objectivity may be compromised.

4   Familiarity threats – may occur when, because of a close relationship, an individual within the practice becomes too sympathetic to the interests of others.

5   Intimidation threats – these may occur when an IP may be deterred from acting objectively by threats, actual or perceived.

3.3 Safeguards

IP's should ensure that safeguards are in place to reduce the level of any threat. These may include:

▸   Leadership that stresses the importance of compliance with the fundamental principles

▸   Policies and procedures to implement and monitor quality control of engagements

▸   Documented policies regarding the identification of threats to compliance with the fundamental principles, the evaluation of the significance of these threats and the identification and the application of safeguards to eliminate or reduce the threats, other than those that are trivial, to an acceptable level

▶ Documented internal policies and procedures requiring compliance with the fundamental principles

▶ Policies and procedures to consider the fundamental principles of the Code before the acceptance of an insolvency appointment

▶ Policies and procedures regarding the identification of interests or relationships between individuals within the practice and third parties

▶ Policies and procedures to prohibit individuals who are not members of the insolvency team from inappropriately influencing the outcome of an insolvency appointment

▶ Timely communication of a practice's policies and procedures, including any changes to them, to all individuals within the practice, and appropriate training and education on such policies and procedures

▶ Designating a member of senior management to be responsible for overseeing the adequate functioning of the safeguarding system

▶ A disciplinary mechanism to promote compliance with policies and procedures

▶ Published policies and procedures to encourage and empower individuals within the practice to communicate to senior levels within the practice and/or the IP any issue relating to compliance with the fundamental principles that concerns them.

Safeguards specific to an appointment may include:

▶ Involving and/or consulting another IP from within the practice to review the work done

▶ Consulting an independent third party, such as a committee of creditors, a licensing or professional body or another IP

▶ Involving another IP to perform part of the work, which may include another IP taking a joint appointment where conflict arises during the course of the appointment

▶ Seeking directions from the court.

▶ Obtaining knowledge and understanding of the entity, its owners, managers and those responsible for its governance and business activities

▶ Acquiring an appropriate understanding of the nature of the entity's business, the complexity of its operations, the specific requirements of the engagement and the purpose, nature and scope of the work to be performed

▶ Acquiring knowledge of relevant industries or subject matters

▶ Possessing or obtaining experience with relevant regulatory or reporting requirements

▶ Assigning staff with the necessary competencies

▶ Using experts where necessary

▶ Complying with quality control policies and procedures designed to provide reasonable assurance that specific engagements are accepted only when they can be performed competently.

Where a threat cannot be eliminated the IP should evaluate the significance of such a threat and apply necessary safeguards to reduce them to an acceptable level.

In situations where no safeguards can mitigate a threat, the IP should conclude that it would not be appropriate to accept the insolvency appointment.

The IP should always be aware of how his actions will be perceived by others. Sometimes the mere perception of risk or conflict will undermine confidence in the practitioner's objectivity. In such circumstances, acceptance of an insolvency appointment would be unwise.

IPs should document their consideration of the fundamental principles and the reasons behind their agreement or otherwise to accept an insolvency appointment.

3.4 Fees and other types of remuneration

The special nature of insolvency appointments makes the payment or offer of any commission for, or the furnishing of any valuable consideration towards, the introduction of insolvency appointments inappropriate. This does not, however, preclude an arrangement between an IP and a bona fide employee whereby the employee's remuneration is based in whole or in part on introductions obtained for the practitioner through the efforts of the employee.

3.5 Significant professional and personal relationships

The environment in which IPs work can lead to threats to the principles of objectivity and integrity. The most common threats arise from ongoing and previous relationships.

▶ 'Self review threats' – where the practitioner has had a significant professional relationship with the company or individual in relation to which or whom an appointment is taken, and

▶ 'Self interest threats' – threats which refer to personal relationships which may affect the reasoning the practitioner applies.

The IP should identify and analyse the significance of any professional or personal relationship which may affect compliance with the fundamental principles. The IP should consider whether any individual within the practice, or the practice itself, has or had a professional or personal relationship with a principle or employee of an entity for which an insolvency appointment is being considered, or any business controlled by or under the same control as the entity or part of it.

A professional relationship includes where an individual within the practice is carrying out or has carried out audit work or any other professional work. A professional relationship may also arise from an individual within the practice having an interest in an entity.

An IP should not accept an insolvency appointment in relation to an entity where any personal, professional or business connection with a principle is such as to impair or reasonably appear to impair the IP's objectivity.

In assessing whether a relationship is significant the IP should consider:

▶ How the relationship will be viewed by others

▶ How recently any work was carried out

▶ Whether the fee received for the work by the practice is or was significant to the practice itself or is or was substantial

▶ The impact of the work conducted by the practice on the financial state and/or the financial stability of the entity

▶ The nature of the previous duties undertaken by a practice or an individual within the practice during an earlier relationship with the entity

▶ The extent of the insolvency teams familiarity with the individuals connected with the insolvency appointment

If there is a significant relationship, the IP should consider whether that relationship gives rise to any particular threat. In situations where no threat arises, an IP will be able to undertake or continue the insolvency appointment.

Where a threat arises from a significant relationship, and the threat cannot be overcome by safeguards, the professional work cannot be undertaken or continued.

3.6 Audit work previously undertaken for a company or individual to which an appointment is being sought

Where the IP or a practice has previously carried out audit work within the previous 3 years for a company or individual to which the appointment is being considered, the IP should not accept an appointment.

Where the audit work was conducted over three years ago, the IP should still consider whether any self review threats may arise and impose any necessary safeguards before the appointment is accepted.

3.7 Professional work undertaken by an individual within the practice for an entity or any principle of an entity to which an insolvency appointment is being considered

Where an individual within the practice is undertaking professional work (eg. tax work) for an entity or any principle of an entity to whom an insolvency appointment is being considered, this will give rise to a threat to independence. The nature of the professional work will have to be considered. For example, basic tax work for the director of an entity may not be regarded as so significant as tax planning work undertaken for the entity.

3.8 Appointment as Nominee and/or Supervisor of a Company Voluntary Arrangement, Administrator or Administrative Receiver or other receiver

Where there has been a significant professional relationship with a company or a personal relationship with a director, former director or shadow director of a company, no individual within the practice should accept appointment as nominee or supervisor of a voluntary arrangement, administrator or administrative or other receiver in relation to that company.

3.9 Appointment as Investigating Accountant at the instigation of a creditor

A significant professional relationship would not normally arise following the appointment of the practice by a creditor of a company to investigate its affairs provided that:

(a)   There has not been a direct involvement by an individual within the practice in the management of the company, and

(b)   The practice continues to have its principle client relationship with the creditor, rather than the company and the company is aware of this.

Where an IP or the practice has undertaken an investigation into the financial affairs of the company at the request of a secured creditor of the company, and is asked, as a consequence, by that creditor to accept appointment as administrator or administrative receiver, the IP should be satisfied that the company (acting by its board of directors) does not object to the acceptance of the appointment.

IPs may be called upon to justify the propriety of acceptance where the circumstances of the initial appointment are such as to prevent open discussion of the financial affairs of the company with the directors.

3.10 Administration following appointment as supervisor of a voluntary arrangement

Appointment as administrator may be accepted where an individual in the practice has acted as the supervisor of a voluntary arrangement, provided the appointment is made by the holder of a floating charge and consideration has been given to the principles set out in the Code.

3.11 Administrator, nominee and/or supervisor of a voluntary arrangement following appointment as administrative receiver or LPA or other receiver

Appointment should not be accepted where an individual within the practice is, or in the previous three years has been an administrative or other receiver of a company or a LPA receiver unless the previous appointment was made by the court.

3.12 Audit following appointment as supervisor of a voluntary arrangement, administrator or administrative or other receiver

Appointment as auditor of a company should not be accepted for any accounting period during which an individual within the practice has acted as supervisor of a voluntary arrangement, administrator or administrative or other receiver of a company.

3.13 Liquidation following appointment as supervisor of CVA or administrator

Appointment as liquidator can be accepted where administration is followed by compulsory winding up, however the administrator should not accept appointment as liquidator unless he has the agreement of the creditors' committee or of a meeting of creditors. Appointment as liquidator following a voluntary arrangement is acceptable.

Where an individual within the practice is, or in the previous three years has been, administrative receiver of a company, or a receiver under LPA 1925 or otherwise, of any of its assets, no individual within that practice should accept appointment as liquidator of the company in an insolvent liquidation. This does not apply however where the previous appointment was made by the court.

3.14 Pre-agreed business sales

Where the assets and business of an insolvent company are sold by an IP shortly after appointment on pre agreed terms, this could lead to an actual or perceived threat to independence. To reduce the threat the IP should obtain an independent valuation of the assets and seek to identify other potential purchasers.

3.15 Relationships between insolvent individuals and insolvent companies

An IP, or an individual within the practice, who acts as an IP in relation to an individual may be asked to accept an insolvency appointment in relation to a company of which the debtor is a major shareholder or creditor or where the company is a creditor of the debtor. Acceptance should not be taken unless the IP is satisfied that steps can be taken to minimise problems of conflict and the IP's overall integrity and objectivity are, and are seen to be, maintained.

3.16 Joint appointments

Where an IP is specifically precluded by the guidance given in the Code from accepting an appointment as an individual, a joint appointment will not render the appointment acceptable.

3.17 Relationship with a debenture holder

An IP should, in general, decline to accept an insolvency appointment in relation to a company if an individual within a practice has such a personal or close and distinct business connection with the debenture holder as might impair or appear to impair the IP's objectivity. It is not considered likely that a close and distinct business connection would normally exist between an IP and a clearing bank or other major financial institution.

3.18 'Independent trustees' of Pension schemes

The Pensions Act 1995 (brought into force on 6 April 1997) requires the IP or OR to ensure that the trustee is independent. Where there is no independent trustee, one should be appointed as soon as reasonably practicable.

In corporate insolvency, members should not appoint a principal or employee of their firm (or connected parties) as independent trustee of a pension scheme of a company in respect of which they are the responsible IP.

The guide warns of the threat to objectivity posed by reciprocal arrangements in respect of these appointments with other firms.

Interactive question: Biome Limited

One of the partners in the accountancy firm you work for has been approached to act as administrator to Biome Limited. You will be the manager with day-to-day responsibility for the assignment.

Requirement

List the practical steps to be taken regarding conflicts of interest and qualification to act as administrator, before your partner accepts the appointment.

See **Answer** at the end of this chapter.

4 Money Laundering

Section overview

▶ There are a number of Acts that contain law relating to money laundering. The main ones are:

- Money Laundering Regulations 2007

- Part 7 Proceeds of Crime Act 2002 (Money Laundering) (POCA 2002)

- s18 and s21A Terrorism Act 2000 (TA 2000)

▶ Compliance with the 2007 Money Laundering Regulations is a legal requirement. The regulations came into force on 15 December 2007 and apply to all appointments held by an IP at that date.

Definition

Money Laundering: a number of offences involving the proceeds of crime (including tax evasion and fraud) or terrorist funds. It is the process by which the identity of dirty money (ie. The proceeds of crime and the ownership of those proceeds) is changed so that the proceeds appear to originate from legitimate sources. It includes possessing, dealing with or concealing the proceeds of any crime or similar activities in relation to terrorist funds, which includes funds from legitimate sources which are likely to be used for terrorism, as well as the proceeds of terrorism.

4.1 Money laundering process

Money laundering is conventionally described as being a three stage process:

▶ Placement – where cash (literally money in the form of coins and banknotes) is deposited into the banking system. Serious and organised criminals need access to the international banking system due to the practical difficulties in using cash to settle large transactions.

▶ Layering – a series of transactions designed to disguise the audit trail.

▶ Integration – whereby the now apparently cleaned funds are invested in the legitimate economy.

An Insolvency Practitioner can be targeted at any of the three stages, for instance:

▶ Placement – A potential purchaser of a business who wishes to pay for assets in cash

▶ Layering – A criminal sends a cheque made payable to a liquidator of a company purporting to be in payment of a debt owed to the company which is being wound-up. The liquidator pays the cheque into an account maintained in the name of his firm in compliance with SIP 11. The debtor ledger is then checked and when it becomes apparent that the debt in question does not exist a cheque in the name of the firm is sent to the criminal. The funds appear legitimate.

▶ Integration – A criminal acquires a business through an office–holder using funds which have already passed through a money laundering process and now appear to be legitimate.

4.2 Offences

There are a wide range of offences under POCA 2002, TA 2000 and 2007 Regulations. The main ones relate to where a person:

▶ Conceals, disguises, converts or transfers criminal property from the UK

▶ Enters into or becomes concerned in an arrangement which he knows or suspects facilitates the acquisition, retention, use or control of criminal property by or on behalf of another person

▶ Acquires, uses and/or possesses criminal property

A second tier of offences relate to the regulated sector and relate to where a person:

▶ Fails to disclose knowledge or suspicion of money laundering to the nominated officer or Serious Organised Crime Agency (SOCA)

▶ Tips off any person that such a disclosure has been made.

4.3 IP's obligations re money laundering

IP's are required to:

▶ Establish procedures to identify customers and verify their identities

▶ Carry out ongoing monitoring of business relationships

▶ Appoint a nominated officer called a 'Money Laundering Reporting Officer' (MLRO) to whom principals and employees must make money laundering reports. This does not apply to sole practitioners who do not employ any staff or act in association with any other parties.

▶ Establish internal systems, procedures, policies and controls to forestall and prevent money laundering

▶ Provide relevant individuals with training on Money Laundering

▶ Maintain records of client identification and of business relationships for at least 5 years

▶ Report suspicions of money laundering to SOCA

4.4 Identification procedures

Reg 5 Money Laundering Regulations 2007 details identification procedures which IP's must have in place for identifying the customer and verifying their identity on the basis of documents, data or information obtained from a reliable and independent source.

Identification procedures are required when:

- Entering a business relationship
- Carrying out an occasional transaction
- Where there is suspicion of money laundering or terrorist financing
- Where there are doubts concerning the validity of previous identification evidence

Definition

Occasional transaction: a transaction amounting to 15,000 euros or more. (This would include the sale of assets of an insolvent involving the paying of 15,000 euros or more to the IP).

Identification procedures for an individual would include the IP seeing and taking copies of evidence establishing the applicants full name and address ie. Passport, photo driving licence, recent utility bill, Inland Revenue Tax notification, Benefits Agency benefits book.

Identification procedures for a company may also involve identifying the controllers of the company. Suitable evidence for a company includes:

- Certificate of incorporation
- Evidence of company's registered address
- Copy of company's annual return

4.5 Reporting suspicions of money laundering

Internal reports of money laundering should be made to the MLRO who is required to decide whether to report the matter on to the SOCA. If in doubt, the MLRO should seek legal advice. Reports should be made as soon as possible, irrespective of the amounts involved.

There are two types of form for reporting to the SOCA:

- Standard Disclosure Form
- Limited Intelligence Value Report Form.

Care must be taken that a money launderer is not tipped off (this constitutes an offence under POCA 2002 and TA 2000).

Having made the report, no action that would assist the launderer or otherwise constitute money laundering by the IP may take place for 7 working days, unless SOCA gives consent for it to go ahead. This may impact on a potential sale in which case reports to SOCA may be marked urgent.

4.6 High Value Dealers

High value dealers are required to register with the Commissioners of HM Revenue & Customs.

Definition

High value dealer: the activity of dealing in goods whenever a transaction involves accepting a total cash payment of 15,000 euros or more in one operation or several if they are linked.

5 The EC Regulation on Insolvency Proceedings 2000

Section overview

▶ The EC Regulation on Insolvency Proceedings 2000 (The "EC Regulation") was adopted by the Council of Ministers of the European Union on 29th May 2000 and came into force on 31st May 2002.

▶ The EC Regulation applies throughout the European Union with the exception of Denmark which exercised its right of opt - out.

▶ Note that although the European Community has become the European Union it is still usual to refer to EC legislation. This is because the Legislation is intended to promote the single market rather than other EU aims such as a common foreign and security policy.

5.1 Significance of 'Regulation' status

A Regulation is an item of European secondary legislation (as opposed to primary legislation such as the Treaty of Rome). A Regulation is said to be "directly applicable" i.e. on coming into force it is automatically part of the law of each member state without the need for (in the UK) an implementing statute or piece of delegated legislation.

This should be contrasted with Directives which are not directly applicable. For example the 1977 European Acquired Rights Directive designed to protect an employees rights on transfers of undertakings was enacted in UK law by the Transfer of Undertakings (Protection of Employment) Regulations 1981 (TUPER).

European law is normally broadly drafted and a purposive rather than literal approach to interpretation will be taken by the courts. For instance in *Litster v Forth Dry Dock and Engineering Co. Ltd 1989* where staff had been dismissed one hour before the transfer in an attempt to evade the effect of TUPER, mentioned above, the House of Lords interpreted the words "immediately before the transfer" as meaning "or would have been so employed if not unfairly dismissed before the transfer".

Under the European Community Act 1972 European Law has supremacy over UK made law and it follows that courts will not be bound to follow UK law which is inconsistent with the EC Regulation.

5.2 The UK under the EC Regulation

The UK is treated as one jurisdiction i.e. Scotland and Northern Ireland where insolvency law differs from that in England and Wales are not considered separate territories.

Gibraltar is included within the UK.

5.3 Application of the EC Regulation

The EC Regulation will apply to a debtor company or individual where its' Centre of Main Interests ("COMI") is within the European Union (para 14 of the Recitals: "This Regulation applies only to proceedings where the centre of the debtors main interests is located in the community").

Definition

Centre of main interests: this is the place of command or control, the place where the debtor conducts the administration of its business on a regular basis. This could be where the registered office is, but may not always be so.

If the COMI is outside the EU the EC Regulation will not apply. Where a company has its' COMI in the US for instance and that company has assets in the UK, domestic UK law and not the EC Regulation will apply to those UK assets.

Paragraph 1 of Article 3 of the EC Regulation provides that in the case of a company the registered office shall be presumed to be the COMI in the absence of proof to the contrary. However

▶ Paragraph 13 of the Recitals provides that the COMI "should correspond to the place where the debtor conducts the administration of his interests on a regular basis and is therefore ascertainable by third parties".

▶ In *Re Brac Rent-a-car Ltd* concerning a company registered in *Delaware* the High Court held that the EC Regulation applied as the company's operations were conducted almost entirely in the UK and the COMI was therefore also situated in the UK.

▶ The Eurofoods decision of the European Courts of Justice (02.05.06) emphasised that:

– The EC Regulation is to be applied separately to each company in a group;

– The registered office presumption can only be rebutted by objective evidence ascertainable by creditors. A parent-subsidiary relationship or evidence that a parent determined the economic choices of a subsidiary was insufficient on its own to rebut the presumption.

– Where a party disagreed with the decision of a national court in relation to the opening of main proceedings the appropriate remedy was to appeal through the national courts not to appeal to the ECJ.

▶ In *Geveran Trading v Skjevesland* the court held that the EC Regulation did not apply as the debtors COMI was in Switzerland, and commented that a company's head office was more likely to correspond to its COMI than the registered office which in the UK might simply be the address of a firm of accountants.

5.4 Types of insolvency procedure governed by the EC Regulation

Article 1 of the EC Regulation provides that it applies to "collective insolvency proceedings which entail the partial or total divestment of a debtor and the appointment of a liquidator".

"Collective insolvency proceedings" consist in the UK of (see Article 2(a) and Annex A):

▶ Winding up by the court

▶ Creditors voluntary winding-up. However here, as a CVL is not a court procedure, "confirmation by the court" is required.

▶ Administration – and the EC Reg will also apply to subsequent insolvency proceedings such as a CVL under para 83 of Schedule B1 of the Insolvency Act 1986.

▶ IVAs and CVAs

▶ Bankruptcy.

Those who qualify as "liquidators" are listed in annex C and include liquidators, administrators, supervisors, the OR and a trustee in bankruptcy, i.e. the term "liquidator" in the EC Regulation is used loosely to mean the office holder in an annex A insolvency proceeding.

There are some notable omissions from the annex A list

▶ Members voluntary liquidations (EU cross-border issues here are covered by the Brussels Convention).

▶ Administrative receivership or receivership under a fixed charge. The EC Regulation is concerned with processes designed to deal with creditors generally. Receiverships concern the enforcement of private contractual rights by a secured creditor. Administrators will therefore have advantages over administrative receivers where there are assets outside the UK in more readily being able to "export" their powers to other EU jurisdictions.

▶ S895 CA 2006 Schemes of arrangement.

Article 1 (2) excludes insurance undertakings, credit institutions, investment undertakings holding funds or securities for 3rd parties and collective investment undertakings (e.g. unit trusts). These financial services sector businesses have their own separate European regulatory framework.

5.5 Main proceedings

(i) **Concept of 'main proceedings'**

Article 3(1) "The courts of the Member State within the territory of which the centre of a debtor's main interests is situated shall have jurisdiction to open insolvency proceedings." These proceedings will be "main proceedings" (see next section for significance of the expression).

Remember that the COMI will not necessarily be the same as the jurisdiction of incorporation or the domicile of the registered office of the company. In the Daisytek case for instance both the UK High Court and the French Court of Appeal held that the COMI of a French subsidiary of a UK holding company was in the UK, the courts being presented with evidence that the French company was managed from the UK (following Eurofoods this would need to be ascertainable by creditors). The UK High Court was able to make separate, UK administration orders in relation to both the holding and subsidiary companies.

(ii) **Significance of 'main proceedings'**

All other Member State courts must recognise the judgment of the court opening main proceedings (this is the court in the territory of the COMI of the relevant debtor. (Article 16(1)).

Courts in other Member States may not open main proceedings in relation to the same debtor i.e. there can only be one set of main proceedings in relation to a company or individual.

The rights of courts in other Member States to open any other form of insolvency proceeding are restricted. By Article 3(2) these (non-main) proceedings

▶ Can only be opened in another Member State if the debtor possesses an "establishment" within that territory

▶ An 'establishment' is defined as 'any place of operations where the debtor carries out a non-transitory economic activity with human means and goods'

▶ And the effect of those proceedings is restricted to the assets of the debtor situated in the territory in which the non-main proceedings are opened.

Where main proceedings have been opened any proceedings opened subsequently in another member state are termed 'secondary' proceedings. Secondary proceedings must be 'winding-up' proceedings, defined in annex B as a winding-up by the court, CVL or bankruptcy.

Proceedings which were opened prior to the opening of main proceedings in another member state are called 'territorial' proceedings in the Regulation. Territorial proceedings can only be opened if

▶ Opening of main proceedings in the jurisdiction of the debtors COMI is not possible under that jurisdictions' law or

▶ The territorial proceedings are opened at the request of a creditor who is domiciled, habitually resident or has its registered office in that jurisdiction or whose claim arises from the operation of that establishment (Article 3(4)).

By Article 18 'The liquidator appointed by a court which has jurisdiction' to open main proceedings may exercise all the powers conferred on him by the law of the state of the opening of proceedings.

▶ If a UK court opens main administration proceedings therefore the administrators powers are 'exportable' to other EU states where the debtor company has assets or interests.

▶ These powers would include the power to challenge voidable transactions and the power to enforce co-operation under Ss 234-237 of the Act.

Summary and self-test

Summary

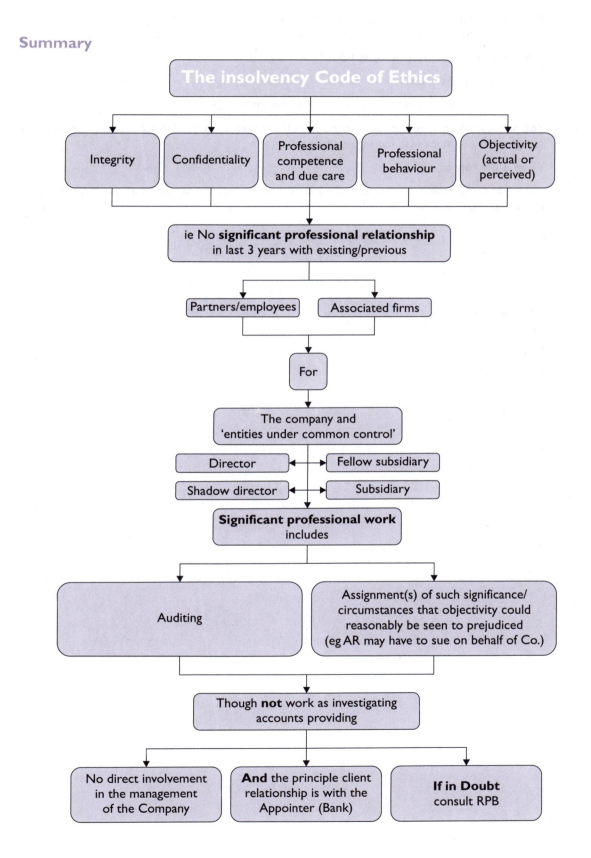

Self-test

Answer the following questions.

1   What are the five fundamental principles?

2   If you were asked to act as administrator of a company, what practical steps would you take to establish whether there were any ethical reasons why you should not accept the appointment?

3   What is a 'centre of main interests (COMI)' ?

4   What is an 'establishment'?

5   To what insolvency procedures do the EC Regulations not apply?

6   You have just been appointed administrator of Parry Stationers Ltd. How can you ensure that you comply with the money laundering regulations?

7   What is the role of a MLRO?

Now, go back to the Learning Objectives in the Introduction. If you are satisfied that you have achieved these objectives, please tick them off.

Answers to Self-test

1   – Integrity

        – Objectivity

        – Professional competence and due care

        – Confidentiality

        – Professional behaviour

2   Obtain company search (including for any associated or connected companies) to identify the directors of the company.

        Prepare group structure chart and identify directors and shareholders to check if conflicts exist.

        Ask the directors if they are aware of any involvement of my firm with them or the company.

        Do I have a personal connection with any of the directors of the company?

        Circulate partners, managers etc in my firm and ask them if they are aware of any previous professional involvement with the company or directors.

        Ensure that my firm has not acted as auditors of the company within the last three years.

        Check own practice management system/ client lists for details of any involvement.

        Ensure my firm has not acted as administrative receivers or LPA receivers of the company within the last three years.

        Consider the nature and impact of any advice given to the directors pre insolvency by my firm.

        Consult my professional body for advice.

        Ensure that I am duly qualified to act as administrator.

        Ensure that I hold the required general penalty bond.

3   **Centre of main interests**: this is the place of command or control, the place where the debtor conducts the administration of its business on a regular basis. This could be where the registered office is, but may not always be so.

4   **Establishment**: Any place of operations where the debtor carries out a non-transitory economic activity with human means and grounds.

5   Members' voluntary liquidation.

        Administrative receivership.

        Fixed charge receivership.

        S425 scheme of arrangement.

6   (i)   Obtain satisfactory evidence of the identity of the business and of any individual business who expresses an interest in purchasing the assets of the company in administration ie. Passport, photo driving licence, credit card bill, bank statement, utility bill;

                ▶   Evidence of major shareholders and directors, company search, latest accounts.

        (ii)   Ensure office:

                ▶   Has appointed a MLRO (money laundering reporting officer)
                ▶   Has procedures in place for reporting suspicious transactions
                ▶   Carries out staff training re money laundering issues
                ▶   Keeps records of checks made

(iii)   If become suspicious re any transaction, must report suspicions to the MLRO who will then make a suspicious activity report to SOCA. The transaction will be halted until permission is received from the SOCA (should receive within 7 working days or if no response after 7 days transaction may continue).

7   He is a nominated officer to whom principals and employees report suspicions of money laundering. He decides whether matters need reporting on to the SOCA.

Answers to interactive question

Interactive question: Biome Limited

The following practical steps should be taken relating to conflicts of interest:

- Circulate partners, managers etc in own firm to ask if any previous professional or personal involvement with the company or the directors (asking for nil returns as well)

- Check own practice management system/ client lists etc for details on any such involvement

- Check company search to see if your firm is auditor of the company (or has been during previous three years)

- Ask the directors if they are aware of any involvement of your firm with them or the company

- Consider the nature and impact of any advice that your firm has given to the directors pre-insolvency

- Make a file note evidencing that you have considered all the above factors and concluding that it is in order for you to accept the appointment

In relation to qualifications:

- Ensure that you have current authorisation to accept insolvency appointments
- Ensure that you have a self-certification borderau limit sufficient to bond the case
- If the limit is too low, contact the bond provider before accepting the appointment.

2

Statements of Insolvency Practice

> > > > > > > > > > > > > > >

Introduction

Learning objectives

Tick off

▶ Understand what a Statement of Insolvency Practice (SIP) is, who produces them and why they are important ☐

▶ Learn relevant SIP numbers and names ☐

▶ Understand what a Technical Release is ☐

▶ Understand what an Insolvency Guidance Paper (IGPs) is, who produces them and why they are important ☐

Working context

Due to the differing nature of insolvency appointments there is a need to co-ordinate and promote best practice amongst insolvency professionals. Statements of Insolvency Practice outline best practice and basic principles which must be followed by insolvency professionals. A good knowledge of the SIPs is therefore fundamental to ensure that all areas of your work are carried out with the appropriate levels of competence and skill.

Stop and think

Why do office holders need a uniform approach to practical issues relating to insolvency appointments? Why are there only 15 SIPs?

Examination context

It is unlikely in the exam that a question will appear testing your knowledge of a particular statement in its own right. However a good, detailed knowledge of the SIPs are required in order to pass the exam, for example, a question regarding CVA's would require a detailed knowledge of the content of SIP 3 and a question re director's disqualification will require a detailed knowledge of SIP 4.

Past exam questions to look at include:

2005	Question	1
2003	Question	2
2002	Question	4(d)
2001	Question	2(c), (d), (e)
2001	Question	3
2001	Question	4(d)
1998	Question	2

1 Statements of Insolvency Practice and Technical Releases

Section overview

▶ Statements of Insolvency Practice (SIPs) set out basic principles and essential procedures with which office holders are required to comply.

1.1 SIPs

Statements of Insolvency Practice (SIPs) are produced by R3 (the Association of Business Recovery Professionals). SIPs should be used as guidance only and should not be relied upon as definitive statements. The introduction to each SIP details who it is issued by and sets out the context in which it is to be used.

1.2 Technical Releases

SIP 5 and SIP 6 were withdrawn by the Society of Practitioners of Insolvency in August 1999 and replaced by Technical Releases. These apply in exactly the same way as the original SIPs.

2 List of SIPs

Section overview

▶ The following is a list of SIPs in force at January 2009. Where a detailed knowledge of the content of the SIP is required reference is made to the relevant chapter in this text.

2.1 Summary of SIPs

SIP	Name	Chapter
1	An administrative receiver's responsibility for the company's records	8
2	A liquidator's investigation into the affairs of an insolvent company	
3	Voluntary arrangements	13
4	Disqualification of directors	11
5	Non preferential claims by employees dismissed without proper notice by insolvent employers (replaced by Technical Release 5)	10
6	Treatment of director's claims as employees in insolvency administrations (replaced by Technical Release 6)	10
7	Preparation of insolvency office holder's receipts and payments	12
8	Summoning and holding meetings of creditors convened pursuant to s98 IA	
9	Remuneration of insolvency office holders	
10	Proxy forms	
11	The handling of funds in formal insolvency appointments	
12	Records of meetings in formal insolvency proceedings	13
13	Acquisition of assets of insolvent companies by directors	10

SIP	Name	Chapter
14	A receiver's responsibility to preferential creditors	8
15	Reporting and providing information on their functions to committees in formal insolvencies	11

3 Insolvency Guidance Papers

Section overview

▶ Insolvency Guidance Papers (IGPs) are developed and approved by the Joint Insolvency Committee and are issues to insolvency practitioners to provide guidance on matters that may require consideration in the conduct of insolvency work or in an insolvency practitioner practice.

▶ Unlike SIPs, which set out required practice, IGPs are purely guidance and practitioners may develop different approaches to the areas covered by the IGPs.

3.1 List of IGPs

The following IGPs have been issued to date:

▶ Control of cases
▶ Succession planning
▶ Bankruptcy – family homes

Appendix 1

Insolvency Guidance Paper – Control of cases

Introduction

Insolvency appointments are personal to an individual practitioner, who has an obligation to ensure that cases are properly controlled and administered at all times. However, issues can arise when an insolvency practitioner delegates work to others, or takes appointments jointly with other practitioners. In such circumstances, a practitioner's planning and administrative arrangements will need to consider how best to ensure that cases are properly controlled at all times, and that proper regard is paid to the interests of creditors and other affected parties.

Delegation

Given the wide variation in the size of firms dealing with insolvency work, each practitioner will have different case loads and resources and thus a different requirement to delegate work. Delegation can take on a number of forms, including

▶ Delegation of work to staff in the practitioner's own office or to sub-contractors

▶ Delegation of work to staff within a firm but in another location

▶ Taking a reduced role on an appointment taken jointly with an insolvency practitioner in the practitioner's office

▶ Taking a reduced role on an appointment taken jointly with an insolvency practitioner within the same firm but in another location

▶ Allowing a specialist insolvency practitioner within a firm to take responsibility for all work of a specific type

▶ Allowing a specialist within a firm to handle work of a specific type (eg tax)

▶ Sharing work on an agreed basis on an appointment taken jointly with a practitioner from another firm

▶ Employing another firm to give specialist advice (eg tax) or to undertake specific work (eg an investigation) and

▶ Allowing a practitioner in a former firm (following either the practitioner's move to another firm or retirement) to take responsibility for appointments for a short time pending the transfer of cases

For each of the above examples (and in other cases where delegation takes place) the practitioner must be satisfied at all times that work is being carried out in a proper and efficient manner, appropriate to the case.

Control

In determining the procedures to be put in place to ensure that an appropriate level of control can be established in relation to delegated work, it is recommended that a practitioner have regard to the following matters:

▶ The structure within a firm, and the qualifications and experience of staff

▶ The need for the practitioner to be involved in setting case strategy at the outset, depending on the nature, size and complexity of the case

▶ The procedures within a firm to ensure consultation by joint appointees, other practitioners and staff

▶ The extent to which levels of responsibility are defined, and the circumstances in which a reference to, or approval by, the practitioner is required

- ▸ Whether there are clear guidelines within a firm to deal with the administration of cases at locations remote from the practitioner

- ▸ The ways in which compliance and case progress are monitored, and then reported to the practitioner

- ▸ The frequency of case reviews, and who carries them out

- ▸ The systems for dealing with correspondence received and, in particular, complaints

- ▸ The process by which work is allocated on a joint appointment with a practitioner from another firm, the rationale for that split, and the controls to be put in place, subject always to statutory requirements and

- ▸ The way in which specialist advisers (including agents and solicitors) and sub-contractors are chosen and engaged, and how their work is monitored

Insolvency practitioners are aware that they may be required to justify their decisions and demonstrate that appropriate levels of control have been established. It is recommended that for firm wide procedures guidance is set out in writing, and that on a case by case basis contemporaneous working papers or file notes are prepared.

Appendix 2

Insolvency Guidance Paper – Succession planning

Introduction

Insolvency appointments are personal to an insolvency practitioner, who has an obligation to ensure that cases are properly managed at all times, and to have appropriate contingency arrangements in place to cover a change in the insolvency practitioner's circumstances. The over-riding principle is that the interests of creditors and other stakeholders should not be prejudiced.

Continuity

It is important for insolvency practitioners to consider on a regular basis the arrangements in place to ensure continuity in the event of death, incapacity to act, retirement from practice, or the practitioner otherwise retiring from a firm.

Sole practitioners

A sole practitioner should consider the steps necessary to put a workable continuity agreement in place, although there may well be considerations as to whether a sole practitioner's cases would be accepted by another insolvency practitioner. The full consequences, both practical and financial, of the relationship with another insolvency practitioner have to be recognised by both the office holder and the nominated successor, so that continuity can be achieved and the interests of creditors and other stakeholders safeguarded. In particular, the nominated successor would have to consider whether the obligations arising from a successor arrangement can be discharged properly and expeditiously, having regard to the number and nature of cases to be taken over.

A retiring office holder should normally make arrangements for the transfer of cases (including, where appropriate, an application to Court) in sufficient time to ensure that the cases are transferred before the retirement takes place.

The nominated successor may need to make an application to Court for the transfer of cases as soon as possible after the other office holder's death, incapacity or, if no other arrangements have been made, retirement.

The arrangements with the nominated successor will need to be reviewed as circumstances dictate, but preferably at least annually.

The principal matters that might routinely be dealt with in a continuity agreement are set out in the Appendix to this paper.

Firms

Every insolvency practitioner in a firm (whether a principal or employee) should consider the comments made above regarding sole practitioners, and should discuss with the firm the arrangements for succession planning, to cover death, incapacity to act, retirement, or leaving the firm. It is recommended that this is reflected in the partnership agreement or in a separate insolvency practice agreement.

In a firm with other insolvency practitioners, it is likely that the arrangements would include, at the least, an understanding that another insolvency practitioner will take over open cases, and make an application to court for the transfer of those cases, if the office holder is unable to do so. It will be the professional responsibility of the remaining partners (as insolvency practitioners) to take prompt action to safeguard the interests of creditors and other stakeholders.

When an office holder retires from a firm, it may be acceptable for the office holder to remain in office for a short period, with an insolvency practitioner in the firm dealing with the administration of cases. However, there the office holder needs to receive appropriate information on the progress of cases, and be consulted when decisions are to be made; the office holder is likely to require unrestricted access to case files. Such an arrangement, however, is unlikely to be appropriate other than for cases that are clearly in their closing stages. In normal circumstances, the retiring office holder should be replaced within a reasonable period, likely to be within 12 months of retirement.

Where there are no other insolvency practitioners in a firm, and in the absence of any contractual arrangements to deal with death, incapacity to act, or retirement, the remaining partners (presumably themselves members of professional bodies) should consider their own professional obligations to ensure the proper management of their practice, including making arrangements for another insolvency practitioner to step in as office holder. The firm may have to procure an application to court for the transfer of cases as soon as possible after the office holder's death, incapacity or retirement.

The principal matters that might routinely be dealt with in an insolvency practice agreement (or a partnership agreement) are set out in the Appendix to this paper.

Disputes

There can be disputes between firms and partners (and employees who are office holders) who leave the firm, principally arising from the personal nature of insolvency appointments. However, commercial disputes should not be allowed to obscure the over-riding principle set out at the beginning of this paper - that the interest of creditors and other stakeholders should not be prejudiced.

It is important therefore, that the contractual arrangements referred to above should provide for the (essentially) mechanistic and financial consequences of an office holder leaving the firm (or upon incapacity to act). There will be similar considerations when an office holder (either partner or employee) is suspended by a firm, or is otherwise excluded from the firm's offices.

Where there are no contractual arrangements, or where a dispute arises, both parties should consider their professional obligations, and the standard of conduct required by their professional bodies. Further, an office holder must have regard to the statutory obligations of the offices held.

If there is a dispute, it is for the office holder to decide how best to ensure that the obligations of office can be discharged; an application to court may be the only means of finding a solution. It is always open to an office holder to consult with his or her authorising body.

As noted above, there may be professional obligations on remaining partners to arrange for the proper management of their practice, and so ensure that they do not bring their own professional bodies into disrepute.

Appendix

Principal matters that might be dealt with in a continuity agreement

1   A clear statement of the circumstances upon which the agreement would become operative, and also the circumstances in which the nominated successor can decline to act.

2   The extent and frequency of disclosure to the nominated successor of case details and financial information.

3   Detailed provisions to provide for:

   ▸   The steps to be taken by the nominated successor when the agreement becomes operative
   ▸   Ownership of, or access to, case working papers
   ▸   Access to practice records
   ▸   Financial agreements

Principal matters that might be dealt with in an insolvency practice agreement (or in a partnership agreement)

1   Clear statements of what happens in the event of an insolvency practitioner (whether partner or employee)

   ▸   Dying, or being otherwise incapable of acting as an insolvency practitioner
   ▸   Retiring from practice
   ▸   Being suspended or otherwise excluded from the firm's offices or
   ▸   Leaving the firm

2   Where the agreement provides for another insolvency practitioner (whether in the firm or in another firm) to take over appointments

- The time within which transfers of cases will take place and the arrangements for the interim period, including provisions for access to information and files
- The obligations placed on the practitioner, the firm and the successor practitioner, both in the interim period and thereafter
- Professional indemnity insurance arrangements and
- Financial arrangements

3   Where the insolvency practitioner is to remain as office holder following retirement or leaving the firm

- Ownership of, or access to, case working papers
- Access to practice records
- Professional indemnity insurance arrangements and
- Financial arrangements

Self-test

Now answer the following questions.

1   You have just been appointed administrative receiver of Whole Foods Limited. To which SIP would you look to for guidance regarding your responsibility for the company's records?

2   What matters are dealt with by SIP 7?

3   What matters are dealt with by SIP 13?

4   As an administrator of a company, to which SIP would you look to for guidance on drawing your remuneration?

5   Which SIP deals with a receiver's responsibility to preferential creditors?

6   As an administrator, to which SIP would you look for guidance when reporting to a creditors' committee?

7   What matters are dealt with by SIP 10?

8   What matters are dealt with by SIP 11?

9   What matters are dealt with by SIP 12?

Now, go back to the Learning Objectives in the Introduction. If you are satisfied that you have achieved these objectives, please tick them off.

Answers to Self-test

1 SIP 1

2 Preparation of insolvency office holders' receipts and payments accounts

3 Acquisition of assets of insolvent companies by directors

4 SIP 9

5 SIP 14

6 SIP 15

7 Proxy forms

8 The handling of funds in formal insolvencies

9 Records of meetings in formal insolvencies

3

Introduction
to administration

➤ ➤ ➤ ➤ ➤ ➤ ➤ ➤ ➤ ➤ ➤ ➤ ➤ ➤ ➤ ➤

Contents

Introduction

Learning objectives

▶ Qualifications of an administrator ☐

▶ Purposes of administration ☐

▶ Who may initiate administration ☐

▶ How an administrator may be appointed and the procedures to be followed ☐

▶ Status, duties and powers of an administrator ☐

Working context

Since the introduction of new administration procedures on 15 September 2003 many more companies have entered into administration. It is likely therefore that in a work environment you will be asked to assist in an administration. It is important to understand how the process of administration works and the powers and duties of an administrator.

Stop and think

What is administration? How does it differ from liquidation? Why is the court involved? What are the duties and powers of an administrator, how do they differ from those of a liquidator?

Do differences between AR & Administrator

Examination context

Administration is a popular topic for the JIEB exam. You should ensure that you are familiar with the routes to place a company into administration and that you can state the powers, duties and status of the administrator.

Past exam questions to look at include:

2007	Question 3
2006	Question 4(a)
2005	Question 4(a) and (b)
2002	Question 3(a) and (b)
1998	Question 3
1992	Question 2(iv)
1990	Question 2(b)(i)

1 Introduction to administration

Section overview

▶ Administration orders were introduced into UK law by the Insolvency Act 1986. The Enterprise Act 2002 introduced new legislation into the Act for administrations initiated on or after 15.09.03. The new reforms were designed to make administrations the corporate recovery procedure of choice for floating charge holders. The legislation governing administrations can be found in Schedule B1 of the Act and Part 2 of the Rules (Insolvency (Amendment) Rules 2003). (For administrations prior to 15.09.03 the procedure can be found in ss8 to 27 IA 1986). The Sch B1 procedure may also be applied to both limited liability partnerships and also old style 1890 Act partnerships.

1.1 Advantages of administration

▶ Administrative receivership is generally not available to a floating chargeholder where the charge was created on or after 15.09.03, leaving administration as the 'single gateway' corporate recovery procedure.

▶ An administrator can be appointed post 15.09.03 merely by filing certain documentation with the court. This includes provision for filing out of court hours in cases of urgency by faxing documents to a designated fax number. Administration now shares many of the ease and speed of initiation advantages of administrative receivership.

▶ There may be less reputational risk in appointing an administrator in that the administrator acts for all the creditors and may be less linked in the (informed) public eye with the appointing bank than a receiver would be. This may be important where the chargeholder is seeking to avoid any perception of "pulling the plug" on a company in which there is significant local or public interest (e.g. a pensions provider or football club).

▶ Administrations are recognised under the EC Regulation whilst administrative receiverships are not. Where there are assets located in other EU jurisdictions and where the IP wishes to exercise his or her powers in those territories administration has the advantage that the regulation requires overseas courts to co-operate with the IP.

▶ Where there are multiple floating chargeholders it may be easier for the holder of the senior charge to appoint an administrator rather than for all the chargeholders to negotiate for a single AR to represent their collective interests.

▶ An administrator has the benefit of a moratorium an administrative receiver does not. In cases where the company depends on leased or HP equipment this will provide a useful breathing space in which the administrator can arrange for the continued financing of the various contracts.

▶ An administrator has the same powers to trade, manage and sell the business as a going concern as an administrative receiver. Where such a sale is likely and the chargeholders security covers the amount due, the chargeholder may be content to allow the directors to appoint an administrator.

▶ A chargeholder has no potential liability to indemnify an administrator. There may be such a liability where an AR has succeeded in negotiating an indemnity with the appointing debentureholder.

▶ An administrator can challenge antecedent transactions.

▶ There are many flexible exit routes out of administration.

▶ The introduction on 1 April 2008 of Reg 4(1) of The Non-Domestic Rating (Unoccupied Property) (England) Regulations 2008 reversed the decision in *Trident* regarding rates as an expense of administration and put rates in administration in the same position as liquidation.

1.2 Disadvantages of administration

- Corporation tax on a capital gain will be an expense of the administration.
- New tax period will commence which will prevent the bringing forward of tax losses to reduce any tax liabilities on a capital gain.
- Administrator's duty is to achieve one of the three para 3 Sch B1 IA purposes.
- Administrator's duty is owed to the court and to the creditors generally.
- There is an automatic termination of the administration after 12 months, unless it is extended by the creditors or the court.
- Administrator is required to seek approval to proposals from creditors.

1.3 Qualifications to act as administrator

Definition

Administrator: a person appointed under Schedule B1 to manage the affairs, business and property of a company (Sch B1 para 1(1)).

A person may be appointed as administrator of a company only if he is qualified to act as an Insolvency Practitioner (IP) in relation to the company (Sch B1 para 6). To be qualified to act as an IP the following must apply:

- Must be an individual
- Must be authorised to act by virtue of membership of a professional body recognised under the IP (Recognised Professional Bodies) Order 1986.
- Must hold relevant security (see 1.4 below)
- Must not be an undischarged bankrupt
- Cannot be subject to a disqualification order or undertaking under CDDA 86
- Cannot lack capacity to act as an IP within the meaning of the Mental Capacity Act 2005

An administrator is an officer of the court (whether or not he is appointed by the court) (para 5 Sch B1 IA).

1.4 Bonding

Administrators are required to hold security (Sch 2 IP Regs 2005). Office holders must have in force a bond in a form approved by the Secretary of State which:

(a) Contains provision whereby a surety or cautioner undertakes to be jointly and severally liable for losses in relation to the insolvent caused by:

    (i) The fraud or dishonesty of the IP whether acting alone or in collusion with one or more persons

    (ii) The fraud or dishonesty of any person committed with the connivance of the IP and,

(b) Otherwise conforms to the requirements of this Part.

    The administrator must hold:

    (i) A general penalty bond in the sum of £250,000, and

    (ii) A specific penalty bond. This should be equal at least to the value of the estate in the administration, as estimated by the IP as at the date of his appointment, but ignoring the value of any assets charged to a third party or held on trust. This is subject to a minimum specific penalty bond sum of £5,000 and a maximum of £5,000,000.

Interactive question 1: Bonding

A company enters administration with the following assets and liabilities:

	£
Fixed charge assets	65,000
Floating charge assets	120,000
Amount due to fixed charge holder	48,000
Amount due to floating charge holder	140,000
Amount due to preferential creditors	20,000
Amount due to unsecured creditors	195,000

Calculate the sum for which the administrator should bond.

See **Answer** at the end of this chapter.

2   Purpose of administration

Section overview

▶ The purposes of administration are set out in para 3(1) of Schedule B1 to the Act. The administrator must perform his functions as quickly and efficiently as is reasonably practicable (para 4 Sch B1 IA).

The administrator of a company must perform his functions with the objective of:

▶ Purpose (1)(a) "rescuing the company as a going concern". The administrator must perform his functions with this objective unless he thinks either:

    (a)   That it is not reasonably practicable to rescue the company as a going concern or

    (b)   That the objective in sub-paragraph (1)(b) would achieve a better result for the creditors as a whole.

▶ Purpose (1)(b) "achieving a better result for the company's creditors as a whole than would be likely if the company were wound up (without first being in administration)".

▶ Purpose (1)(c) "realising property in order to make a distribution to one or more secured or preferential creditors". This may only be pursued if:

    (a)   the administrator thinks that it is not reasonably practicable to achieve either objective (1)(a) or (1)(b) and

    (b)   he does not unnecessarily harm the interests of the creditors of the company as a whole".

The administrator must perform his functions in the interests of the company's creditors as a whole.

▶ Purpose para 3(1)(a) emphasises the rescue of the "company" i.e. of the legal person itself rather than the rescue of the "business" or "undertaking". It has been argued that it would have been more appropriate to focus on survival of the business as it is this which would result in saving jobs and minimising losses to creditors. The government counter-argument, however, was that it is the company to whom directors and employees owe their loyalty and therefore to maximise the "buy-in" of these key stakeholders it is essential to make survival of the company itself the administrator's primary goal.

▶ An administrator's sale of the assets and undertaking followed by a winding-up of the corporate shell that is left would not satisfy para 3(1)(a). However such a sale might well satisfy para 3(1)(b) and it should be noted that under para 3(3) an administrator is entitled to pursue objective 3(1)(b) if either rescue of the company is impossible or if para 3(1)(b) appears to promise a better outcome for creditors generally. Essentially an administrator is not forced to rescue the company if some other strategy is likely to be of more benefit to creditors.

▶ Achieving the approval of a CVA or the sanctioning of a s 425 IA Scheme are no longer statutory purposes of administration. However both procedures can still be used by the administrator as techniques to aid in achieving any of the three new objectives.

▶ Objective 3(1)(c) (realisation followed by distributions to secured/preferential creditors) may prove useful to administrators appointed by QFC holders, where there are insufficient assets to pay any sort of a dividend to unsecured creditors.

3   Routes into administration

Section overview

▶   A person may be appointed as administrator of a company:

–   By administration order of the court under para 10 Sch B1 IA

–   By the holder of a floating charge under para 14 Sch B1 IA

–   By the company or its directors under para 22 Sch B1 IA

Definition

Administration order: an order appointing a person to act as the administrator of a company (para 10 Sch B1 IA)

3.1   Application to the court

Application to the court for an administration order may be made by the following persons or by any combination of them (para 12(1) Sch B1 IA):

▶   The company

▶   The directors

▶   Justices chief executive for a magistrates court (this is in relation to enforcement of fines against a company)

▶   One or more creditors of the company

▶   The supervisor of a CVA (not mentioned in para 12(1) but see s7(4)(b) of the Act)

▶   A liquidator where the company is in voluntary or compulsory liquidation

▶   A qualifying floating chargeholder where the company is in compulsory winding-up (Para 8(3) and para 37). In voluntary winding-up the qualifying floating chargeholder will have an opportunity to appoint an administrator prior to the shareholders meeting (s84 (2A) IA).

The court will make an administration order in relation to a company if it is satisfied:

▶   The company is or is likely to become unable to pay its debts, and

▶   The administration order is reasonably likely to achieve the purpose of the administration.

Company may not already be in administration or in voluntary or compulsory liquidation.

However if the company is in compulsory liquidation, any QFC holder or the liquidator may still make an application for administration.

If the company is in voluntary liquidation, the liquidator may still make an application for administration. Notice that where the company is in voluntary liquidation only the liquidator (and not the QFC holder) is entitled to apply to the court for an administration order. This is because the QFC holder must by s84(2A) IA already have been notified of the proposed resolution to wind-up and has therefore already had an opportunity to appoint an administrator rather than allowing the company to go into liquidation.

Where the company is in liquidation and an application is made for an administration order the court has wide powers including:

- To discharge the winding-up
- To make modifications to the Schedule and to make consequential provisions
- To specify which Schedule B1 powers shall be exercisable by the administrator.

Where a company is in liquidation the affidavit in support of the administration application must detail (rule 2.11):

- Full details of the liquidation including name and address of the liquidator, date of appointment and by who appointed

- Reasons why it has subsequently been considered appropriate that an application should be made

- Other matters which would in the opinion of the applicant assist the court in considering the need to make provision in respect of matters arising in connection with the liquidation

- Plus the matters in rule 2.4(2) and (4) which have to appear in all other affidavits in support of administration applications.

It may seem strange that the directors would apply to the court for an administration order even though they have the power to appoint an administrator out of court.

Para 25 Schedule B provides that an administrator cannot be appointed out of court by the directors or the company where:

▸ A petition for winding up has been presented and has not yet been disposed of
▸ An application to court for an administration order has been made and has not yet been disposed of
▸ An administrative receiver of the company is in office.

In these situations the directors or the company will need to apply to court for administration. However, the court cannot make an administration order where an administrative receiver is in office unless:

▸ The appointing debentureholder consents, or

▸ The charge or charges would be voidable under ss238, 239 or 245 IA if an administration order were made. This is a judgment which must be made by the court hence the need for the directors to apply rather than relying on their para 22(1) Sch B1 IA power to appoint an Administrator out of court.

Creditors (other than qualifying floating chargeholders) may only put a company in administration by applying to the court.

Procedure for appointment by the court:

Application to the court for an administration order is made in Form 2.1B (rule 2.2(1)). Applications by the directors (stating that it is made under para 12) or a supervisor are treated as applications by the company (see rules 2.2 (4) and 2.3 (2). In all these cases the application must state the name of the company and its address for service (which in the absence of "special reasons to the contrary" will be the address of the registered office)

▸ Applications by more than one creditor are treated as an application by one creditor on behalf of the other applicants (rule 2.3(4)). Whether the application is by one or multiple creditors an address for service must be stated.

▸ Unless the applicant is a QFC holder, a statement of the applicant's belief that the company is or likely to become unable to pay it's debts must be made (rule 2.4(1))

The application must include a written statement, in Form 2.2B from the proposed administrator stating:

- ▸ That the IP consents to the appointment
- ▸ Details of any prior professional relationships
- ▸ IPs opinion that it is reasonably likely that the purpose of the administration will be achieved.

The application must be accompanied by an affidavit in support (r2.2(1)).

- ▸ Application by directors – one director or the company secretary swears on behalf of the board

- ▸ Application by the company – although the authority to apply derives from a resolution of the members, the affidavit will also be sworn by a director or company secretary acting on behalf of the company

- ▸ Application by the creditors – no restriction on who swears the affidavit providing that they are authorised to do so and that they swear to the means by which they have knowledge of the matters stated in the affidavit.

Content of affidavit (rule 2.4(2)):   *— how do creditors know?*

- ▸ A statement of the company's financial position, specifying (to the best of the applicant's knowledge and belief) the company's assets and liabilities, including contingent and prospective liabilities;

- ▸ Details of any security known or believed to be held by creditors of the company, and whether in any case the security is such as to confer power on the holder to appoint an administrative receiver or to appoint an administrator under para 14 Sch B1 IA. If an administrative receiver has been appointed, that fact shall be stated;

- ▸ Details of any insolvency proceedings in relation to the company including any petition that has been presented for the winding up of the company so far as within the immediate knowledge of the applicant;

- ▸ Where it is intended to appoint a number of persons as administrators, details of the matters set out in para 100(2) Sch B1 IA regarding the exercise of the function of the administrators; and

- ▸ Any other matters which, in the opinion of those intending to make the application for an administration order, will assist the court in deciding whether to make such an order, so far as lying within the knowledge or belief of the applicant.

The affidavit will also state whether the *EC Regulation* applies and if so whether the proceedings will be main (i.e. the Centre of Main Interests of the company is in the UK) or territorial (i.e. the COMI is in another member state.)

The application, administrator's statement and affidavit must be filed in court with sufficient copies for service. The court seals the copies, endorsing date and time of filing, fixes venue for the hearing endorsing this on the copy applications, and returns the documents to the applicant, whilst keeping one copy for the court file.

The application and supporting documents must now be served on:

- ▸ Any person who has appointed an AR (para 12(2)(a) Sch B1 IA), any AR (rule 2.6(3)(a)) and any person who is or may be entitled to appoint an AR (para 12(2)(b) Sch B1 IA) or administrator under para 14 (para 12(2)(c) Sch B1 IA)

- ▸ Any petitioner for winding-up and any provisional liquidator (rule 2.6(3)(b))

- ▸ The proposed administrator (rule 2.6(3)(d))

- ▸ Any supervisor of a CVA (rule 2.6(3)(f))

- ▸ If the application is by the creditors or a QFC holder, on the company (rule 2.6(3)(e))

- ▸ In addition notice of filing of the application must be given to any enforcement officer charged with execution and any person who has distrained against the company or its property (rule 2.7)

The applicant must file an affidavit of service in Form 2.3B confirming that the above rules have been complied with. Filing must be at least one day pre-hearing (r 2.9).

QFC holders, ARs, supervisors, the directors, the company, the applicant and the proposed administrator may all appear or be represented at the hearing. Assuming that the court makes an order the applicant will be sent 2 copy orders and sends one to the newly appointed administrator.

The court has wide powers and by para 13 Sch B1 IA can make any of the following orders:

▸ Make an administration order

▸ Dismiss the application

▸ Adjourn the hearing conditionally or unconditionally

▸ Make an interim order which can restrict the powers of the directors and confer a discretion on the part of the court or the IP

▸ Treat the application as a winding-up petition and make any s 125 IA order.

▸ Make any other order which the court thinks appropriate.

3.2   Out of court appointment by the holder of a qualifying floating charge (QFC)

Definition

Qualifying floating charge holder: A QFC is effectively the type of chargeholder who can appoint (or could have appointed) an administrative receiver.

The statutory definition is in Schedule B para 14(2) – "a floating charge…created by an instrument which"

▸ States that para 14 applies to it or

▸ Purports to empower the chargeholder to appoint an administrator or

▸ Purports to empower the floating chargeholder to make an appointment which would be the appointment of an AR

The debentures must be secured by (para 14(3) Sch B1 IA)

▸ A QFC or QFCs which relate to the whole or substantially the whole of the company's property or

▸ By charges and other forms of security which together relate to the whole or substantially the whole of the company's property and at least one which is a QFC.

There are a number of pre-conditions which must be met when applying out of court:

The floating charge on which the appointment relies must be enforceable. On normal principles this means that there has been default under the terms of the debenture. With an overdraft this will consist of:

▸ A valid demand for re-payment and a failure to re-pay
▸ The company being given time for the mechanics of repayment.

Notice there is no requirement for the company to be unable to pay its debts on a QFC holder filing for appointment of an administrator.

The company may not already be in administration (para 7 Sch B1 IA) – subject to provisions allowing for replacement administrators.

The company may not be in administrative receivership (para 17(b) Sch B1 IA).

No provisional liquidator appointed (para 17(a) Sch B1 IA).

The company is not in liquidation (voluntary or compulsory).

Procedure for a QFC to appoint an administrator:

► The QFC holder must give at least 2 business days written notice to any prior QFC holder. The idea is to always give the most senior floating chargeholder the opportunity to take the initiative and appoint their own choice of IP as administrator. (Para 15(1) Sch B1 IA)

    – Notice is in prescribed Form 2.5B.

    – A copy of Form 2.5B must at the same time be filed in court (R2.15(2)).

    – On usual principles a QFC holder is "prior" either because their floating charge was created first or because a deed of priority so provides.

    – Filing Form 2.5B in court triggers an interim moratorium which lasts until an administrator is appointed or for 5 business days if no administrator appointed (para 44(2) Sch B1 IA).

    – The prior QFC holder may now:

       ► Consent to the appointment of an administrator by the QFC holder who served notice on them. They can consent either by filling in the box on form 2.5B itself and returning it to the serving chargee or by giving consent in writing (see para (iii) below) which complies with rule 2.16(5).

       ► Do nothing in which case the serving QFC holder will be entitled to appoint an administrator at the expiry of the 2 business days. Para 96 Sch B1 IA gives the prior QFC holder the right to apply to the court later for replacement of the administrator with their own nominee.

       ► Take steps to appoint their own choice of administrator.

► Para 15(1)(a) and (b) make it clear that there is no need to give 2 business days notice in Form 2.5B if the QFC holder already has the written consent of the prior chargeholder.

► Written consents of prior QFC holders (other than those endorsed on the prescribed Form 2.5B itself) must comply with para 2.16(5) of the rules and must contain:

    – Name, address, registered office, registered number of the company

    – Details of the (prior QFC) holders charge including date of registration and where applicable any financial limit or deed of priority

    – Prior QFC holders name and address

    – Name and address of the QFC holder proposing to make the appointment

    – Date that notice of intention to appoint was given

    – Name of proposed administrator

    – Statement of consent to the proposed appointment

    – The consent should be signed and dated.

► The QFC files in court 3 copies of a notice of appointment in Form 2.6B (para 18(1)(a) Sch B1 IA). The notice of appointment must include a statutory declaration which must have been made not more than 5 business days before being filed in court (r2.16(3)). The content of the statutory declaration confirms (para 18(2) Sch B1 IA):

    – That the appointor of the administrator is a QFC holder

    – That each floating charge relied on in making the appointment is or was enforceable on the date of the appointment

    – That the appointment is compliant with Schedule B1.

► The notice of appointment must identify the administrator and must be accompanied by a (Form 2.2B) statement by the administrator:

    – That he consents to the appointment
    – That in his opinion the purpose of the administration is likely to be achieved.

▶ Form 2.5B (notice to prior QFC holder), Form 2.6B (notice of appointment) and Form 2.2B (administrators statement) must be accompanied by:

– Evidence that any prior QFC holder has consented (as explained above this could consist of the endorsement on Form 2.5B itself or a written statement containing the rule 2.16(5) details)

– If joint administrators are to be appointed a statement as to what functions can be conducted by any of them individually as opposed to functions which must be exercised jointly (rule 2.16(2)(c) and para 100(2) Sch B1 IA).

▶ The court will now seal the Form 2.6B notices of appointment and endorse date and time of filing (r2.17(1)). It will then issue two sealed copies to the appointor who will transmit one to the administrator (r2.17(2)).

Interactive question 2: Green Engineering Limited

Barwest Bank PLC hold fixed and floating charges over the property and assets of Green Engineering Limited. The company has been experiencing severe cash flow problems for a number of months and the directors have recently advised the bank that they are unable to meet the current repayment terms on their loans. The local bank manager, Mr Jones, is uncertain what to do and has approached you for some advice. The directors of the company have mentioned administration as a possible option but he is not sure exactly what this is or how it would affect the bank.

Requirement

Write a letter to the bank outlining:

(a) The advantages to the bank of appointing an administrator rather than an administrative receiver.
(b) The procedure to be followed by the bank in order to appoint an administrator.

See **Answer** at the end of this chapter.

3.3 Out of court appointment by the company or its directors

An administrator may not be appointed where:

▶ The company is already in administration (again subject to provisions re replacement administrators)

▶ The company is in liquidation (either voluntary or compulsory). However whilst liquidators may apply for an administration order, and QFC holders may so apply in the case of a compulsory winding up, the directors/company have no power to apply where a company is in liquidation of either kind

▶ An administrative receiver of the company is in office (para 25(c) Sch B1 IA).

Unlike QFC holders directors/the company may not appoint an administrator out of court where:

▶ The company has been in administration in the previous 12 months (see para 23 Sch B1 IA)

▶ A schedule A1 CVA small company moratorium was obtained in the previous 12 months and

– No CVA came into force or
– The CVA ended prematurely (see s7B)

▶ A petition for winding-up has been presented and is not yet disposed of

Note: In these three cases the directors/company retain their right to apply to the court for an administration order.

Procedure for appointment:

▶ The directors/company must give 5 business days written notice of their intention to appoint a named administrator (Form 2.8B) to the following:

- Para 26 Sch B1 IA – any person entitled to appoint an administrative receiver or an administrator under para 14 (i.e. any debentureholder with a QFC). The intention here is to give the debentureholder the opportunity to intervene at this stage and appoint their own choice of IP as administrator or to appoint an administrative receiver where the floating charge was created pre 15.09.03

Notice should also be given to the following:

- Any enforcement officer charged with execution or other legal process against the company (r2.20(2)(a))

- Any person who has distrained against the company or its directors (r 2.20(2)(b))

- Any supervisor of a CVA (r 2.20(2)(c))

- The company (assuming it is the directors and not the company which is proposing to make the appointment) (r 2.20(2)(d)).

▶ The directors/company file a copy of the notice of intention to appoint together with any documents accompanying it in court (para 27(1) Sch B1 IA). The notice of intention will include a statutory declaration (see next para). The documents to file are:

- Appointment by directors – a valid board resolution authorising appointment

- Appointment by company – an ordinary resolution in G.M. authorising named shareholders to appoint administrator

▶ The copy notice of intention to appoint must be accompanied by a statutory declaration (made not more than 5 business days pre-filing (r 2.21)) made by the directors/company. Contents (para 27(2) Sch B1 IA):

- Company is or is likely to become unable to pay its debts

- Company is not in liquidation

- Appointment is not prevented by paras 23 to 25 Sch B1 IA (i.e. existing administrator or administrative receiver in office, CVA moratorium or administration in previous 12 months, outstanding petition for winding up or application for administration)

- The R3 Technical Bulletin issue number 65 points out a problem arising from the wording of Form 2.8B. The form contains a statement that it has been sent to the persons set out in rule 2.20(2) (these are listed in para (i) above). However directors cannot swear that this is so in the attached statutory declaration because the notice has not been sent to those parties at the time of the completion of the declaration. The Insolvency Service have agreed that pending issue of a new Form 2.8B it is acceptable to amend it to read 'Note: A copy of this form will be given to all those persons to whom it is required to be given under Rule 2.20(2)'.

▶ The directors/company may not make an appointment:

- Until the 5 business days notice to QFC holders mentioned in para (i) above has expired and

- Not after 10 business days beginning with the day of filing of the notice of intention to appoint in court (para 28(2) Sch B1 IA)

- If there are no QFC holders entitled to appoint an AR or administrator, no notice of intention need be filed and the directors/company can go straight to the next stage.

▶ Directors/company now file 3 copies of a notice of appointment in court (para 29(1)(a) Sch B1 IA):

- Prescribed Form 2.9B must be used, unless no notice of intention was served in which case Form 2.10B is used (& includes the statutory declaration which normally accompanies the notice of intention to appoint)

- The notice must identify the Administrator

- The notice includes a statutory declaration by the appointor (made not more than 5 business days pre filing of notice by rule 2.24) stating that:

  ▶ Appointor is entitled to make a para 22 appointment

> ▸ Appointment is in accordance with Schedule B1
>
> ▸ So far as the appointor is able to ascertain the statements made and information given in the statutory declaration filed with the notice of intention to appoint remain accurate.

▸ Also filed with notice of appointment

- Administrator's statement in Form 2.2B (consents to appointment and purpose of administration likely to be achieved)

- Written consents of QFC holders unless the 5 business day notice period has expired

- A statement re joint administrator appointments

- Where no notice of intention to appoint filed, copy board resolution/G.M. resolution authorising the appointment of an administrator.

3.4 Effect of administration

The granting of an administration order will have the following effect:

▸ Any AR will vacate office.

▸ Receivers, other than ARs must vacate office if the administrator requires.

▸ No resolution may be passed for the winding up of the company.

▸ No order may be made for the winding up of the company.

▸ No steps may be taken to enforce security over the company's property except with the consent of the administrator or the permission of the court.

▸ No steps may be taken to repossess goods in the company's possession under a HP agreement, chattel leasing agreement or ROT agreement (see Chapter 10 for more details).

▸ Landlords may not exercise right of forfeiture by peaceable re-entry except with the consent of the administrator or with permission of the court.

▸ No legal process, including legal proceedings, distress and executions, may be instituted or continued with against the company without the consent of the administrator or permission of the court.

4 Status and duties of the administrator

Section overview

▸ The administrator is an officer of the court (whether or not he is appointed by the court). As an officer of the court he owes duties to both the court and to creditors generally and in particular he is required to act fairly and impartially in dealing with creditors. He must perform his functions as quickly and efficiently as is reasonably possible (para 4).

4.1 Duties of the administrator

The administrator must perform his functions with the three objectives listed in para 3(1) Sch B1 IA. The administrator must perform his functions in the interests of the creditors of the company as a whole (para 3(2) Sch B1 IA) although this duty is modified where objective 3(1)(c) is being pursued, which envisages only secured or preferential creditors being paid.

The administrator owes his duties to the company and to the general body of creditors and not to any individual creditor (*Oldham v Kyrris 2003*)

On appointment the administrator must take custody or control of all the property to which he thinks the company is entitled (para 67 Sch B1 IA).

The administrator must manage the affairs, business and property of the company in accordance with the proposals for achieving his para 3 objective (whether as originally approved or later revised).

The administrator must comply with any court directions.

The administrator must submit a D Return on the conduct of directors. (see chapter 11 for details)

4.2 Specific statutory duties of the administrator

1   To publicise his appointment:

To appoint an administrator out of court a QFC holder, or the directors must file three copies of a notice of appointment in court. The court seals these and endorses date and time of filing before returning two copy notices to the appointor who is in turn required to provide the administrator with one copy.

Administrator must now advertise his or her appointment as soon as reasonably practicable (para 46(2)(a) Sch B1 IA and rule 2.27(1)). The advertisement must be placed in the London Gazette and in such newspaper as the administrator thinks most appropriate for ensuring that the appointment comes to the notice of the company's creditors. The advertisement is in prescribed Form 2.11B.

Administrator must also give notice of appointment (prescribed Form 2.12B) as soon as reasonably practicable to:

▶   The company (para 46(2)(a) Sch B1 IA)

▶   (Having obtained a list of the company's creditors) the creditors of whose claim and address he is aware (para 46(3) Sch B1 IA)

▶   The petitioner under any pending winding-up petition, and any provisional liquidator.

▶   Any receiver or administrative receiver who has been appointed (r 2.27(2)(a))

▶   Any enforcement officer who to the administrator's knowledge is charged with execution or other legal process against the company (r 2.27(2)(c))

▶   Any person who to the administrator's knowledge has distrained against the company or its property (r 2.27(2)(d))

▶   Any supervisor of a CVA (r 2.27(2)(e))

Note: The court can relieve the administrator of the duty to give notice of appointment or give more time in all the above cases except that of notifying the company (see para 46(7) Sch B1 IA).

The administrator shall send notice of his appointment to the registrar of companies within 7 days

'7 days' and 'as soon as reasonably practicable' are calculated from when the administrator receives from the appointor the sealed copy of the notice of appointment. In cases where an application to court is necessary the date of the administration order is taken.

2   To require a Statement of Affairs (para 47 Sch B1 IA and rules 2.28 – 2.32)

(Para 47(1) Sch B1 IA) as soon as reasonably practicable the administrator shall by notice require one or more 'relevant persons' to provide a statement of affairs. Relevant persons are persons who are or have been officers of the company or those who in the previous year have been promoters or employees of the company or officers or employees of the company.

The relevant person(s) have 11 days in which to submit a statement although the administrator has power to extend this period even after its expiry or even to revoke the demand for a statement of affairs altogether. *When received file in Court + with Registrar*

Rule 2.30 gives the administrator the power to apply to the court for an order of limited disclosure in respect of the statement of affairs, on the grounds that disclosure would prejudice the conduct of the administration. The court can order that all or part of the statement 'shall not be filed with the registrar of companies'. Creditors may, on three days notice to the administrator, apply to court for an order of disclosure. Any such order may be subject to conditions regarding confidentiality. The administrator has a duty to apply to court for an order rescinding the original order wherever there is a change of circumstances such that the limit on disclosure is no longer necessary.

3   To make a statement setting out proposals for achieving the purpose of the Administration (para 49(1) Sch B1 IA)

The proposals must, where appropriate, explain why the administrator believes that the para 3(1)(a) or (b) objectives are not achievable (para 49(2)(b) Sch B1 IA).

Para 49 Sch B1 IA specifically provides that the proposals can propose a s425 IA Scheme or CVA.

Detailed contents of the proposals are set out in rule 2.33.

Para 73 Sch B1 IA provides that an administrators proposals may not have any negative impact on secured or preferential creditors unless they consent.

A copy of the proposals must be sent to the registrar of companies and to all creditors and members of whose address the administrator is aware:

▶   As soon as reasonably practicable

▶   In any event within 8 weeks from the date the company entered administration (administrator can apply to court for extension of time).

As an alternative to sending proposals to members the administrator can advertise in a newspaper, providing an address to which members can write for a copy of the proposals (para 49(6) Sch B1 IA and rule 2.33(7))

4   To call a meeting of creditors to consider the administrator's proposals (para 51 Sch B1 IA and rules 2.34 to 2.48)

(a)   **Convening the meeting**

This is referred to in the Act and rules as the 'initial creditors meeting'.

The administrator's proposals must be accompanied by an "invitation" to the initial creditors meeting (para 51(1) Sch B1 IA). Rule 2.35(2) provides that this invite should (as with all creditors meetings in administration) be in Form 2.20B. The notice specifies the purpose of the meeting, sets out requisite majority rules and contains a proxy form.

In three situations no initial meeting of creditors to approve proposals is required and therefore no notice in Form 2.20B need be included with the proposals sent to the creditors (see para 52 Sch B1 IA):

▶   Where proposals state that the company has sufficient property to enable each creditor to be paid in full

▶   Where proposals state that the company has insufficient property to enable a distribution to be made to unsecured creditors (except under prescribed part rules)

▶   Where neither of the objectives in para 3(1)(a) or (b) Sch B1 IA can be achieved. Remember this would leave only para (c) which envisages a distribution only to preferential or secured creditors – so that as in the previous paragraph – ordinary, unsecured creditors would effectively have no interest in the outcome of the administration.

Even in the three circumstances mentioned above, the creditors (10% by value) can requisition an initial meeting of creditors. The request for a creditors meeting must be made within 12 days of the date on which the administrator's proposals are sent out (rule 2.37). The requisitioned meeting itself must be held within 28 days of the administrator receiving the requisition. The costs of summoning and holding the meeting:

▶   Shall be paid by the creditor(s) requesting the meeting who must deposit with the administrator such sum as 'administrator may determine'

▶   The meeting, once held, can resolve that the costs are paid out of the assets of the company.

The initial meeting must be held as soon as reasonably practicable, in any event within ten weeks of the company going into Administration. Again the administrator can apply under para 107 Sch B1 IA for an extension of time.

14 days notice of the meeting is required. Those who should be notified are:

▶ All creditors known to the administrator and who had claims against the company at the date it entered administration. Any creditor who has subsequently been paid in full, does not, however, have to be notified

▶ Directors or officers (including past directors or officers) whose presence at the meeting is in the administrator's opinion required.

Notice of the meeting must be advertised in the same newspaper in which the administrator's appointment was advertised – plus other newspapers if the administrator thinks it appropriate.

(b) **Function of the meeting**

The function of the initial meeting is to approve the administrator's proposals, together with any modifications. The rules are:

▶ The administrator must consent to any proposed modification (para 53(1)(b) Sch B1 IA).

▶ The proposals, whether or not modified are approved by a simple majority in value of those present and voting in person or by proxy (r2.43(1)).

▶ However such a resolution will be invalid if those voting against include a simple majority of notified unconnected creditors.

▶ If the administrator's proposal includes the setting up of a CVA the 'initial meeting' can also perform the function of a s3 IA meeting to approve the CVA proposal but s3 IA approval requires over 75% by value to vote in favour.

▶ If a resolution approving the administrator's proposal is not passed, the chairman can adjourn the meeting, once, for up to 14 days. The administrator should then notify the creditors of the venue of the adjourned meeting as soon as reasonably practicable (rules 2.34(4) & 2.35(6) & (7)).

(c) **Voting**

There are detailed rules on entitlement to vote in rules 2.38 to 2.42.

The deadline for proofs and proxies is 12.00 noon on the business day preceding the day of the meeting, although the chair has a discretion to allow a creditor to vote where their failure to lodge a claim on time was 'due to circumstances beyond the creditors control'.

In quantifying a claim, the value at the date the company went into administration is taken less:

▶ Any set-off
▶ Any amounts paid to the creditor since that date

Secured creditors can only vote for the unsecured element of their claim. However in one situation they will be entitled to vote for the full value of their debt without deduction of the value of their security;

▶ Where the administrators proposals state that there is insufficient property to pay a dividend to unsecured creditors (other than under 'prescribed part rules')

▶ And creditors have requisitioned an 'initial meeting'

HP, chattel lease and conditional sale agreement creditors are entitled to vote for the amount due and payable to them at the date the company entered administration

A creditor shall not vote in respect of unliquidated or unascertained claims unless the chair agrees to put upon the debt an estimated minimum value for the purpose of entitlement to vote (rule 2.38(5)). The wording of this rule is as in the equivalent rules in liquidation and bankruptcy, and NOT as in VAs where a chair is now expressly entitled to value such claims at £1 (see for instance rule 1.17(3) on CVAs).

Where a chair is in doubt regarding validity:

▶ He may require the creditor to produce documents or evidence to substantiate the claim (rule 2.38(3))

▶ He should allow the creditor to vote marking the claim as 'objected to' (rule 2.39(3))

▶ The creditor can appeal against the chair's determination on validity or quantum but at an 'initial' meeting only has 14 days from the administrator's report on the meeting to do so.

(d) **Reporting the outcome of the meeting**

Para 53(2) Sch B1 IA requires the administrator to report the decision of the initial meeting, as soon as reasonably practicable, to:

▶ Every creditor who received notice of the meeting (rule 2.46(1))

▶ Any other person who received a copy of the original proposals (this might include the members)

▶ The court

▶ The registrar of companies

▶ Any creditors who did not receive notice of the meeting or of whose claim the administrator has become subsequently aware.

The report of the decision of the initial meeting referred to in para 53(2) Sch B1 IA is a Form 2.23B "notice of result" of the meeting. In the case of the court, registrar and any new creditors it must be accompanied by a copy of the proposals. *already has proposals*

If the administrator reports that his proposals have not been approved the court may:

▶ Provide that the administrator's appointment shall cease to have effect from a specified time

▶ Adjourn the hearing conditionally or unconditionally

▶ Make an interim order

▶ Make an order on a petition for winding up (these are "suspended" (see para 40(1)(b) Sch B1 IA) on appointments of administrators by QFC holders)

▶ Making any other order as the court thinks appropriate.

In order to streamline the procedure as much as possible para 58 Sch B1 IA and rule 2.48 provide for all meetings of creditors, including the initial meeting to take place by correspondence. The administrator will send notice in Form 2.25B to the same creditors entitled to notice of the meeting. Creditors must have at least 14 days to submit their votes although the administrator has a discretion to specify a longer period. At least one valid Form 2.25B must be received by the administrator:

▶ If no Form 2.25B received a meeting of creditors must be called

▶ If 10% or more by value require the administrator to call a meeting of creditors within 5 business days of receiving the Form 2.25B from the administrator – a meeting of creditors must be called

▶ The administrator may call a meeting of creditors where the 2.25B procedure results in rejection of his proposals.

5 IP Case Records

IP Regs 2005 require the administrator to maintain a record of the appointment. The form is prescribed in Schedule 3 of the Regs (See chapter 11 for more details).

6 Duty to account

R2.47 requires the administrator to send the requisite of his receipts and payments to:

- ▸ Court
- ▸ Registrar of Companies
- ▸ Creditors

Accounts should be submitted on Form 2.24B and sent, within one month of the expiration of 6 months from the date of appointment and every 6 month period and within one month of the administrator ceasing to act.

(See chapter 12 for details re preparation of receipts and payments accounts).

5 Powers of the administrator

Section overview

▸ The administrator has a general power to do anything necessary or expedient for the management of the affairs, business and property of the company (para 59(1) Sch B1 IA). He also has the same Schedule 1 powers as an administrative receiver ie. The administrator has statutory powers to manage and trade the business of the company.

5.1 Other general powers of the administrator

To remove a director of the company and to appoint a director to the board of the company (para 61 Sch B1 IA) (NB officers can only exercise management powers with the consent of the administrator)

To call a meeting of members or creditors

To apply to the court for directions

To make a distribution:

- ▸ To secured or preferential creditors
- ▸ With the courts permission, to an ordinary unsecured creditor.

To dispose of floating charge assets as if they were not subject to the charge. The chargeholder will have the same priority in respect of the 'acquired' property (usually the sale proceeds) as he had in respect of the property disposed of. 'Acquired' property means property directly or indirectly representing the property disposed of.

Para 71 Sch B1 IA applies to security other than floating charge security. The administrator is empowered to apply to the court for an order to enable him or her to dispose of the (fixed) charge property.

(i) The disposal must be likely to promote the purpose of the administration

(ii) And it must be a condition of the order that the chargeholder receives

- ▸ The net proceeds of sale

- ▸ Plus any additional money so as to produce the amount determined by the court as the net market value of the property.

The administrator has a similar power in para 72 Sch B1 IA to apply to the court for an order authorising disposal of "goods" under an "HP agreement". Para 111 Sch B1 IA defines "HP agreement" (as under the old legislation) as including a conditional sale, chattel leasing or ROT agreement.

An administrator has similar powers to bring actions against directors and others as a liquidator in that he or she can;

(i) challenge transactions at undervalue (s238 IA), preferences (s239 IA), extortionate credit transactions (s244 IA), and s245 IA floating charges (see Chapter 14 for more details). For ss.238, 239 and 245 IA 'relevant time' is calculated

- In appointments out of court, from the date of filing of notice of intention to appoint an administrator. In addition the period between filing of this notice and the appointment of the administrator is also a relevant time.

- In cases where an application to court for an administration order is made, the date of the application is taken. Again the period between the application and the order is also a relevant time.

(ii) Administrators may use ss234 – 237 IA to enforce compliance of directors and others.

(iii) Administrators are not empowered to bring actions under s212 IA (Misfeasance), s213 IA (Fraudulent Trading) s214 IA (Wrongful Trading) or s216 IA (Phoenix Companies) although these provisions will become available if a company in administration is subsequently liquidated.

An administrator has the power in s233 IA to require supplies from utility providers.

As agent of the company the administrator can bind the company to contracts with third parties.

Appendix

R2.33 content of administrator's proposals:

(a) Details of the court where the proceedings are and the relevant court reference number

(b) The full name, registered address, registered number and any other trading names of the company

(c) Details relating to his appointment as administrator, including the date of appointment and the person making the application or appointment and, where there are joint administrators, details of the matters set out in para 100(2) Sch B1 IA

(d) The names of the directors and secretary of the company and details of any shareholdings in the company they may have

(e) An account of the circumstances giving rise to the appointment of the administrator

(f) If a statement of the company's affairs has been submitted, a copy or summary of it, with the administrator's comments, if any

(g) If an order limiting disclosure of the statement of affairs has been made, a statement of this fact, as well as:

    (i) Details of who provided the statement of affairs
    (ii) The date of the order of limited disclosure
    (iii) The details or a summary of the details that are not subject to that order

(h) If a full statement of affairs is not provided, the names, addresses and debts of the creditors including details of any security held

(j) If no statement of affairs has been submitted, details of the financial position of the company at the latest practicable date, a list of the company's creditors including their names, addresses and details of their debts, including any security held, and an explanation as to why there is no statement of affairs

(k) The basis upon which it is proposed that the administrator's remuneration should be fixed

(l) To the best of the administrator's knowledge and belief:

    (i) An estimate of the value of the prescribed part and an estimate of the value of the company's net property

    (ii) Whether, and if so why, the administrator proposes to make an application to court under s176A(5) IA

(m) How it is envisaged the purpose of the administration will be achieved and how it is proposed that the administration will end

(n) Where the administrator has decided not to call a meeting of creditors, his reasons

(o) The manner in which the affairs and business of the company:

    (i) Have, since the date of the administrator's appointment, been managed and financed, including, where any assets have been disposed of, the reasons for such disposals and the terms upon which such disposals were made; and

    (ii) Will, if the administrator's proposals are approved, continue to be managed and financed

(p) Whether the EC Regulation applies and if so, whether the proceedings are main proceedings or territorial proceedings

(q) Such other information as the administrator thinks necessary to enable creditors to decide whether or not to vote for the adoption of the proposals

Summary and self-test

Summary

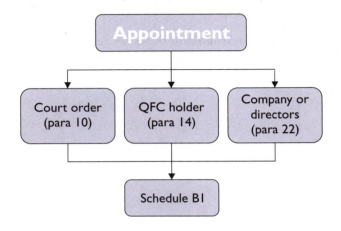

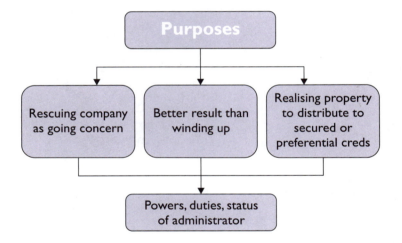

Self-test

Answer the following questions.

1 How many days notice must the directors give to a QFC holder of their intention to appoint an administrator?

2 What are the purposes for which an administration order may be sought under para 3(1) Schedule B1 of the Act?

3 The administrator has a number of statutory duties to comply with following his appointment. What are these?

4 Within what time period must the administrator send a copy of his proposals to the Registrar of Companies, creditors and members?

5 Within what period must the administrator hold a meeting of creditors to consider his proposals?

6 Where an administrator requests that an officer of a company submit a statement of affairs, within how many days must he comply?

7 Within how many days of his appointment must the administrator send notice to the Registrar of Companies?

8 What is the function of the initial meeting of creditors?

9 Outline the powers of an administrator.

Now, go back to the Learning Objectives in the Introduction. If you are satisfied that you have achieved these objectives, please tick them off.

What are the advantages + disadvantages of Administration

What are the routes into Administration?

Answers to Self-test

1   5 business days.

2   (a)   Rescuing the company as a going concern, or

       (b)   Achieving a better result for the company's creditors as a whole than would be likely if the company were wound up (without it first being in administration), or

       (c)   Realising property in order to make a distribution to one or more secured or preferential creditors

3   (i)   Advertise his appointment as soon as reasonably practicable in London Gazette and one other newspaper

       (ii)   Give notice of his appointment to:

- The company
- Creditors
- Any receiver or administrative receiver who has been appointed
- The petitioner under any pending winding-up petition
- Any Court Enforcement Officer who is charged with execution or other legal process against the company
- Any provisional liquidator
- Any person who has distrained against the company or its property
- Any supervisor of a CVA
- Registrar of companies

       (iii)   Obtain Statement of Affairs

       (iv)   Set out proposals for achieving the purpose of the administration

       (v)   Call a meeting of the company's creditors to consider his proposals

4   As soon as reasonably practicable and in any event, within 8 weeks from the date the company entered administration.

5   As soon as reasonably practicable and in any event, within 10 weeks of the company entering administration.

6   Within 11 days.

7   Within 7 days from the receipt of the notice of appointment from the appointor.

8   To approve the administrator's proposals, together with any modifications.

9
- To do anything necessary or expedient for the management of the affairs, business and property of the company (para 59(1) Sch B1 IA)
- Powers listed in Schedule 1 ie. To manage and trade the business of the company
- Remove a director of the company and appoint a director to the board of the company
- Call meetings of members or creditors
- Apply to court for directions
- Make a distribution to secured or preferential creditors and (with court permission) unsecured creditors
- Dispose of floating charge assets as though they are not subject to the charge

- Apply to court for an order authorising disposal of goods under an HP agreement
- Bring actions against directors and others under s238, 239, 244 and 245 IA
- Enforce compliance of directors and others under s234, 235, 236 and 237 IA
- Require supplies from utilities s233 IA
- Bind the company to contracts with 3rd parties

Answers to Interactive questions

Interactive question 1: Bonding

The administrator should bond for the value of assets which are available for the unsecured creditors ('unsecured' includes preferential creditors in this regard).

	£
Fixed charge assets	65,000
Less Fixed charge holder	(48,000)
	17,000
Floating charge assets	120,000
	137,000

The administrator should bond for £137,000.

Interactive question 2: Green Engineering Limited

Letter format

(Note: easy marks are available for presentation and layout. Ensure you follow any requirements of the question as regards presentation).

(a) Advantages of administration for the bank:

- If the banks floating charge was created after 15 September 2003, then administration is the only choice for the bank, they will be unable to appoint an administrative receiver.

- Quick and easy to appoint.

- Less reputational risk for the bank, administration is seen as a 'rescue' rather than 'pulling the plug'.

- Administrations are recognised under EC regulations.

- Benefit of a moratorium.

- Administrator has powers to trade and manage the business.

- No potential liability to indemnify the administrator.

- Bank will retain priority over charged assets sold. Fixed charge assets can only be sold with the bank's consent.

(b) Procedure to appoint administrator by QFC holder:

1   The bank must give at least two business days notice to any prior QFC holder in Form 2.5B.

2   A copy of Form 2.5B must be filed in court (this will trigger an interim moratorium).

3   Copies of a notice of appointment must be filed in court in Form 2.6B. The notice must include a statutory declaration (made not more than five working days before being filed in court) that:

- The appointor of the administrator is a QFC holder

- That each floating charge relied on in making the appointment is or was enforceable on the date of the appointment

- That the appointment is compliant with Schedule B1

4   The notice of appointment must identify the administrator and must be accompanied by a statement by the administrator on Form 2.2B:

- That he consents to the appointment

- That in his opinion the purpose of the administration is likely to be achieved.

5   Form 2.5B, Form 2.6B and Form 2.2B must be accompanied by:

▶   Evidence that any prior QFC holder has consented

▶   If joint administrators are to be appointed a statement as to what functions can be conducted by any of them individually as opposed to functions which must be exercised jointly.

6   The court will seal the Form 2.6B notices of appointment and endorse the date and time of filing. It will issue two sealed copies to the appointor, who will send one copy to the administrator.

7   The administrator must now advertise his appointment as soon as reasonably practicable.

Administrations

4

Conduct
of administration

⋗ ⋗ ⋗ ⋗ ⋗ ⋗ ⋗ ⋗ ⋗ ⋗ ⋗ ⋗ ⋗ ⋗ ⋗

Contents

Introduction

Learning objectives

▶ The effect of the moratorium ☐

▶ How to deal with creditors seeking leave to enforce security ☐

▶ Statutory returns to be submitted by the administrator and to whom ☐

▶ Administrators' duties re pension schemes ☐

▶ The process of making dividend payments to creditors ☐

Working context

In a work environment you may be asked to prepare a progress report for creditors, you may also be asked to assist in agreeing creditors' claims and making a dividend payment ensuring that all statutory matters have been complied with.

Stop and think

What is the purpose of the moratorium? Why should creditors be prevented from taking enforcement action? How do creditors receive a dividend in administration?

Examination context

The majority of topics covered in this chapter are not regularly tested in the JIEB exam however it is still important to know the effects of administration and how administrators deal with creditors seeking leave to enforce security.

Past exam questions to look at include:

2006   Question 4(b)

2002   Question 3(b)

1993   Question 2(a) and (b)

1991   Paper I Question 3

1 The moratorium

Section overview

▶ During the administration the moratorium prevents secured and other duress creditors from exercising their rights without the leave of the administrator or the court. The moratorium provides a breathing space within which the administrator can put together a strategy to take the company forward.

1.1 The interim moratorium (para 44 Sch B1 IA)

An 'interim moratorium' applies in three situations

▶ Where there has been an application to the court (para 10 Sch B1 IA) but the application has not yet been granted or dismissed, or it has been granted but has not yet 'taken effect'. By para 13(2) Sch B1 IA an administration order takes effect at a time appointed in the order (and in default at the time of making of the order itself).

▶ Where a QFC holder has filed notice of intention to appoint, (Form 2.5B) an interim moratorium will come into effect and will last until the earlier of the expiry of 5 business days or the appointment of an administrator.

▶ Where the directors/company have applied for an administration order (Para 22 Sch B1 IA) an interim order will come into effect and will last until the earlier of the expiry of 10 business days or the appointment of the administrator.

The terms of the interim moratorium are set out in paras 42 and 43 Sch B1 IA and are the same as the terms that apply once a company is in administration.

The interim moratorium does not prevent

▶ The presentation of a winding-up petition by the Financial Services Authority or by the Secretary of State on public interest grounds.

▶ The appointment of an administrative receiver. If an AR is appointed he or she can carry out their functions in the usual way, including realising the charged assets. The interim moratorium will not come into effect unless and until the appointer consents to the AR stepping down.

1.2 The paragraph 42 and 43 Sch B1 IA moratorium

This applies where administration takes effect.

1   Impact on administrative receivership (AR):

▶ Any AR vacates office (remember this will be either because the appointer consents or because the court finds that the charge or charges on which the appointment depends are potentially voidable under ss.238, 239 or 245 IA.)

▶ ARs "remuneration" is charged on and paid out of any property of the company which was in his custody or control immediately before vacation of office, in priority to the appointor.

▶ "Remuneration" includes expenses properly incurred as well as the ARs indemnity out of company assets (in relation to contracts entered into and adopted employment contracts).

Receivers other than ARs must vacate office if the administrator requires. Even if the receiver is allowed to remain in office he will be unable to enforce the appointer's security without the consent of the administrator or the permission of the court.

2   Impact on winding-up:

▶ No resolution may be passed for winding up the company.

▸ No order may be made for the winding up of the company. This does not apply to orders made on public interest or FSA petitions. If such a petition is presented the administrator should apply to the court for directions.

3 Impact on creditors with proprietary rights (all subject to consent of administrator or permission of the court)

▸ No step may be taken to enforce security.

▸ No step may be taken to repossess goods in the company's possession under an HP agreement. By para 111(1) Sch B1 IA this includes a conditional sale agreement, a chattel leasing agreement and a retention of title agreement.

▸ Landlords may not exercise a right of forfeiture by peaceable re-entry.

4 No legal process including legal proceedings and executions may be instituted or continued against the company without consent of the administrator or permission of the court.

1.3 Applications by creditors for leave to enforce security

Creditors with proprietary rights may only take steps to enforce their security with the consent of the administrator or the court. *Re Atlantic Computers* provides guidelines for administrators to follow when dealing with applications by creditors for leave to enforce security.

The administrator is an officer of the court, when a creditor applies to him for leave he should:

▸ Act speedily (if necessary making an interim decision – e.g. retaining the goods/machinery etc. but meeting current payments as an expense of administration)

▸ Act 'responsibly'

▸ Not use moratorium as a bargaining counter

▸ Give succinct reasons for his decision

The Court will not adjudicate on disputes on the existence or validity of security … unless it is a short issue of law which it is convenient to decide.

▸ The onus is on the applicant for leave to make out their case.
▸ The court considers all relevant matters including the conduct of the parties.
▸ The court has a broad discretion unfettered by rules of rigid application.

If granting leave was unlikely to impede the achievement of the s 8(3) IA purpose – leave should normally be granted (more likely to now be para 3(1) Sch B IA purpose).

If granting leave will impede the court must carry out a 'balancing exercise':

▸ Court/administrator must balance the legitimate interests of the applicant against the interests of the creditors generally.

▸ Great importance is attached to the proprietary interests of the applicant:

– Administration for the benefit of unsecured creditors should not be conducted at the expense of those who have proprietary rights.

– The purpose of the power to give leave is to enable the court to relax the moratorium where it would be inequitable for the prohibition to apply.

Therefore if significant loss would be caused by refusal leave will normally be granted.

▸ If substantially greater loss would be caused to others by granting leave which is out of all proportion to the loss to the applicant – leave may be refused.

▸ In assessing losses the court will look at the financial position of the company and specifically its capacity to pay on-going interest or rental payments under the agreement.

> A likely compromise is for the administrator to retain the goods equipment etc. but subject to the condition that rental and other payments during the period for which the order is in force are paid as an expense of the administration.

Interactive question 1: Farm Feeds Limited

You were appointed administrator of Farm Feeds Limited on 2 March 2009 by Northern Bank PLC the holders of a qualifying floating charge. The company operates from freehold premises in Bolton importing and supplying animal feeds throughout the UK.

The purpose of the administration is to rescue the company as a going concern and to this end you have decided to continue trading the company until a sale as a going concern can be achieved. A number of parties have expressed an interest in the company however to date no firm offers have been received.

You have been notified by JD Leasing Limited that the company's entire computer system is leased and that the agreement is currently 3 months in arrears. They intend to remove the computer system next week if the arrears are not immediately settled in full. The directors advise you that the company would be unable to continue trading if the computer system was removed as it is automatically linked into the warehouse operated by the company in Oxford from where all orders are dispatched.

Requirement

State what action you would take, as administrator, in response to the leasing company's demands.

See **Answer** at the end of this chapter.

2 Statutory returns

Section overview

> The administrator is required under r2.47 to submit accounts of his dealings in the administration.

The administrator must send a progress report, attached to Form 2.24B, within one month of the end of each period to:

(i) The creditors
(ii) The court
(iii) The Registrar of Companies

The progress report shall cover the period of 6 months commencing on the date that the company entered administration and every subsequent period of 6 months.

The report should include the following details:

(i) The court and court reference number
(ii) The company's name, address of registered office and registered number
(iii) The administrator's name and address, date of appointment, name and address of appointor
(iv) Details of any extensions to the initial period of appointment
(v) Details of progress during the period of the report, including a receipts and payments account
(vi) Details of any assets that remain to be realised
(vii) Any other relevant information to the creditors.

The receipts and payments account shall state what assets of the company have been realised, for what value, and what payments have been made to creditors or others.

3 Taxation

Section overview

▶ The administrator should be aware of the tax implications of trading and selling assets during the administration.

Where an administrator causes the company to sell its assets or trade, the corporation tax consequences will be an expense of the administration r2.67(1)(J).

If assets are sold prior to administration the tax liability will rank as an ordinary unsecured liability of the company in a subsequent administration.

Administration begins a new tax period so that earlier losses cannot be carried forward to set against a capital gain incurred.

Corporation tax will be payable as an expense of the administration in priority to the administrator's own remuneration.

Interest earned on cash balances in the administration will be taxable as an expense of the administration.

4 Distribution to creditors

Section overview

▶ Schedule B1 para 65 now provides the administrator with an express power to make distributions.

No sanction of the court is needed if the payment is to a secured or preferential creditor, however sanction of the court is required if the payment is to ordinary unsecured creditors. Para 65 Sch B1 IA expressly states that s 175 of the Act applies to an administrator's distributions. In other words, as in winding-up the preferential creditors will take priority to the holders of floating charges.

The rules relating to distributions to creditors by an administrator are found in Chapter 10, r2.68 – r2.105.

There are many circumstances other than the making of distributions (which carries the same connotations as paying a dividend) where an administrator is entitled to make payments.

▶ Under Schedule 1 IA para 13 an administrator is empowered to make any payment which is necessary or incidental to the performance of his functions and under para 65 of Schedule B1 itself can make a payment other than a distribution or under para 13 if he thinks it likely to assist the achievement of the purpose of the administration.

▶ An administrator will usually continue to trade the business and in doing so will cause the company to pay employees and suppliers in the usual way. On vacating office any liabilities on contracts entered into by the administrator or for wages or salary for the period of the administration (after the first 14 days) must be paid by the administrator in priority both to his or her own remuneration and to any floating chargees.

▶ Where an administrator realises fixed charge or HP assets with sanction of the court it will be a condition of the court order that he pays the chargee the higher of the sale proceeds or the market value of the assets.

4.1 Proofs of debt

A person wishing to be a creditor of the company and recover his debt in whole or in part must submit his claim in writing to the administrator.

Definition

Proof: a document by which a creditor seeks to establish his claim

Proving: a creditor who claims is referred to as 'proving'

The proof must be signed by the creditor, or a person authorised by him and must contain the following information (r2.72(3)):

(i) The creditor's name and address

(ii) The total amount of his claim as at the date on which the company entered administration, less any payments that have been made to him after that date in respect of his claim and any adjustment by way of set off in accordance with r2.85

(iii) Whether or not the claim includes outstanding uncapitalised interest

(iv) Whether or not the claim includes value added tax

(v) Whether the whole or any part of the debt falls within any, and if so, which categories of preferential debts under s386 IA

(vi) Particulars of how and when the debt was incurred by the company

(vii) Particulars of any security held, the date on which it was given and the value which the creditor puts on it

(viii) Details of any reservation of title in respect of goods to which the debt refers

(ix) The name, address and authority of the person signing the proof (if other than the creditor himself)

The proof should specify details of any documents by which the proof can be substantiated. The administrator may call for any document or other evidence to be produced to him where he thinks it necessary for the purpose of substantiating the whole or any part of the claim.

The administrator can require a claim to be verified by affidavit in Form 2.29B (r2.73(1)).

The following people can inspect the proofs lodged with the administrator on any business day:

▸ Any creditor who has submitted a proof of debt which has not been wholly rejected for the purposes of dividend or otherwise

▸ Any contributory of the company

▸ Any person acting on behalf of either of the above

4.2 Admission/ rejection of proofs

It is for the administrator to admit or reject a creditor's claim. A proof may be admitted for dividend either for the whole amount claimed by the creditor or for part of that amount. The administrator must deal with all claims within 7 days of the last date for proving.

If the administrator rejects a proof in whole or in part, he must send to the creditor a written statement of his reasons for doing so. If the creditor is dissatisfied with the administrator's decision he may apply to court, within 21 days of his receiving the statement, for the decision to be reversed or varied.

Any other creditor may, if dissatisfied with the administrator's decision admitting or rejecting the whole or any part of a proof, make such an application within 21 days of becoming aware of the administrator's decision.

A creditor's proof may, at any time, by agreement between himself and the administrator, be withdrawn or varied as to the amount claimed.

4.3   Treatment of special cases

1   **Debt payable at a future time:**

For the purpose of dividend only the amount of the creditor's claim must be reduced by applying the following formula (r2.105):

$$\frac{x}{1.05^n}$$

Where   x is the value of the admitted proof

n is the period beginning with the relevant date and ending with the date on which payment of the debt would otherwise be due in years and months in a decimalised form.

2   **Discounts:**

All trade and other discounts should be deducted from the claim except for any discount for immediate, early or cash settlement.

3   **Secured creditors:**

A secured creditor can prove for any balance after deducting any amounts realised for the security.

4   **Mutual credit and set-off:**

An account should be taken as at the date of the notice of what is due from each party to the other in respect of mutual dealings, any balance of the account owed to the creditor may be proved for in the administration.

5   **Debt in foreign currency:**

The amount of the debt must be converted into sterling at the official exchange rate on the date when the company entered administration.

6   **Payments of a periodical nature:**

In the case of rent and other payments of a periodical nature, the creditor may prove for any amounts due and unpaid up to the date when the company entered administration.

7   **Interest:**

Interest is provable as part of a debt up to the date the company entered administration. Post administration interest is not provable.

4.4   Notice of proposed distribution

The administrator must give 28 days' notice to creditors of his intention to declare and distribute a dividend.

The notice must be sent to all creditors whose addresses are known to the administrator and must state:

▸   Whether the dividend is to preferential creditors or preferential and unsecured creditors

▸   Where the dividend is to unsecured creditors, the value of the prescribed part.

▸   That the dividend will be made within 2 months from the last date for proving

▸   Whether the dividend is interim or final

▸   Specify a date up to which proofs may be lodged, being not less than 21 days from the date of the notice.

The notice must also be given by public advertisement.

4.5 Declaration of dividend

Within the 2 month period referred to in the notice the administrator must proceed to declare the dividend. He must give notice to all creditors who have proved their debts (r2.98).

The notice must include the following details:

▶ Amounts raised from the sale of assets indicating (so far as practicable) amounts raised by the sale of particular assets

▶ Payments made by the administrator

▶ Where the dividend is to unsecured creditors, the value of the prescribed part

▶ Provision (if any) made for unsettled claims and funds retained for particular purposes

▶ The total amount of the dividend and the rate of dividend

▶ How he proposes to distribute the dividend

▶ Whether, and if so when, any further dividend is expected to be declared

Payment of the dividend may be distributed simultaneously with the notice declaring it.

4.6 Notice of no dividend, or no further dividend

If the administrator gives notice that he is unable to declare a dividend or any further dividend, the notice shall contain a statement that no funds have been realised or that the funds realised have already been distributed or used or allocated for defraying the expenses of the administration (r2.100).

4.7 Proof offered after payment of dividend

If, after the dividend has been paid, the creditor increase the amount claimed in his proof, he is not entitled to disturb the distribution of the dividend. He is however entitled to be paid, out of any money for the time being available for the payment of further dividend, any dividend or dividends which he has failed to receive.

If, after a creditor's proof has been admitted, the proof is withdrawn or expunged, or the amount is reduced, the creditor is liable to repay to the administrator any amount overpaid by way of dividend (r 2.101).

Interactive question 2: Bean & Sons Limited

You were appointed administrator of Bean & Sons Limited eight months ago. The following claims have been received:

1 Plymouth Trading Limited has submitted a claim in the sum of £4,780. The usual trading terms allow for a prompt payment discount of 10% and a regular customer discount of 5%. The claim submitted has not been discounted.

2 Barby Bank PLC hold a fixed charge over the company's retail premises to secure an outstanding debt. Since the bank's claim was submitted in the sum of £186,000 the premises have been sold and the sum of £112,000 paid to the bank.

3 Paris Designs Limited has submitted a claim in the sum of 498 euro. Exchange rate details are as follows:

Date debt incurred	£1:1.49 euro
Date of administration	£1:1.64 euro
Today's date	£1:1.87 euro

4 Foale Industries Limited has submitted a claim in the sum of £14,890. The claim includes interest of which £486 represents interest claimed for the period from the date the company entered administration to the date the claim was submitted.

5   K Etherton Limited submitted a claim in the sum of £8,790 in respect of supplies made. The company successfully recovered stock valued at £2,600 under a ROT agreement. No adjustment has been made to their claim.

6   The company's landlord, JB Properties Limited has submitted the following claim:

	£
Dilapidations	13,780
Rent arrears	28,000
Rent to end of lease	119,000

You are aware that the landlord has re-let the premises and the property was actually only empty for a period of two months. The monthly rental cost of the property is £7,000.

7   The company regularly traded with its wholly owned subsidiary supplying stocks of raw materials and purchasing finished goods back. At the date of administration the subsidiary, Bean Limited, was showing as a debtor in the sum of £13,780 and a creditor in the sum of £29,400.

Requirement

Adjudicate on the claims received to date giving full reasons for your treatment of each claim.

See **Answer** at the end of this chapter.

5 Creditors' committee

The creditors may establish a committee, of at least three and not more than five, creditors at the para 51 Sch B1 IA meeting, to exercise the functions conferred upon it by or under the Act. The rules relating to the committee may be found in r 2.50 – r 2.65 and are substantially the same as the rules governing committees in liquidation and administrative receivership.

See Chapter 11, section 3 for more details.

Summary and self-test

Summary

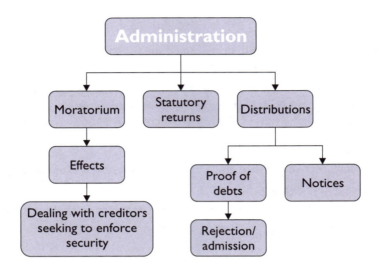

Self-test

Answer the following questions.

1   Where a qualifying floating charge holder files notice of intention to appoint an interim moratorium comes into effect. For how long will this moratorium last?

2   How long will the interim moratorium last if the administrator is appointed out of court by the company or the directors?

3   What is the effect of the moratorium on a creditor with a valid ROT claim?

4   How often should the administrator send a progress report to creditors?

5   The administrator sells property of the company which gives rise to a taxable charge. How should this tax liability be treated by the administrator?

6   How would the tax position differ if the asset had been sold prior to the administrator's appointment?

7   Within how many days of the last date for proving must the administrator deal with claims received?

8   How many days notice must be given to creditors of the administrator's intention to declare and distribute a dividend?

9   What matters must be stated in the notice of intention to declare a dividend?

10   What matters must be stated in the notice of declaration of dividend under r2.98?

Now, go back to the Learning Objectives in the Introduction. If you are satisfied that you have achieved these objectives, please tick them off.

How often must a statutory return be made, to whom, + what are the contents?

What information must a proof of debt contain?

LEARNING MEDIA

Answers to self-test

1   It will last until the earlier of the expiry of five business days or the appointment of the administrator.

2   Until the earlier of the expiry of ten business days or the appointment of the administrator.

3   The creditor will be unable to take steps to recover goods supplied under the ROT agreement without the agreement of the administrator or the court. However, the administrator is also unable to use the goods subject to a valid ROT agreement without the consent of the supplier or if he applies to the court under para 71 Sch B1 IA for an order enabling him to dispose of the goods as though they were not subject to the ROT claim.

       The disposal must be likely to promote the purpose of the administration and the supplier must receive the net proceeds of sale/market value for the goods.

4   Within one month of the end of the first period of six months since the company entered into administration and every subsequent period of six months.

5   The administrator will have to pay the tax arising as an expense of the administration r2.67(1)(j). Under para 99 Sch B1 IA the corporation tax will be payable in priority to the administrator's own remuneration.

6   The tax liability would rank as an ordinary unsecured liability of the company.

7   Within seven days.

8   28 days' notice.

9   Whether the dividend is to preferential creditors or to preferential and unsecured creditors.

       Where the dividend is to unsecured creditors, the value of the prescribed part.

       That the dividend will be made within two months from the last date for proving.

       Whether the dividend is interim or final.

       A date up to which proofs may be lodged (not less than 21 days from the date of the notice).

10   Amounts raised from the sale of assets indicating amounts raised from the sale of particular assets.

       Payments made by the administrator.

       Value of the prescribed part (where the dividend is to unsecured creditors).

       Provision for unsettled claims and funds retained for particular purposes.

       Total amount and rate of dividend.

       How the dividend is proposed to be distributed.

       Whether and if so when, any further dividend is expected to be declared.

Answers to interactive questions

Interactive question 1: Farm Feeds Limited

Moratorium is in place so no steps can be taken by the leasing company to repossess the computers without the consent of the administrator or permission of the court.

The administrator should advise the leasing company of this fact and request a copy of the lease and full details of amounts outstanding.

The administrator should seek to negotiate with the leasing company for use of the computer system during the administration. Advise them that ongoing rentals will be paid as an expense of the administration (do not agree to pay arrears). Advise them that the administrator is seeking a buyer for the business which would provide longer term security. It is therefore in the interests of the lease company to allow continued use of the system. The second hand value of the computers is likely to be low.

It is for the lease company to make out the case for giving leave to repossess the equipment. If granting leave was unlikely to impede the purpose of the administration then leave should normally be given.

However, in this case, the purpose of the administration is to rescue the company as a going concern. It would appear that repossession of the computer system would impede this as trade would have to cease.

The court would balance the interests of the leasing company and the interests of other creditors.

It would normally be sufficient grounds to grant leave if a significant loss would be caused to the lease company by refusal. However, if the administrator pays current rentals, the loss to the lease company is likely to be small.

The court will have regard to the conduct of the parties and whether the administrator has dealt with the leasing company in a timely manner. The administrator should:

▶   Act speedily
▶   Act responsibly
▶   Not use the moratorium as a bargaining tool
▶   Give succinct reasons for his decision

It is likely that as long as the administrator continues to pay current rentals, he will be able to continue using the computer system and achieve a sale as a going concern.

Interactive question 2: Bean & Sons Limited

1   **Plymouth Trading Limited £4,780**

    All usual discounts should be applied but not a prompt payment discount.

    Admit claim £4,541.

    (£4,780 less regular customer discount of 5%).

2   **Barby Bank PLC £186,000**

    The bank can claim for any balance of its debt after deducting amounts realised for the security.

    Admit claim £74,000.

    (£186,000 less sale proceeds £112,000).

3   **Paris Designs Limited 498 euro**

    Foreign debts must be converted into sterling at the official exchange rate on the date the company entered into administration.

    Admit claim £304.

    (498 euro @ £1:1.64 euro).

4 **Foale Industries Limited £14,890**

Interest may only be claimed up to the date the company entered administration.

Admit claim £14,404.

(£14,890 less post administration interest of £486).

5 **K Etherton Limited £8,790**

Need to adjust claim for amounts received under ROT agreement.

Admit claim £6,190.

(£8,790 less stock received £2,600).

6 **JB Properties Limited £160,780**

The landlord may claim rent arrears in full. Future rent may also be claimed however the landlord has a duty to mitigate his claim ie. By re-letting the property. Dilapidations may be claimed under the terms of the lease.

Admit claim:

	£
Rent arrears	28,000
Dilapidations	13,780
Future rent	14,000
(2 months' rent re empty property)	
Total claim	55,780

7 **Bean Limited £29,400**

Where there has been mutual dealings with another company, an account should be taken of what is owed to and by each company and only the balance claimed for in the administration.

Admit claim £15,620.

(£29,400 - £13,780 = £15,620).

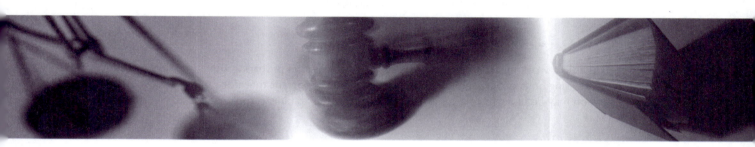

5

Ending administrations

➤ ➤ ➤ ➤ ➤ ➤ ➤ ➤ ➤ ➤ ➤ ➤ ➤ ➤ ➤

Contents

Introduction

Learning objectives

▶ Learn the various options available to exit administration ☐

▶ Understand how an administrator may vacate office and obtain his release ☐

▶ Learn the duties of the administrator when vacating office ☐

Working context

It is likely that in a work environment you may be asked to assist in preparing administration cases for closure or advising on appropriate exit routes available. It is important therefore to know how an administration may be brought to a close and the duties of the administrator on closure.

Stop and think

Why is there more than one way to exit an administration? How can an administrator vacate office? How can he be replaced if the administration has not yet ended?

Examination context

Closure of administration and exit routes are regularly tested in the JIEB exam and should be learnt thoroughly.

Past exam questions to look at include:

2007   Question 1

2004   Question 1

2004   Question 2

2003   Question 3(c)

2000   Question 1(b)

1999   Question 2(a)

1994   Question 4

1990   Question 2 (b)(ii)

1 Exit routes from administration

Section overview

There are a number of options available to the administrator for exiting administration, these include:

- Handing the company back to the directors.

- Petitioning the court for compulsory winding-up.

- Filing to place the company into a creditors voluntary liquidation.

- Having distributed realisations filing for the dissolution of the company.

- Obtaining the creditors approval to a CVA and ending the administration.

- Obtaining the creditors approval and sanction of the court to a s895 CA 2006 Scheme and ending the administration.

- Allowing the administration to lapse through expiry of the 12 month fixed period.

- Applying to the court for the ending of the administration.

1.1 Handing the company back to the directors

This is an option available where the administrator has achieved a para 3(a) Sch B1 IA purpose, ie rescuing the company as a going concern. Schedule B1 para 65 now provides the administrator with an express power to make distributions. No sanction of the court is needed if the payment is to a secured or preferential creditor. However sanction of the court is required if the payment is to ordinary unsecured creditors. Para 65 expressly states that s 175 of the Act applies to an administrator's distributions. In other words, as in winding-up the preferential creditors will take priority to the holders of floating charges.

1.2 Petitioning the court for compulsory winding up

In most cases administrators will prefer to use the creditors voluntary winding-up route. However, petitioning for compulsory winding-up may be appropriate where the creditors want a thorough investigation into allegations of fraud against the directors.

An administrator has a specific power to present a winding-up petition (Schedule 1 para 21) By R4.7(7) the petition must be expressed to be the petition of the company by its administrator and must:

- State the name of the administrator

- State the court case number

- State the date the company entered administration

- Contain an application under para 79(2) Sch B1 IA requesting that the appointment of the administrator ceases to have effect. Para 79(2) Sch B1 IA envisages applications to court to end administration being made where:

  - The company should not have entered administration; or

  - The creditors' meeting requires the administrator to apply to end the administration (and here the administrator should attach a statement indicating with reasons whether he agrees with the creditors requirement); or

  - The administrator thinks that the purpose of the administration cannot be achieved.

- Applications under para 79 Sch B1 IA must be accompanied by a progress report from the date the company entered administration or from the last progress report.

R2.114 requires the petitioning administrator to give seven days notice to the appointing creditor(s) or the applicant(s) for the administration order of his intention to apply to court under para 79 Sch B1 IA and also of whether he intends to seek appointment as liquidator. The administrator's petition containing para 79(2) Sch B1 IA statement should also state that he has complied with the requirement to notify creditors and should have any response from the creditors attached to it. Notice to creditors is not required if it is the creditors themselves who have made the administrator apply to court.

The court makes the winding-up order and (s 140(1) IA) may now appoint the administrator as liquidator of the company, in which case the OR will not become the liquidator and therefore will not have a duty to consider whether or not to call a meeting of creditors.

Where the administrator becomes the liquidator any creditors' committee in the administration will continue in being as the liquidation committee for the purposes of the winding-up (R4.174).

In practice, situations will arise where it will be inappropriate for the court to appoint the administrator as liquidator eg:

▶ The creditors are unhappy with the conduct of the administration, and have required the administrator to apply to court for the ending of the administration perhaps with the intention that in a subsequent compulsory liquidation there will be an investigation of the administrator's conduct;

▶ The administrator declines to accept the appointment because of concerns over potential conflict of interests.

In this situation the OR will become the liquidator. Rule 4.174 will not apply so that the committee in administration will NOT become the liquidation committee.

1.3 Filing to place the company into creditors' voluntary liquidation (para 83 Sch B1 IA)

The administrator sends a notice to the Registrar of Companies that para 83 Sch B1 IA applies (Form 2.34B) attaching a final progress report detailing assets to be dealt with in the CVL.

▶ A copy of the notice must also be filed with the court (para 83(5) Sch B1 IA).

▶ A copy of the notice must also be sent to each creditor of whose claim and address the administrator is aware (para 83(5) Sch B1 IA) as well as to all those who received notice of the administrator's appointment (Rule 2.117(2)).

▶ The registrar registers the para 83 Sch B1 IA notice and from this time:

– The appointment of the administrator ceases to have effect and

– The company shall be wound-up as if a resolution for voluntary winding-up under s 84 IA were passed on the day on which the notice is registered.

Notice that there is no requirement for a board meeting, meeting of shareholders, nor for a s 98 IA meeting of creditors. Case law has confirmed that there is no requirement to separately apply to court under para 79 Sch B1 IA to end the administration.

By R2.33(2)(m) an administrator must state in the proposals "how it is proposed that the administration shall end". If a CVL is proposed:

▶ Details of the proposed liquidator (usually the administrator) must be provided

▶ And a statement that (in accordance with para 83(7) Sch B1 IA and R2.117(3)) creditors may nominate a different person as the proposed liquidator, provided that the nomination is made after the receipt of the proposals and before the proposals are approved.

▶ If no other liquidator is appointed the administrator will be the liquidator (para 83(7) Sch B1 IA).

The committee in the administration will become the liquidation committee in the CVL (para 83(8)(f) Sch B1 IA).

The para 83 Sch B1 IA CVL route can only be used if two pre-conditions are met:

▶ Total amount which each secured creditor of the company is likely to receive has been paid or set aside and

▶ A distribution to unsecured creditors will be made (para 83(1) Sch B1 IA).

The CVL route has a number of advantages:

- Any problems in respect of completing the administration within 12 months or having to obtain an extension of time from creditors or the court are pre-empted.

- As liquidator the IP has enforcement powers which are not available to an administrator e.g. to bring actions against directors for misfeasance, wrongful and fraudulent trading. When challenging voidable transactions relevant time will be calculated from the commencement of the administration not from the resolution to wind-up.

- A liquidator has a statutory power to disclaim onerous property – an administrator does not.

- The liquidator has full powers to compromise claims with creditors and the lack of a 12 month time limit provides time to negotiate and settle complex claims.

A disadvantage of either liquidation route is that since the House of Lords decision in *Leyland Daf* the liquidator (in contrast to an administrator) cannot pay general costs of winding-up out of floating charge realisations. The CA 2006 introduced a new s176 ZA into IA 86 with the effect (from 6 April 2008) of reversing the decision in Leyland Daf. (See Chapter 6, section 5.3.)

1.4 Moving from administration to dissolution (para 84 Sch B1 IA)

As with para 83 Sch B1 IA the procedure is straightforward and consists of filing a notice with the registrar and with the court and with every creditor of whose claim and address the administrator is aware. On registration of the notice the administration ceases to have effect, and in a further three months the company is deemed dissolved.

This exit route is only available where the administrator thinks that the company has no property which might permit a distribution to its creditors. This provision (para 84(1) Sch B1 IA) has caused some controversy. Does para 84(1) Sch B1 IA mean that the company never had property which might permit a distribution or does it simply mean that at the time of filing the para 84 Sch B1 IA notice the administrator must believe there are no available realisations for unsecured creditors?

- The former view (never was anything to distribute to unsecured creditors) seems to have been the view of the Judge, expressed obiter, in *Ballast PLC and others (2004)*.

- However, the Insolvency Service have expressed the view that the para 84 Sch B1 IA procedure is available where the administrator

  - Has distributed realisations under para 65 Sch B1 IA

  - And having no further property to distribute, now files under para 84 Sch B1 IA to dissolve the shell of the company.

- *GHE Realisations* confirms that the dissolution route is available where a paragraph 65 Sch B1 IA distribution has been made.

Again no application to court is required to end the administration.

1.5 Company voluntary arrangement

Attempting to obtain agreement to a proposal for a CVA would be consistent with the ostensible statutory purpose of administration to secure the rescue of the company as a going concern.

Schedule B1 para 49(3) expressly states that the administrator's proposals may include a proposal for a CVA. The proposals can be put to creditors at the same time as the meeting to approve the administrator's proposals for achieving this para 3 Sch B1 IA purpose.

The disadvantages of following the CVA route are:

- Supervisor has no power to challenge antecedent transactions (other than under s423) and has no power to enforce the directors co-operation under ss.234-237. An administrator does have these powers but once the CVA has been approved may well have achieved the purpose of the administration and will therefore be obliged to take steps to end the administration.

- ▶ At the end of the CVA further steps may have to be taken to dissolve or liquidate the company if the CVA has not resulted in the survival of the company.

- ▶ Like administrators, supervisors have no power to bring actions under ss.212-214 IA nor can they disclaim onerous assets. *fraudulent or wrongful trading.*

The advantages of the CVA route are that:

- ▶ The proposal can contain detailed provisions on the agreement and compromising of claims against the company.

- ▶ Directors will remain involved in management of the company and this may maximise the 'buy-in' of the current management team.

1.6 Administration comes to an end through the passage of time

By para 76(1) Sch B1 IA the appointment of an administrator ceases to have effect at the end of one year beginning when the administration takes effect.

On the application of the administrator the court can extend this for a specified period. The court must order extension prior to the expiring of the administrators term of office.

The creditors can also extend the administration for a maximum period of six months by consent. By para 78 Sch B1 IA 'consent' means consent of

- ▶ Each secured creditor or

- ▶ If the administrator thinks that a distribution may be made to preferential creditors, consent of:
  - (i) each secured creditor, and
  - (ii) preferential creditors whose debts amount to more than 50% of the preferential debts of the company, disregarding debts of any creditor who does not respond to an invitation to give or withhold consent.

  iii) *unsecured creditors 50% unless Para 52 applied for.*

If the administrator however has made a para 52(1)(b) Sch B1 IA statement (i.e. insufficient assets to pay a dividend to unsecured creditors other than under prescribed part rules), then only secured creditors need give consent.

Creditors must be given at least 14 days' notice of a resolution to extend administration. The request must be accompanied by a progress report for the period since the last report.

There are restrictions on the creditors power to extend the administrators term of office:

- ▶ Can only be extended once

- ▶ Cannot extend if the court has previously granted an extension. Note that the court *can* grant a further extension where either creditors or the court itself have previously granted an extension.

Where a term of office is extended by consent the administrator must notify both the court and the registrar of companies.

1.7 Termination of administration where objective achieved

Para 80 Sch B1 IA provides a procedure where an administrator appointed out of court under para 14 or 22 Sch B1 IA has achieved the objective of the administration, the administrator files notice with the court and the registrar of companies and the administrator's appointment then ceases to have effect.

It might be appropriate to use this procedure where for instance:

- ▶ The administrator has succeeded in securing the survival of the company as a going concern or

- ▶ The administrator's proposals for a CVA have been approved by the creditors.

1.8 Other options

An administration can also come to an end where:

Administrator applies to the court under para 79(2) Sch B1 IA (see earlier).

Administrator appointed by the court applies to the court under para 85 Sch B1 IA for discharge of the order.

A creditor applies to the court under para 81 on the grounds that the appointors (appointments out of court) or applicants (appointments by the court) had an 'improper motive'. In addition under para 74 Sch B1 IA creditors can apply to the court on the basis that their interests are being or will be unfairly harmed by the administrator. One of the courts powers under para 74 Sch B1 IA is to end the administration.

2 Vacation of office and release

Section overview

The administrator can vacate office in a number of ways:

▶ Resignation
▶ Removal by the court
▶ Ceases to be qualified to act as an administrator
▶ Death

2.1 Resignation

The administrator may only resign on the following grounds (r2.119):

▶ Ill health
▶ Intends ceasing to practice as an IP
▶ Conflict of interest

Permission of the court is required if the administrator wishes to resign on other grounds.

The administrator must give at least seven days' notice in Form 2.37B of his intention to resign to (r2.120(1)):

▶ Any continuing administrator of the company
▶ Creditors' committee
▶ The company and creditors (if no continuing administrator or creditors' committee)
▶ Member state liquidator (if applicable)

Where the administrator was appointed by administration order, notice in writing must also be given to the court.

If the administrator was appointed by the holder of a qualifying floating charge under para 14 Sch B1 IA, notice of intention to resign must also be given to all holders of prior qualifying floating charges and to the persons who appointed the administrator.

Where the administrator was appointed by the directors or the company under para 22 Sch B1 IA, a copy of the notice of intention to resign must also be sent to the appointor and all holders of a qualifying floating charge.

Notice of resignation on Form 2.38B must, within five days of the notice of ~~intention to resign~~ being given, be:

▶ Sent to Registrar of Companies
▶ Filed with the court
▶ Sent to all those who received notice of intention to resign

2.2 Application to court for removal

Application may be made to court under para 88 Sch B1 IA for the removal of the administrator. The application should state the grounds upon which it is requested that the administrator be removed from office.

Not less than 5 days before the date fixed for the application to be heard, notice of the application must be served on (r2.122):

▶ The administrator

▶ The person who made the application for the administration order or who appointed the administrator

▶ The creditors' committee (if any)

▶ Joint administrator (if any)

▶ If no creditors' committee or joint administrator, the company and the creditors, including floating charge holders

Where the court makes an order removing the administrator it shall give a copy to the applicant, who must send a copy to the administrator.

A copy of the order must also be sent to all those who received notice of the application, within five business days of the order being made.

A copy of the order must be sent to Registrar of Companies on Form 2.39B within five business days of the order being made.

2.3 Ceases to be qualified to act

If an administrator ceases to be qualified to act he must vacate office (para 89 Sch B1 IA). He must give notice, in writing, to whoever appointed him and the Registrar of Companies on Form 2.39B (r 2.123).

The criteria to be qualified to act are set out in s390 IA.

2.4 Duties on vacating office

The administrator must, as soon as reasonably practicable, deliver to his successor:

▶ The assets (after deduction of any expenses properly incurred and distributions made by him)
▶ The records of the administration including correspondence, proofs and other related papers
▶ The company's books, papers and other records

Within one month of ceasing to act he must send a final progress report on Form 2.24B , detailing matters since the last progress report until he ceased to act, to:

▶ The creditors
▶ The court
▶ The Registrar of Companies

The final progress report must include a summary of (r 2.110):

▶ The administrator's proposals
▶ Any major amendments to or deviations from these proposals
▶ The steps taken during the administration
▶ The outcome
▶ SIP 9 disclosure report for remuneration and category 2 disbursements
▶ Authorising body of the IP

The report should also include:

▶ Details of the court, court reference number, company name, registered office and registered number

- Administrator's name, address and the date of appointment

- A receipts and payments account stating what assets have been realized, for what value and payments made, to include a statement as to the amount paid to unsecured creditors by virtue of the application of s176A IA

- Any other relevant information for the creditors

2.5 Discharge from liability

Where an IP ceases to be the administrator (however he ceases to act) he is discharged from liability in respect of any action of his as administrator (para 98(1) Sch B1 IA) however discharge is not automatic.

Discharge takes effect:

- In the case of death, on the filing with the court of notice of his death

- In the case of an administrator appointed under para 14 or 22 Sch B1 IA, at a time appointed by the resolution of the creditors' committee or creditors or in any case, at a time specified by the court.

Interactive question: Mattisons Limited

Mr Jones was appointed administrator of Mattisons Limited on 2 June 2007 by the directors of the company.

He has recently been diagnosed with a serious illness and now wishes to resign as administrator.

Requirement

Write a memo to your principal detailing:

(a)   The steps to be taken by Mr Jones to resign as administrator
(b)   His duties upon vacating office.

See **Answer** at the end of this chapter.

Summary and Self-test

Summary

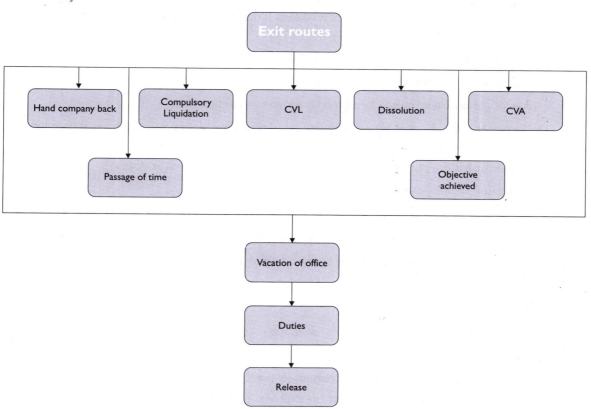

Self-test

Answer the following questions.

1   In what circumstances is an administrator likely to petition for the compulsory liquidation of a company as an exit route from administration?

2   Can the administrator be appointed liquidator when compulsory liquidation is used as an exit route?

3   What pre-conditions must be met before a CVL can be used as an exit route?

4   What are the advantages of using CVL as an exit route from administration?

5   What are the disadvantages of using a CVA as an exit route from administration?

6   After what period of time will an administration automatically come to an end?

7   In what ways may an administrator vacate office?

8   What are the administrator's duties on ceasing to act?

9   If an administrator was appointed by a holder of a qualifying floating charge to whom must he give notice of his intention to resign?

Now, go back to the Learning Objectives in the Introduction. If you are satisfied that you have achieved these objectives, please tick them off.

Answers to Self-test

1   When creditors want a thorough investigation into the conduct of the directors.

2   Yes, the administrator may be appointed liquidator but he should have the agreement of the creditors' committee or a meeting of creditors. If there is likely to be a conflict of interests, the administrator should not accept the appointment.

3   The total amount which each secured creditor is likely to receive has been paid or set aside.

    A distribution to unsecured creditors will be made.

4   Avoids the problems caused by 12 month administration time limit.

    Liquidator has enforcement powers which an administrator does not ie. To bring actions for wrongful/ fraudulent trading.

    Liquidator has the power to disclaim onerous property (administrator doesn't).

    Liquidator has full powers to compromise creditors' claims.

5   Supervisor has no power to challenge antecedent transactions or bring actions under s212 – 214 IA.

    At end of CVA, further steps may be required to dissolve or liquidate the company.

6   At the end of one year beginning when the administration takes effect (para 76(1) Sch B1 IA).

7   Resignation

    Removal by the court

    Ceases to be qualified to act

    Death

8   The administrator must, as soon as reasonably practicable, deliver to his successor:

    –   The assets (after deduction of any expenses properly incurred and distributions made by him)
    –   The records of the administration including correspondence, proofs and other related papers
    –   The company's books, papers and other records

    Within one month of ceasing to act he must send a final progress report on Form 2.24B , detailing matters since the last progress report until he ceased to act, to:

    –   The creditors
    –   The court
    –   The Registrar of Companies

    The final progress report must include a summary of (r 2.110):

    –   The administrator's proposals
    –   Any major amendments to or deviations from these proposals
    –   The steps taken during the administration
    –   The outcome

9   Any continuing administrator of the company

    Creditors' committee

    If none of the above, the company and creditors

    All holders of QFCs

    QFC who appointed the administrator

Answers to Interactive Question

Answer to Interactive Question: Mattisons Limited

Memo format

(a)   Mr Jones may resign on the grounds of ill health (r2.119).

He must give seven days' notice of his intention to resign on Form 2.37B to:

–   Any continuing administrator of the company

–   Creditors' committee

–   (if none of the above) the company and creditors

–   The directors who appointed him

–   All holders of a qualifying floating charge

Then, within five days of the notice of intention to resign being given to the directors, he must give notice of resignation, on Form 2.38B, to:

–   Registrar of Companies

–   The court

–   All those who received notice of intention to resign.

(b)   Duties on vacating office:

The administrator must, as soon as reasonably practicable, deliver to his successor:

–   The assets (after deduction of any expenses properly incurred and distributions made by him)

–   The records of the administration including correspondence, proofs and other related papers

–   The company's books, papers and other records

Within one month of ceasing to act he must send a final progress report on Form 2.24B , detailing matters since the last progress report until he ceased to act, to:

–   The creditors

–   The court

–   The Registrar of Companies

The final progress report must include a summary of (r 2.110):

–   The administrator's proposals

–   Any major amendments to or deviations from these proposals

–   The steps taken during the administration

–   The outcome

6

Charges

> > > > > > > > > > > > > > > > > >

Contents

Introduction

Learning objectives

▶ Identify the key features of a fixed and floating charge ☐

▶ Understand the priority of charges ☐

▶ Calculation of preferential creditors and receiver's duties to the preferential creditors ☐

▶ Calculation of the prescribed part ☐

Working context

Understanding what fixed and floating charges are and the priority of payment of funds coming into the hands of an IP are very important in a work environment when dealing with matters from preparing an estimated outcome statement to making dividend payments.

Stop and think

What is a charge? What does it do? Why are preferential creditors paid in priority to floating charge holders? What is the prescribed part?

Examination context

The topics covered in this chapter give basic background knowledge which is essential for the JIEB exam. Whilst the topics covered are unlikely to form the basis of an exam question in their own right an understanding of the principles are required in order to answer other questions, for example, preparing a distribution statement requires an understanding of the priority of charges.

Past exam questions to look at include:

2002   Question 4(d)

1994   Question 5(a)

1993   Question 4(c)

1 Charges

Section overview

▶ A charge is an interest in a company's property created in favour of a creditor. Where a company issues a debenture in favour of a bank it will be secured by fixed and floating charges. It is important to be able to distinguish between what property is covered by a fixed charge as opposed to a floating charge for the statement of affairs or preparing an estimated outcome statement.

1.1 Fixed charge

A fixed charge is a charge over assets of the company which are *(Illingsworth v Houldsworth)*:

▶ ascertained and definite or
▶ capable of being ascertained and defined.

A fixed charge will usually cover assets such as:

▶ land and buildings
▶ fixed plant (i.e. affixed to the fabric of the building such as a central heating system)
▶ intellectual property rights such as patents
▶ uncalled share capital

A fixed charge attaches to the charged property on creation (providing validly registered etc.) The effect of this is:

▶ that the company is no longer free to dispose of the charged property.
▶ and will need to seek authorisation of the charge holder before realising the charged property.

1.2 Floating charges

A floating charge has, according to Lord Justice Power in *Re Yorkshire Woolcombers Association Ltd*, three characteristics:

▶ a charge over a class of assets present and future

▶ changing from time to time in ordinary course of business

▶ the company remaining free to carry on business in the usual way in relation to those assets (until 'crystallisation').

Stock and non-fixed plant and machinery would normally be covered by a floating charge and debtors.

In practice the security documentation will often provide for a fixed charge on the assets listed in 1.1 above and a floating charge on the rest of the company's property.

The possession of a floating charge (even where the assets covered are of negligible value) has a number of advantages for a debenture holder:

▶ If the charge was created prior to 15.09.03 and providing the charge or charges cover the whole or substantially the whole of the company's assets, the chargee will be able to appoint an administrative receiver.

▶ An administrative receiver has wide statutory powers to trade, manage and sell the business, to enforce co-operation of directors and to apply to court to over reach the rights of any prior charge holders.

▶ An administrative receiver appointment prevents an administrator being appointed to the company. Effectively the charge can 'veto' the administration process.

▶ The holder of a 'Qualifying Floating Charge' as defined in the Act can make an appointment of an administrator out of court. This is so whether or not the charge was created prior to 15.09.03.

▶ Holding charges over all the assets of a company may facilitate a going concern sale which should in turn maximise the return to the holder of the charge.

1.3 'Legal' and 'equitable'

Charges may also be described as 'legal' or 'equitable'. The significance of the distinction is that;

▶ in English law generally legal charges are 'good against the world' whereas an equitable charge is not good against a bona fide purchaser for value without notice of the charge.

▶ Only holders of legal charges have a statutory right to appoint a receiver in certain circumstances, as set out in the *Law of Property Act 1925*. Holders of equitable charges will only be able to appoint where their charge gives them a contractual right to do so.

A fixed charge may be legal or equitable. A floating charge is always equitable.

A legal charge will be executed formally in a deed.

An equitable charge will be executed in a less formal way e.g. in a signed contract (executed 'under hand') or in the case of land by a deposit of title deeds.

1.4 Priority – preferential creditors

The holder of a fixed charge has no duty as such to pay preferential creditors in priority to itself.

S40 IA provides that a receiver appointed by holders of charges which as created were floating charges does have a duty to pay the preferential creditors in priority to his appointor.

In administration para 65 Sch B1 IA empowers an administrator to make a distribution to preferential creditors without the need to apply to the court for permission. The paragraph specifically incorporates s175 IA into the regime for administrators. S175(2)(b) IA gives the preferential debts priority over holders of floating charges.

1.5 s245 IA – validity of floating charge

This rule only applies to floating charges. It provides that a floating charge:

▶ created within 12 months of:

– date of application for an administration order or the filing of a notice of intention to appoint an administrator (out of court appointments) or in other cases the appointment of an administrator or

– date of 'commencement' of liquidation

▶ at a time when the company is insolvent

▶ is invalid except to the extent that fresh consideration is provided for it.

Where the charge is given to a connected party:

▶ the relevant time is extended to 2 years

▶ and there is no requirement that the company be insolvent at the time of the giving of the charge.

Fresh consideration will often have been provided by the bank merely by the turnover of the company's bank account.

Notice that s245 IA is only triggered by liquidation or administration and *not* by the appointment of an administrative receiver. S245 IA has no retrospective effect therefore and does not invalidate the acts of an administrative receiver up to the date of commencement of administration or liquidation.

1.6 Fixed charge over book debts

There are clear advantages to a lender if a valid fixed charge over book debts can be created.

(i)   Book debts may be one of the only assets which are readily realisable by a receiver – a welcome source of liquidity which can be used to make an early distribution to the lender.

(ii)   Fixed charge assets are not subject to:

  ▸   The claims of preferential creditors

  ▸   The prescribed part rules which apply to floating charges created on or after 15 September 2003.

The 1979 case of *Siebe Gorman v Barclays Bank* established that it was possible for a borrower to create a fixed charge over future book debts and their proceeds, where such proceeds were paid into an account with and controlled by, the lending bank.

To establish a charge over debtors as fixed it was necessary for the chargee to demonstrate that they had a degree of control over the debts. In order to do so, the security documentation usually provides for:

(i)   An express provision stating that the charge is a fixed charge

(ii)   A requirement that the company pays the book debts receipts into the company's account with the bank

(iii)   The company is prohibited from charging or assigning the book debts in favour of another person.

The *New Bullas* Principle

In 1994 in the case of *New Bullas Trading Ltd* the Court of Appeal recognised that it was possible to treat book debts and their proceeds differently so that the debenture took effect as a hybrid: as a fixed charge whilst the book debts were uncollected and as a floating charge over their proceeds once collected. However, it made no commercial sense to distinguish between the debt itself and its proceeds. A fixed charge on debts and a floating charge on proceeds are in reality a single floating charge.

The *Brumark* Case (*Agnew v Commissioner of Inland Revenue*)

The Judicial Committee of the Privy Council delivered a landmark decision on 5 June 2001 on an appeal from a decision of the New Zealand Court of Appeal in *Re: Brumark Investments*. It held that in the case of a New Bullas type debenture, the charge over book debts and their proceeds should properly be considered as a floating charge since the commercial reality of the charging provisions, taken as a whole, is that the company has unrestricted right to make use of the assets charged in order to run its business. Book debts are part of the circulating capital of the business and are a class of assets constantly changing as new debts are created and old ones received. To this extent, book debts are the natural subject of a floating charge.

After the *Brumark* decision

The *Brumark* case gave rise to a great deal of debate with the banks being reluctant to concede that their fixed charges over debtors were in reality floating.

The matter was decided in the *Spectrum Plus Ltd (2004)* case. In this case, whilst the bank had required the company to pay book debt proceeds into an account with the bank, there were no further restrictions on the use of the account and therefore the court held that the proper categorisation of the charge was that it was a floating charge.

The bank appealed and the Court of Appeal allowed the banks appeal and found that the charge was a fixed charge.

The Court of Appeal's decision was appealed to the House of Lords. The judgement immediately held that *Siebe Gorman* was wrong and should be overruled. The Lords found that the bank's debenture created a floating charge (not a fixed charge) over book debts.

It is possible to create a fixed charge over book debts by preventing the charger company from dealing with book debts so that they were preserved for the benefit of the security. This can be done by:

(i)   Assigning the book debts to the charge

(ii)   Requiring the borrower to pay the proceeds of book debts to the charge in reduction of the borrower's outstanding debt

(iii)   Requiring the borrower to pay the collected proceeds into a separate account with a third party over which the charge has a fixed charge

The important point to note is that existing charges over book debts, in standard form (where the company remains free to deal with the proceeds of book debt realisations in the ordinary course of business) will be interpreted as creating a floating charge over book debts.

If you are uncertain in the exam whether to treat book debts as a fixed or floating charge asset you should clearly state what assumptions you have made in determining the treatment of book debts in your answer. If the exam question states that the bank has a valid fixed charge over book debts, you may assume that this is so and treat the book debts as a fixed charge asset. Otherwise treat book debts as a floating charge asset and state clearly why you are doing so (ie following the decision in *Spectrum Plus Ltd (2004)*).

2 Priority of charges

Section overview

▶   It is possible for a company to issue fixed and floating charges to secure debts owed to more than one lender. It is important therefore to know the order in which they rank so that correct payments may be made from the realisation of charged assets.

2.1 Contract

Where there is more than one secured creditor they may always agree between themselves as to the order in which they will rank should the company default on its loans.

Similarly a bank may always make it a condition of granting a loan that a company does not create charges ranking in priority to its own security. It may require, for instance, that no subsequent fixed charges are created taking in priority to its own floating charge (a negative pledge). Note that:

▶   Registration of a floating charge does not constitute constructive notice of the terms and conditions in the security documentation.

▶   Details of the negative pledge clause itself should therefore also be provided to Companies House on registration.

In ascertaining the order of payment in the exam therefore check whether any deed of priority has been entered into or whether any negative pledge clause has been registered.

It is of course possible for a floating charge to rank ahead of a fixed charge.

2.2 Validity

For a lender to rank as other than unsecured the charge must be valid.

Both fixed and floating charges must be registered at Companies House under s395 Companies Act 1985.

S395 CA 1985 requires that charges are registered within 21 days of creation. If it is not so registered it is void against:

▶   the liquidator
▶   administrator
▶   or any creditor

of the company.

If, however, the Registrar of Companies does permit registration outside the 21 day period, the charge *is* none the less validly registered (*Re Esal Commodities*). This is because the Registrars certificate of registration is conclusive evidence of compliance with s395 CA 1985

In theory it is the obligation of the Company (acting through its directors) to register the charge, but registration may be effected by any person interested in the charge, and in practice the banks solicitors will register the charge.

The validity of a floating charge may be challenged under s245 IA (see earlier). Although there is no similar 12 month rule in relation to fixed charges – such a charge created within six months of liquidation or administration could be challenged as a preference (see chapter 14 for more details). However:

▶ it would need to be shown that the company was insolvent at the time of the giving of the charge and

▶ that there was a 'desire' to improve the position of the bank. If the granting of a debenture by the directors was motivated, as is often the case, merely by an intention to prevent the bank from calling in the overdraft or taking some other enforcement measure the requisite subjective desire will be absent (*Re M C Bacon*). On the other hand 'desire' will be present where the directors' motive was to reduce their exposure under their personal guarantees.

In theory, a charge could be challenged as a transaction at an undervalue by a liquidator or administrator. (See chapter 14 for more details).

2.3 Fixed charges – priority

▶ fixed charges over land rank in order of registration at the Land Registry not in order of creation or registration at Companies House.

▶ fixed charges over assets other than land rank in order of creation and again not in order of registration at Companies House.

Chargees will receive realisations after deduction of costs, expenses and remuneration properly attributable to the fixed charge assets.

Preferential creditors have no priority over fixed charge assets. If there is a fixed charge surplus therefore this will not in administration or administrative receivership be paid to the preferential creditors. In administrative receivership the surplus will be paid to the company acting through its liquidator or directors.

2.4 Floating charges – priority

Assuming no deed of priority exists, floating charges rank in the order of creation (and not date of registration at Companies House). Preferential creditors rank ahead of all floating charge holders (and not only those who have appointed receivers (*Re H and K Medway 1997*)

Where floating charge assets are realised the office holder must pay out the funds in a certain order of priority. The general position is as follows:

(i) Costs of preserving and realising floating charge assets

(ii) The office holders' remuneration and the proper costs and expenses of the receivership attributable to the floating charge assets.

(iii) Preferential creditors.

(iv) Where the floating charge was created on or after 15 September 2003 the prescribed part which must be made available to the unsecured creditors.

(v) The principle and interest secured by the floating charge.

(vi) Any surplus is payable to the company acting through its directors or liquidator.

3 Preferential creditors

Section overview

The Enterprise Act 2002 amended s386 IA and Schedule 6 of the Act so as to abolish crown preference in cases where after 15 September 2003:

▶   a receiver is appointed by a floating charge

▶   a petition for winding-up or bankruptcy is presented

▶   an application for administration is made

▶   an IVA or CVA has effect

▶   a resolution for winding-up is passed.

Crown preference will still apply therefore to pre 15 September 2003 cases and includes 12 months PAYE/NI, and six months VAT.

3.1   Categories of preferential creditors

In post – 15 September 2003 cases preferential creditors are now restricted to:

▶   contributions to occupational pension schemes by employees and employers

▶   remuneration payable to an employee for the four months prior to the relevant date (restricted to £800 per employee)

▶   all accrued holiday pay owed to an employee

▶   the Redundancy Payment Service to the extent that they have met employees preferential claims and are therefore subrogated to the position of the employees.

▶   European Coal and Steel Community levies.

3.2   Relevant date

The 'relevant date' for calculation of preferential claims is set out in s387

▶   For CVAs this is the date of approval of the proposal unless the directors have applied for a small company moratorium in which case the date of filing for that moratorium is the relevant date (s387(2)(b) and (2A) IA). If the CVA takes effect within administration, the date that the company entered administration is taken.

▶   In administrations the relevant date is, again, the date on which the company enters administration (s387(3A) IA), and this will also be the case in a winding-up which follows on from administration, either

–   where an administration order is discharged and compulsory winding-up follows (s387(3)(a) IA) or

–   where a post 15 September 2003 administration is followed by either a voluntary or compulsory winding-up (s387(3)(ba) IA).

▶   Note that where an administration order (made on a pre 15 September 2003 petition) was or is discharged and a creditors voluntary liquidation is used as the exit route, the relevant date for preferential creditors is the date of resolution to wind-up (s387(3)(c) IA). In order to avoid prejudicing the preferential creditors a direction of the court is required that either the administrator should pay the preferential creditors defined at the date of the administration order or that assets should be passed on trust to the liquidator to pay the preferential creditors at that date.

▶   In receivership the relevant date is the date of appointment of the receiver (s387(4) IA).

3.3 SIP 14 A receiver's responsibility to preferential creditors

SIP 14 ('A receivers responsibility to preferential creditors') applies where any assets of the company are subject to a floating charge and emphasises the importance, not only of the correct categorisation of assets as covered by the fixed or floating charges, but also of correctly allocating costs between the respective 'pools' of fixed or floating realisations.

Where costs are clearly identifiable as applicable to fixed or floating charge assets they should be recorded as such in the receiver's records.

In less clear cut cases the receiver retains a duty to allocate costs appropriately, exercising professional judgment 'made with independence of mind and with integrity'. More specifically the receiver must have regard to:

▶ the objectives for which costs were incurred, it being recognised that certain types of costs may, properly, be allocated to the fixed charge assets in one case and to the floating charge assets in another. In another case such costs may enhance realisations in both categories;

▶ the benefits actually obtained for those financially interested in one or other category of asset in terms of protection of those assets or their value and any augmentation of that value;

▶ whether the benefits to those interested in assets subject to a fixed charge has been enhanced by action which proves to be detrimental to those interested in floating charge assets (for example where trading losses are incurred to protect or enhance the value of property or book debts subject to a fixed charge);

▶ whether the realisation of the undertaking and assets by means of a going concern sale has resulted in a reduction in the quantum of debts which are preferential due to the transfer of employment contracts.

Less clear cut cases include:

▶ costs incurred in trading on with a view to a going concern sale. Profitable trading will augment floating charge assets but effecting a going concern sale may also increase the value of assets subject to fixed charges.

▶ Costs incurred in the AR complying with statutory duties such as preparing a s48 IA report.

3.4 The receiver's duty to pay preferential creditors from floating charge assets

The duty is set out in s40(2) IA and provides that the company's preferential debts 'shall be paid out of the floating charge assets coming into the hands of the receiver in priority to any claims for principal or interest in respect of the debentures'.

The duty applies to any receiver appointed under a floating charge and not just to administrative receivers.

The case law makes it clear that the duty to pay preferential creditors is a positive one (*IRC v Goldblatt*). The receiver may be liable to preferential creditors where his actions have the effect of depleting the assets available to pay preferential creditors. The practical consequences of this are:

▶ where continued trading is loss making but is undertaken to improve the return to the fixed chargee, those losses may have to be made good out of enhanced fixed charge realisations.

▶ where an offer for a company's business and undertaking allocates the consideration in a way which would prejudice preferential creditors an administrative receiver may again need to "make up the difference" to those preferential creditors.

When assets are sold as part of a going concern (or otherwise in parcels comprising both fixed and floating charge assets) the apportionment of the total consideration suggested by the purchaser (for example for his own financial reasons) may not properly reflect the financial interests of the different classes of creditors in the individual assets or categories of assets. In these circumstances the receiver should ensure that he will be able properly to discharge his obligations to account to holders of fixed charges on the one hand and creditors interested in assets subject to floating charges on the other.

In appointments made on or after 15 September 2003 crown preference was abolished and the importance of preferential creditor priority has therefore been diminished. Also, where a receiver affects a going concern sale so that employee's contracts are transferred to the purchaser, there may be no preferential creditors at all.

Interactive question 1: Oddbins Limited

You have been appointed administrative receiver of Oddbins Limited, a company which manufactures storage containers. Your appointor bank, Green Bank PLC is owed the sum of £295,000 which is secured by way of fixed and floating charges over the company's assets. You are aware that the company has granted a number of charges to secure borrowings. A search of the registers reveals the following information:

Type of charge	Date of Creation	Date of registration at Companies House	Land Registry
Green Bank PLC:			
Floating charge	10.03.03	17.03.03	
Fixed charge over 26 Bath Road, Bristol	10.03.03	17.03.03	22.03.03
Yellow Bank PLC:			
Floating charge	2.10.89	19.10.89	
Fixed charge over 26 Bath Road, Bristol	5.02.90	not registered	25.02.90
Blue Bank PLC:			
Floating charge	27.08.04	7.09.04	
Pink Bank PLC:			
Floating charge	24.08.04	18.09.04	
Fixed charge over 26 Bath Road, Bristol	9.11.04	15.11.04	20.11.04

Requirement

List the order in which, as administrative receiver, you would distribute realisations and give your reasons.

See **Answer** at the end of this chapter.

4 The prescribed part

Section overview

▶ The Enterprise Act 2002 introduced provision for part of the pool of floating charge assets to be made available for ordinary unsecured creditors. The rules are contained in s176A of the Act and the Insolvency Act 1986 (Prescribed Part) Order 2003. The rules only apply where the floating charge is created on or after 15 September 2003.

4.1 The prescribed part rules

The purpose of the rule is to make part of the pool of floating charge assets available to ordinary unsecured creditors. The governments hope was that some of the funds released by the abolition of crown preference would trickle-down to ordinary trade creditors. However the rule only applies to floating charges created on or after 15 September 2003 so that holders of pre 15 September 2003 floating charges have effectively received a windfall as:

▶ their charges are not subject to crown preference

▶ and are not subject to prescribed part rules either

The rule applies where a floating charge relates to property of a company which has:

▶ gone into liquidation or administration

▶ or where a provisional liquidator has been appointed

▶ or where a receiver has been appointed. This will include an administrative receiver where, for instance, the floating charge formed part of a capital market arrangement.

The effect of the rule is that the office holder must make a 'prescribed' part of the company's 'net property' available for unsecured creditors and must not distribute this part to the holder of a floating charge.

The prescribed part is:

▶ where the company's net property does not exceed £10,000 – 50% of that property

▶ where it exceeds £10,000

– 50% of the first £10,000 plus

– 20% of the balance over £10,000

– subject to an overall cap on the prescribed part of £600,000.

Exceptions where the prescribed part rules will not apply:

▶ Where the company's net property is below the prescribed minimum of £10,000 and the office holder believes the cost of making a distribution would be disproportionate to the benefits.

▶ Where the court orders, on application by a liquidator, administrator or receiver on the grounds that the cost of making a distribution would be disproportionate to the benefits. A likely scenario here is where there are large numbers of trade creditors or customers each owed relatively small sums of money.

▶ Where a CVA or s895 CA 2006 Scheme (taking effect, for instance, within administration) provides that the rule will not apply. In the case of a CVA R1.3 (ca) provides that the proposal must estimate the value of the prescribed part (whether or not the rule is to be disapplied). Creditors will clearly want to know that they are adequately compensated by enhanced dividends for giving up their prescribed part rights or the proposal is likely to be rejected.

▶ Where there are multiple floating charge holders subsequent holders may achieve a better return by relinquishing their security and obtaining a share in a prescribed part distribution as ordinary unsecured creditors.

Definition

Net property: assets which would have been available for floating charge holders (floating charge realisations less costs and preferential creditors).

Interactive question 2: Bond Limited

Bond Limited entered into administration on 1 March 2009. The company has net property, prior to the payment of any creditors, of £525,000. The company has the following creditors:

	£
First qualifying chargeholder	290,000
Second qualifying chargeholder	83,000
Employee holiday pay claims	29,000
Employee redundancy claims	32,000
Unsecured creditors	420,000

Calculate the required part to be made available to the unsecured creditors.

See **Answer** at the end of this chapter.

5 Priority of liquidation costs – Leyland Daf

Section overview

▶ It had been believed that liquidation expenses were payable out of the proceeds of a floating charge in priority to the floating charge holder *(Re Barleycorn Enterprises Ltd)* , however the House of Lords gave judgement on 4 March 2004 in the appeal against the Court of Appeals decision in *Re Leyland Daf Ltd* and overturned the two decisions of the court on this issue.

5.1 Re Barleycorn Enterprises Limited 1970

The court held that the costs of a winding up were payable out of property comprised in a floating charge (which had crystallised when the company was ordered to be wound up) in priority to the claims of the holder of the charge.

5.2 Leyland Daf Ltd

The ruling in *Leyland Daf* in 2004 altered the way in which liquidators of companies could attempt to recover the payment of liquidation expenses and pay the liquidation preferential creditors where the company had granted floating charges over assets.

If a company is in administrative receivership and liquidation its former assets are comprised in two separate funds. Those which are subject to the floating charge (the debenture holder's funds) and those which are not subject to the floating charge (the company's funds) which are held in trust for the unsecured creditors.

Expenses of the administrative receivership are borne by the debenture holder's funds and the expenses of the liquidation are borne by the company's funds. The debenture holder has no interest in the winding up and the unsecured creditors have no interest in the administrative receivership, so neither should bear each others costs.

It follows therefore, that where the company has granted a floating charge, the costs and expenses of liquidation rank after sums payable to both the preferential creditors and to holders of a floating charge and would not be payable ahead of the floating charge security.

If the liquidator realises an asset forming part of the debenture holder's fund, the debenture holder should pay the costs of realisation (*re Regent's Canal Ironworks Company 1875*) but the debenture holder should have no liability for the general costs of the winding up.

The House of Lords decision in *Leyland Daf* has been much criticised.

▶ The decision creates an anomaly in that administrators may pay their general costs and remuneration out of floating charge realisations (see para 99(3) of Schedule B1) whereas liquidators may not. This is odd because:

– both administrations and liquidations are collective insolvency procedures

– it is possible to convert from administration to liquidation and vice versa

– the statutory provisions which apply to administrator's remuneration were modelled on the pre-*Leyland Daf* rules which, it was believed at the time, applied to liquidators i.e. parliament intended the rules applying to liquidation and administration to be the same

– the decision potentially distorts the judgment as to whether a company is more suitable for administration than liquidation. Clearly in the light of the ethical guide an IP should make the judgment based on what is in the best interests of the creditors as a whole NOT on what insolvency procedure best facilitates the payment of his or her remuneration.

5.3 s1282 Companies Act 2006

The Companies Act 2006 introduced a new s176ZA into the Insolvency Act 1986 with the effect of reversing the decision in Leyland Daf so that a liquidator's general costs will be payable as of right out of floating charge assets in defined circumstances.

The Insolvency (Amendment) Rules 2008 came into force on 6 April 2008 and apply to:

▸ Compulsory liquidations where the winding up order was made on or after the commencement date

▸ Voluntary liquidations where the resolution to wind up was passed on or after the commencement date.

The Rules introduce an amended r4.218.

The expenses of the liquidation are payable out of:

(a) The assets held by the liquidator in the course of carrying out his functions in the liquidation

(b) The proceeds of any legal proceedings which he has power to bring or defend, whether in his own name or in the name of the company, and

(c) Subject as provided below, properly comprised in or subject to a floating charge created by the company.

The general priority of the expenses are as shown in r4.218(1) with the following amendments:

(Ai) are properly chargeable or incurred by the Official Receiver or liquidator in preserving, realising or getting in any of the assets of the company or otherwise relating to the preparation and conduct of any legal proceedings which he has power to bring or defend whether in his own name or the name of the company

(s) litigation expenses and property comprised in or subject to a floating charge

Definition

Litigation expenses: those expenses or costs of a liquidation which are properly chargeable or incurred relating to the preparation and conduct of any legal proceedings which a liquidator has power to bring whether in his own name or the name of the company.

Where the assets of a company available for the payment of general creditors are insufficient to meet them, litigation expenses shall not have the priority provided by s176 ZA IA over any claims to property comprised in or subject to a floating charge created by the company and shall not be paid out of any such property save and to the extent provided by rules 4.128B to 4.128 E.

Where the assets will be insufficient to meet the payment of general creditors, the liquidator must seek prior approval or authorisation of such amount for litigation expenses as the liquidator thinks fit. Approval must be sought from relevant creditors or the court.

Relevant creditors: creditors whose claim is to property comprised in or subject to a floating charge out of which the liquidator is seeking to pay litigation expenses.

Summary and self-test

Summary

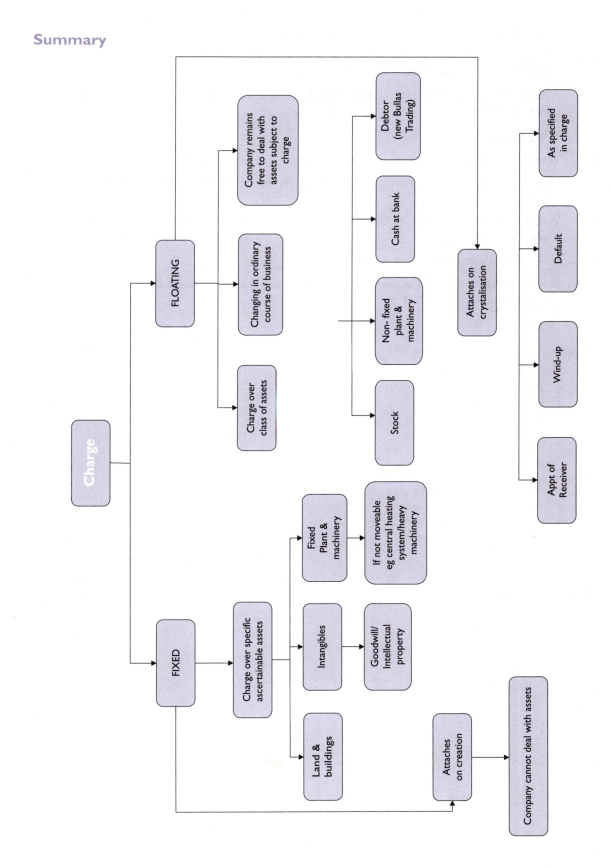

Self-test

Answer the following questions.

1   List three assets which are usually covered by a fixed charge?

2   What are the main characteristics of a floating charge?

3   A floating charge holder has the power to appoint an administrative receiver if his charge was created prior to a certain date. What is this date?

4   A fixed charge attaches to the charged property on creation. When does a floating charge attach to the charged property?

5   When will 'crystallisation' occur?

6   What is the rule in s245 IA?

7   Within how many days of creation must a charge be registered at Companies House for it to be valid?

8   Where there is more than one lender with a fixed charge over the same property, how are the charges given priority?

loose definition.

9   How is the prescribed part calculated?

Now, go back to the Learning Objectives in the Introduction. If you are satisfied that you have achieved these objectives, please tick them off.

Answers to self-test

1   Land and buildings, fixed plant, uncalled share capital, goodwill, intellectual property rights such as patents.

2   Charge over a class of assets present and future.

Changing from time to time in the ordinary course of business.

The company remains free to carry on business in the usual way in relation to those assets.

3   15 September 2003

4   Upon 'crystallisation'.

5   On cessation of a company's business (*Evans v Rivel Granite Quarries Ltd 1910*)

On the liquidation of the company.

On a receiver being appointed under the charge.

On the happening of an event specified in the charge as causing crystallisation.

6   s245 IA provides that a floating charge, created within 12 months of:

▶   date of application for an administration order or filing of notice of intention to appoint an administrator

▶   date of commencement of liquidation at a time when the company was insolvent,

▶   is invalid, except to the extent that fresh consideration is provided for it.

Where the charge is given to a connected party, the relevant time is extended to two years and insolvency of the company at the time of giving of the charge need not be shown.

7   21 days.

8   Fixed charges over land rank in order of registration at the Land Registry.

Fixed charges over assets other than land rank in order of creation.

9   Where the company's net property does not exceed £10,000, 50% of that property.

Where it exceeds £10,000:

▶   50% of the first £10,000 and
▶   20% of the balance over £10,000
▶   Up to a maximum prescribed part of £600,000.

Net property means the amount that would have been available for the floating charge holder ie. Floating charge realisations after deduction of costs, expenses, remuneration, trading losses and after payment of preferential creditors.

Answers to interactive questions

Interactive question 1: Oddbins Limited

Fixed charge realisations:

Yellow Bank Plc's fixed charge is void for want of registration at Companies House. Charges over land rank in order of registration at Land Registry, not in order of creation. A fixed charge will rank ahead of an earlier created floating charge (unless a deed of priority exists).

Distribution of proceeds from the sale of 26 Bath Road, Bristol:

1	Green Bank PLC
2	Pink Bank PLC
3	Preferential creditors
4	Green Bank PLC under its floating charge
5	Pink Bank PLC under its floating charge
6	Unsecured creditors (distributed to company or a liquidator, if appointed)

Floating charge realisations: Pink Bank PLC's charge was not registered within 21 days however the Registrar has registered it therefore it is not void.

Date of creation of the charge is relevant for determining priorities, not the date of registration at Companies House.

Distribution of sale proceeds would therefore be:

1	Preferential creditors
2	Yellow Bank PLC
3	Green Bank PLC
4	Pink Bank PLC
5	Blue Bank PLC
6	Unsecured creditors

Answer to interactive question 2: Bond Limited

	£
Net property	525,000
Less preferential creditors	(29,000)
	496,000
Prescribed part:	
50% × £10,000	5,000
20% × £486,00	97,200
	102,200

7

Introduction to receiverships

> > > > > > > > > > > > > > >

Introduction

Learning objectives

▶ Identify main features of different types of receiver and how they may be appointed

☐

▶ Learn duties and powers of the different types of receiver

☐

Working context

Administrative receiverships are still relevant following the Enterprise Act 2000. It is important to be able to distinguish between an administrative and other receivers and to know when each is likely to be appointed. In a work environment you may be required to liaise with an administrative receiver when acting as liquidator of the same company. It is important therefore that you understand the powers and duties of an administrative receiver.

Stop and think

Why should a receiver appointed under a fixed charge have different powers and duties to a receiver appointed under a floating charge? Why does a LPA receiver not have to be a qualified IP? When would a receiver be appointed by the court?

Examination context

Administrative receiverships still remain relevant for the JIEB exam however it is important to be familiar with all types of receivership and the powers and duties of each type of receiver. Fixed charge and LPA receiverships are less likely to be tested in the exam than administrative receiverships.

Past exam questions to look at include:

2005   Question 1(a)

1999   Question 3(a)

1994   Question 5

1993   Question 1

1992   Question 2

1991   Paper II Question 2(b) (i), (ii), (iii)

1 Introduction

Section overview

There are many types of receiver. However for the purposes of the JIEB exam, there are three types:

▶ Administrative receiver
▶ Receiver appointed by a secured creditor holding a fixed charge only
▶ The receiver appointed by the court

2 Administrative receiver (AR)

Section overview

▶ An administrative receiver (AR) is:

– A receiver or manager of the whole (or substantially the whole) of a company's property appointed by or on behalf of the holders of any debentures of the company secured by a charge which as created was a floating charge, or by such a charge and one or more other securities; or

– A person who would be such a receiver or manager but for the appointment of some other person as the receiver of part of the company's property.

▶ The Government had intended to abolish administrative receiverships however this proposal was dropped and the Insolvency Act 1986, as amended by the Enterprise Act 2002, provided that a floating charge holder remained entitled to appoint an AR where the floating charge was created prior to 15 September 2003 (s72A(4) IA).

2.1 Advantages of administrative receivership

▶ Appointment of an AR is quick, straightforward and relatively inexpensive. However, the importance of this has been diminished by the introduction of the new out of court route into administration for qualifying floating charge holders.

▶ An AR can be appointed whether or not the company is in liquidation.

▶ The appointment of an AR requires no prior notice to be given to any person.

▶ An AR appointment can be made where an administration moratorium has been obtained in the previous 12 months.

▶ An AR has a primary duty to realise charged assets so as to repay the principal and interest to the appointor.

▶ The AR only has a duty of due diligence owed to unsecured creditors and guarantors of the company's debt. In *Silven Properties Ltd v RBS 2003* it was confirmed that the AR owes no duty to unsecured creditors or to the company to delay a sale in the hope of a better price.

▶ The debenture holder can choose which IP acts as AR.

▶ The AR will discuss the strategy for the receivership with the chargeholder, the chargeholder has more ability to influence AR's strategy.

▶ The AR and charge holder are not constrained by any statutory purposes.

▶ Corporation tax on a capital gain is an ordinary unsecured debt.

▶ Administrative receivership does not end a tax period and this facilitates the use of corporation tax losses in reducing taxable profits.

- Business rates will be an unsecured liability of the company rather than an expense of the receivership *Exeter City Council v Bairstow, (Re Trident Fashions) 2007, EWCH 400 (House of Lords)*

- Creditors entitled to appoint a AR can 'veto' the appointment of an administrator (s9 IA).

- No requirement for AR to report to creditors on a periodic basis.

- There is no statutory time limit on administrative receivership.

- AR's have powers specified in Schedule 1 to the IA, LPA receiver's do not.

- AR's may use:

  - s234 IA to get a court order for possession of property, paper, books, records

  - s235 IA to obtain co-operation

  - s236 IA to get a court order for the private examination of officers, debtors and persons suspected to have company property/ persons who have information re promotion, formation, management, dealings, affairs or property of the company.

2.2 Disadvantages of administrative receivership

- AR's have more extensive statutory duties than other types of receiver, which exposes banks to potentially greater costs and liabilities under the usual indemnity:

  - Duty to pay preferential creditors

  - Deal with employee EPA claims

  - Duty to complete D return

- They may only be appointed under a floating charge which was created prior to 15 September 2003

- There is a perception that the bank is pulling the plug - adverse publicity

- Lack of recognition under EC Regs

- Lack of moratorium

- AR may be found liable for misfeasance (LPA receivers cannot).

3   Receiver appointed by holders of fixed charges only

Section overview

A fixed charge receiver may be appointed under:
- The provisions of the LPA 1925
- A power contained in an instrument

3.1 Receiver appointed under LPA 1925

A mortgagee under a legal mortgage (i.e. created by deed) has the right to appoint a receiver (s101 LPA 1925).

However this power only arises:

- After the mortgage money has become due (s101LPA 1925)

- *And* the mortgagee has become entitled to exercise the statutory power of sale (s109 LPA 1925). By s103 LPA 1925 the power of sale arises:

  - Where default in repayment of a loan for three months after a notice requiring it or
  - Interest unpaid for two months after becoming due or
  - Breach of the deed or LPA 1925.

The receiver's powers are limited to collecting rents and income.

Chatsworth Properties Ltd v Effiom - Receiver should make it clear that acting as the mortgagors agent when collecting rents, to prevent any tenancy arising between himself and the tenants.

NB: Receiver has no statutory power to recover possession against the mortgagor (the LPA 1925 does give that power to the mortgagee).

The receiver also has a duty to keep property in repair and to insure.

Liability of LPA receiver:

▶   S 109 LPA 1925 provides that the receiver is the agent of the mortgagor who shall be solely responsible for his acts and defaults. However s 29 IA extends the provisions of s 37 IA to the LPA receiver. By s 37(1) IA receivers or managers (other than administrative receivers who are dealt with in s 44 IA) are:

–   Personally liable on any contract entered into in the performance of their functions

–   And on any contract of employment adopted by them in the performance of those functions (14 day rule applies as with the AR).

–   As in s 44 IA the receiver may seek to exclude liability in the contract and is entitled to an indemnity out of the assets.

▶   The statutory protection afforded the AR by the Insolvency 1986 does not apply to LPA Receivers. They will be personally liable on employment contracts adopted after 14 days.

Mortgagees under an equitable mortgage (i.e. created merely under hand or evidenced by deposit of title deeds) have no statutory power to appoint a receiver.

Byblos Bank SAL v AG Khudairy 1987 - an equitable mortgage created in a written document may contain a valid contractual power to appoint a receiver.

3.2   Receivers appointed under an agreement

There are two drawbacks to relying on the LPA 1925:

▶   Mortgagees power to appoint a receiver is restricted.
▶   Powers of receiver once appointed are limited to collecting rents.

It is common therefore to make express provision in the mortgage.

The mortgage deed commonly gives the receiver:

▶   Power to take possession and sell the property.
▶   Power to borrow money to carry out statutory duties in s 109 LPA 1925 (to insure and repair).

Note. The receivers powers under the deed will now overlap with the mortgagees statutory powers - so receiver and mortgagee should agree on who will exercise each power.

▶   Deed may give the receiver extensive powers to manage the company's business - however trading on may prove difficult in practice as the receiver only has access to the charged assets and would be a trespasser if, for instance, reused stock not covered by his appointors charges.

The deed will commonly shorten the periods of notice required by the LPA for appointment of a receiver.

S 37 IA applies here as for receiver appointed under a statutory power. The receiver is deemed to be personally liable on any contract entered into.

On appointment solicitors advice should be taken to ensure the validity of the borrowing and the charges and also to ensure that the following are co-ordinated:

▶   The property subject to the charge(s)
▶   The property over which the receiver has now been appointed
▶   The powers which the receiver has been granted under the debenture.

3.3   Restriction on appointment of receivers under fixed charges only

S 110 LPA provides that if the mortgagor is in liquidation then the courts permission is required before receiver can be appointed.

Para 43 Schedule B1 IA 86 in relation to administration provides that once the company is in administration:

- ▶   "No steps may be taken to enforce any security over the company's property" except with leave of the court, or the administrator

- ▶   Existing receivers remain in office but may not realise security without the administrator or the courts permission.

- ▶   No receiver may now be appointed, without leave

- ▶   "Any receiver of part of the company's property shall vacate office on being required to do so by the administrator".

Note. Duty to pay preferential creditors is discharged at this point.

- ▶   Para 41 Sch B1 IA provides that if required to leave office the remuneration and expenses of the receiver and his indemnity out of the company's assets (see s37 IA) shall be charged on and paid out of any property of the company which was in his custody or under his control at that time in priority to any security held by the person who appointed him.

3.4   Duties of receivers appointed under fixed charge only

The fixed charge receiver has a number of duties:

To deliver to the registrar accounts of receipts and payments, within one month s38(1) IA:

- ▶   Of the expiration of 12 months from date of appointment, and

- ▶   Of every subsequent period of six months, and

- ▶   Within one month after ceasing to act as receiver and manager, covering the period from the date on which the last abstract made up to the present.

Contravention - receiver liable to fine.

Statement to appear on all letters, invoices etc. that a receiver appointed (s39 IA)

Receiver to pay preferential creditors in priority to holders of floating charges (s40 IA), where appointed under a fixed and floating charge. Such a receiver would normally be an administrative receiver, but can be a 'fixed charge' receiver where the charges do not extend to the 'whole or substantially the whole' of the company's assets.

4   Receiver appointed by the court

Section overview

Under s37 Supreme Court Act 1981, a High Court judge has a power to appoint a receiver where it is 'just and convenient'. Appointments are relatively rare but will typically be made where:

- ▶   Deadlock in management (application by members or directors) and

- ▶   Assets in jeopardy or default.

The receiver is an officer of the court and his powers and duties are set out in the court order. The duties generally are to safeguard and preserve the assets rather than to realise them.

5 Classification of receivers

Section overview

Below is a comparison of receivers appointed out of court.

	Administrative Receiver	Fixed Charge Receiver	LPA Receiver
Status	Must be IP (ss.230(2) IA, and 388(1)(a) IA)	Need not be IP	Need not be IP
Appointment	By chargee in circumstances set out in security documentation	By chargee in circumstances set out in security documentation	By chargee in the limited circumstances set out in the LPA 1925.
Charges	To qualify as A.R, ▸ Must be appointed over whole or substantially whole of company's property ▸ By holders of floating charges (s29(2) IA). ▸ Charge must have been created prior to 15 September 2003 subject to exceptions for bond issues and public finance projects.	Chargee will hold ▸ Fixed charge(s) ▸ And possibly floating charge(s) also	As for Fixed Charge Receiver
Agency	Agent of the company (s44(1)(a) IA)	Security documentation will state agent of company	(s109(2) LPA 1925) Agent of the mortgagor (company)
Liability on contracts	▸ Personally liable on contracts entered into in performance of functions (s44(1)(b) IA) ▸ Subject to indemnity out of assets of company (s44(1)(c) IA)	▸ Personally liable on contracts entered into in performance of functions (s37(1)(a) IA) ▸ Subject to indemnity out of assets of company (s37(1)(b) IA)	▸ S29 IA includes LPA receiver in definition of receiver generally ▸ Therefore s37 IA applies
Liability on adopted contracts of employment	▸ Personally liable on adopted contracts of employment to extent of qualifying liabilities only (s44(1)(b) IA) ▸ Entitled to indemnity out of co's assets ▸ 14 day liability free period	▸ Personally liable on adopted contracts of employment ▸ Not restricted to qualifying liabilities (s37(1)(a) IA) ▸ Entitled to indemnity out of co. assets ▸ 14 day liability free period	As for fixed charge Receiver

	Administrative Receiver	Fixed Charge Receiver	LPA Receiver
Powers	▶ Statutory powers to manage the company (Schedule 1) ▶ Debenture may limit or extend these powers ▶ S 233 IA Power to demand supplies from utilities ▶ Has statutory powers to enforce co-operation of Directors (ss.234-237 IA) ▶ S 43 IA Power to apply to the court for sanction to dispose of property subject to prior charges	▶ Powers set out in the security documentation ▶ Will normally empower receiver to take possession and sell charged assets ▶ No such statutory powers to enforce co-operation ▶ S 43 IA does NOT apply	▶ Statutory powers in LPA limited to (s 109(3) IA) demanding and recovering income and giving receipts. ▶ No power to take possession and sell ▶ No such statutory powers to enforce co-operation ▶ S 43 IA does NOT apply
Duties	▶ (S 40 IA) to pay prefs in priority to holders of floating charges ▶ (S 7(3)(d) CDDA) - to report to Secretary of State on conduct of Directors ▶ (S 48 IA) to report to and call meeting of unsecured creditors ▶ To deal with ERA claims by employees	▶ S 40 IA applies only if receiver also appointed under floating charge ▶ No duty to report ▶ S 48 IA does not apply ▶ N.A	▶ As Fixed Charge Receiver ▶ No duty to report ▶ S 48 IA does not apply ▶ N.A.
Receipts and Payments	(R3.32) Accounts to be delivered to Co's House within two months of ▶ 12 months from appointment ▶ Every subsequent 12 months ▶ Ceasing to act as AR	(S 38) Accounts to be delivered to Co's House within one month of ▶ 12 months from appointment ▶ Every subsequent six months ▶ Ceasing to act as receiver	As for fixed charge receiver
Publicity	(S 39 IA) Statement to appear on all letters invoices etc that a Receiver appointed	As for AR	As for AR

Note. 'LPA Receiver' This book uses this expression to mean a receiver appointed under the statutory power in the LPA and uses 'Fixed Charge Receiver' to mean one appointed under a power in the security documents. In practice 'LPA Receiver' is often used loosely to mean any Receiver appointed under fixed charges.

Interactive question: Surfs Up limited

Your principal, Sally Heyes, has been contacted by Satby Bank PLC. One of the banks customers, Surfs Up Limited, has advised the bank that they are experiencing financial difficulties. The company's only significant asset is its trading premises and debtor ledger.

The bank holds a debenture over the assets of the company which includes a fixed charge over property and goodwill and a floating charge over debtors and all other assets. It is the bank's policy not to become mortgagee in possession.

Requirement

Draft a letter to the bank setting out the alternatives available to it, detailing for each course of action the consequences for the bank and the directors. (Do not consider liquidation as an option).

See **Answer** at the end of the chapter.

6 Remuneration

Section overview

In receiverships, remuneration is a contractual matter between the receiver and the charge holder. There is no statutory criteria to be applied and no provision for dissatisfied office holders to appeal to creditors or the court. A receiver appointed by the court will have his fees determined by the court.

6.1 Dissatisfaction with receiver's fees

The creditors, unlike other insolvency appointments, do not have a say in the level of the receiver's fees. To avoid misuse of such arrangements when a company is wound up following administrative receivership and the administrative receiver was appointed out of court, the liquidator may apply to the court under s36 IA to fix the administrative receiver's remuneration retrospectively, and order him to repay any money he has taken in excess of the amount fixed. This power should only be exercised where the administrative receiver's remuneration is clearly excessive: it is not a procedure for routine taxation of fees: *Re Potters Oils Ltd (No 2)* 1986. An express term in a charge contract providing that the company is liable for the receiver's remuneration precludes any possible liability of the chargee as the beneficiary of the receiver's work: *Hill Samuel & Co Ltd v Laing* 1988.

6.2 Remuneration on vacating office

When an administrative receiver vacates office, his remuneration, expenses properly incurred by him and any indemnity to which he is entitled out of the company's assets are charged on, and must be paid out of, the company's property under his control when he vacated office. This charge has priority over the charge under which the administrative receiver was appointed (s 45(3) IA). It is a form of equitable charge which may be enforced by the court appointing a receiver and ordering sale of the charged assets. If an administrative receiver vacates office on the making of an administration order, then a charge is imposed but it is subject to the general moratorium on enforcement of creditors' securities (s 11(3) and (4) IA).

Summary and Self-test

Summary

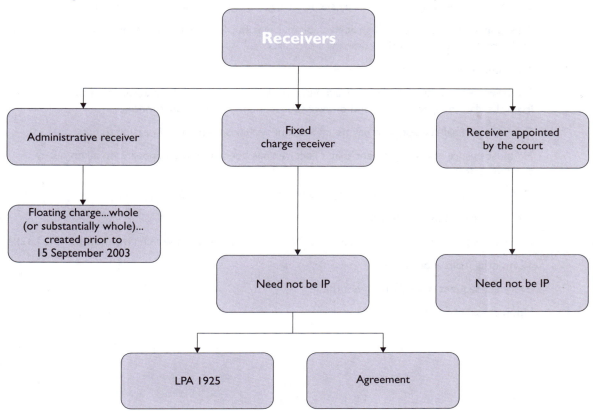

Self-test

Answer the following questions.

1   What is the definition of an administrative receiver?

2   What are the powers of a receiver appointed under LPA 1925?

3   What are the duties of a receiver appointed under a fixed charge only?

4   Which of the following office holders are required to be an IP? Is it:

   A   Administrative receiver
   B   Fixed charge receiver
   C   LPA receiver

5   Which of the following office holders are not required to report on the conduct of the directors under CDDA? Is it:

   A   Administrative receiver
   B   Fixed charge receiver
   C   LPA receiver

6   How often must an administrative receiver submit an account of his receipts and payments to the Registrar of Companies?

Now, go back to the Learning Objectives in the Introduction. If you are satisfied that you have achieved these objectives, please tick them off.

Answers to Self-test

1   A receiver or manager of the whole (or substantially the whole) of a company's property appointed by or on behalf of the holders of any debentures of the company secured by a charge which as created was a floating charge, or by such a charge and one or more securities: or

A person who would be such a receiver or manager but for the appointment of some other person as the receiver of part of the company's property.

2   To collect rents and income.

3   To deliver a receipts and payments account within one month of the expiration of the 12 months from the date of appointment and of every subsequent period of six months.

To deliver a final receipts and payments account within one month of ceasing to act.

He must ensure that a statement that a receiver has been appointed appears on all company documentation.

4   Only an administrative receiver is required to be an IP s230(2), s388(1)(a) IA.

5   Fixed charge receiver, LPA receiver

6   Deliver receipts and payments account to Registrar of Companies within two months of (r3.32):

12 months from appointment

Every subsequent period of 12 months

Upon ceasing to act

Answers to Interactive Question

Answer to Interactive Question: Surfs Up Limited

Letter format.

(Note: It is important to follow instructions in the exam. Marks are awarded for layout/ style which are easy marks to obtain).

Options available to the bank:

(i)   Administration

(ii)   Appoint a fixed charge receiver over property

(iii)   Appoint administrative receiver under floating charge (assumes charge created prior to 15 September 2003)

(i)   Administration:

- Bank will have power to appoint administrator as a holder of a qualifying floating charge

- Banks security remains however rights of enforcement will be lost

- Administrative receiver cannot be appointed

- Administrator acts in interests of creditors generally rather than for charge holder

- Directors' powers cease to the extent that they conflict with powers of the administrator

- Administrator may only realise fixed charge assets with the agreement of the bank or order of the court

- Net proceeds must be paid to the charge holder

- If assets sold at less than market value, the deficiency must be paid to the bank

- Administrator may deal with floating charge assets as if not subject to the charge

- Bank will have no control over actions of the administrator who must act to achieve one of para 3 – objectives.

(ii)   Fixed charge receivership:

- Receiver's powers restricted – can only deal with assets over which specifically appointed

- Can only exercise powers included in LPA 1925 or as extended by the charging document

- Cannot continue to trade

- Directors remain responsible for non charged assets

- Does not stop enforcement action by other creditors

- Receiver's costs will only relate to dealing with charged assets – cheaper

(iii)   Administrative receivership:

- All directors powers over charged assets cease, however they retain responsibility for any assets not covered by the bank's charge

- Director's statutory duties remain

- Bank chooses who will be administrative receiver

- Receiver's first duty is to the bank

- Bank has more control over strategy of the receivership
- Administrative receiver is agent of the company
- Responsible for all assets covered by the floating charge
- Administrative receiver has power to continue trading
- Costs may be higher for the bank
- Administrative receiver has statutory duties including:
  - Dealing with Employment Protection (Consolidation) Act requirements
  - Company Director Disqualification Act requirements
  - Calling creditors meeting under s48 IA.

CVA?
or CVA w'in Receivership
have a view to Cap G.T.

BPP
LEARNING MEDIA

8

Administrative receivership

〉 〉 〉 〉 〉 〉 〉 〉 〉 〉 〉 〉 〉 〉 〉 〉

Contents

Introduction

Examination context

Topic List

1   Appointment

2   Validity of appointment

3   Effect on directors of the appointment of an AR

4   Powers of the AR

5   Agency

6   Property available to an AR

7   Duties of the AR

8   SIP 1 An AR's responsibility for the company's records

9   SIP 14 A receiver's responsibility to preferential creditors

Summary and Self-test

Answers to Self-test

Answers to interactive questions

Introduction

Learning objectives

▶ Matters to be complied with for an AR's appointment to be valid ☐

▶ Powers and duties of an AR ☐

▶ The effect of an AR's appointment on the directors of a company ☐

▶ How an AR should deal with a company's records per SIP 1 ☐

▶ The duties of an AR with respect to preferential creditors ☐

Working context

It is important to know when an AR has been validly appointed, this may be because you have been asked to act as an AR in respect of a company or you may be asked to act as liquidator of a company in respect of which an AR is already acting. It is also important to understand the powers and duties of an AR.

Stop and think

Why should an AR have more onerous duties than any other type of receiver? What are these duties and to whom are they owed? How are the directors of a company affected by the appointment of an AR? Why should the AR not be responsible for the company's statutory records? Why are preferential creditors treated differently to other creditors?

Examination context

Administrative receiverships still remain relevant to the JIEB exam, in particular the duties of the AR and validity of appointment.

Past exam questions to look at include:

2005	Question 1(b)
2002	Question 4(d)
1998	Question 2
1992	Paper 1 Question 3
1991	Paper 1 Question 1

1 Appointment

Section overview

▶ An administrative receiver (AR) is appointed by the holders of a floating charge where there has been a default under the terms of the debenture. The legislation concerning administrative receiverships can be found in s42-49 IA 86 and s72A-72H IA 86 and Part 3 of the Rules, r3.1 – r3.40.

1.1 Restrictions on appointment by IA 86

S72A(1) IA prohibits the holder of a Qualifying Floating Charge from appointing an AR unless the charge was created prior to 15 September 2003.

Further exceptions to s72A(1) IA are set out in ss72B to H IA and Schedule 2A. In these situations an AR can still be appointed even through the floating charge was created after 15 September 2003:

▶ Capital market arrangements involving debt of at least £50 million and where the debentures are rated, listed or traded.

▶ (s72C) IA Public private partnerships (this refers to large government projects where there is collaboration in providing finance between public bodies and the private sector).

▶ (s72D) IA Utility projects

▶ (s72E) IA Large project finance arrangements

▶ (s72G) IA Registered social landlords (this relates mainly to housing associations)

▶ Urban regeneration projects, railway and water companies.

1.2 Qualification to act as AR

Must be a qualified IP (ie hold appropriate licence from RPB/DBERR):

▶ An AR acts as an IP in relation to a company (s388 IA)

▶ It is an offence to act as an IP when not qualified to do so (s389 IA)

▶ Bodies corporate, mental patients, undischarged bankrupts and persons disqualified under CDDA 86 may not be IP's

Receivers who are not administrative receivers don't need to be an IP.

A body corporate may not act as an AR (or liable for a fine) (s30 IA).

An undischarged bankrupt may not act as an AR (or liable to a fine and/ or imprisonment) (s31 IA).

By s1 CDDA 86 any person disqualified under the act may not be an AR.

Note: the rules in s30, 31 and s1 CDDA 86 also apply to non AR receivers.

Must hold relevant security (general penalty bond and specific penalty bond Sch 2 IP Regs)

There must be no ethical reasons why the IP should not act (see Chapter 1 for full guide to ethics). Remember that the main question to ask is :

'Has there been a significant personal or professional relationship with the company or directors within the last three years?'

Note that:

▶ No significant relationship will arise from previous appointment of the IP's firm as investigating accountants. This is providing:

    – There has been no direct involvement in the company's management by any partner or employee of the firm, and

   – The firm's principal client relationship is with the appointing bank rather than with the company (and the company must be aware of this).

▸ Members should decline appointments if they or partners or employees of the firm have such a personal or close and distinct business connection with the debenture holder as might impair or appear to impair the member's objectivity.

The following practical checks should be carried out to prevent an inadvertent breach of the ethical guide:

▸ Request company search in respect of the company over which you are to be appointed, and also other group companies and known associates.

▸ Identify all companies within any group as well as their directors and major shareholders

▸ Check firm's database to ascertain if any partner/employee has conducted significant professional work with any company in the group/director

▸ Check for any potential conflicts of interest (can ask directors to confirm there is none).

▸ Does bank know of any connection between firm and company?

▸ If in doubt consult professional body.

2 Validity of appointment

Section overview

▸ An AR may only be validly appointed if the charge under which he is appointed is itself valid. However the acts of an AR are deemed to be valid despite any defect in his appointment (s232 IA). If there is an invalid appointment of an AR purportedly appointed out of court, then the court may order the person who purported to appoint him to indemnify him against any liability arising solely by reason of the invalidity of his appointment (s34 IA). S232 IA will not however protect an AR where there was no power to appoint in the first place *OBG Ltd v Allen 2005*.

2.1 Validity of debenture and charge

The following points are relevant when considering the validity of a charge:

Has the charge instrument been duly executed?

▸ Executed under seal or as a deed by two directors or a director and the secretary.

▸ If executed under hand cannot create a legal mortgage.

Company Law points:

Was the giving of the security the provision of financial assistance for the purchase of the company's own shares under s143-s154 CA 1985?

Was the giving of the security intra vires the company?

▸ Check objects clause...

▸ ...but under s35 CA 1985 parties are protected where enter into ultra vires transactions in good faith.

Was the giving of the security intra vires the directors? Check:

▸ Effective board resolution authorising the issue of debenture and giving of security.
▸ No reason to suspect that directors acting outside their authority as agents of the company.

Has the charge been registered within 21 days (s385 CA 1985)?

Could the creation of the charge constitute a preference under s239 IA? Remember that the appointment of receiver does NOT trigger s239 IA, (but the company going into liquidation or administration will).

Could the charge (if floating) be invalidated under s245 IA? *(Fresh consideration) P. 279*

▸ Again the section is only activated by the liquidation or administration of the company and not by the appointment of an AR.

▸ Effect of s245 IA is not retrospective *(Mace Builders (Glasgow) Ltd v Lunn (1986)* i.e. the AR's acts prior to the liquidation will be valid, despite fact that charge under which AR appointed has now been invalidated under s245 IA.

Could the charge be invalidated as a transaction at an undervalue under s238 IA? *liq/admin only.*

S. 423 ~~~~~~~~ only on behalf of appointer as victim P 135

2.2 Validity of appointment

The following matters should be dealt with in order to confirm that the appointment itself is valid:

Check that the debenture does authorise appointment of AR in the circumstances that have arisen. Debenture usually provides for appointment on default (and appointment to be made in writing by say "any branch manager").

Note that an overdraft is (unless otherwise agreed) repayable on demand *(Williams & Glyn's Bank Ltd v Barnes 1981)*. However there is no liability to repay until a demand is made and no security can be enforced until a demand has been made and not complied with *(Lloyds Bank Ltd v Margolis 1984)* Therefore check that:

▸ Letter or demand has been sent (although amount demanded in letter does not need to be exact sum due *Bank of Baroda v Panessar)*.

▸ *(Bank of Baroda v Panessar)* time has been given for the mechanics of repayment but

▸ not necessarily for raising capital or seeking to re-finance the loan *(Shamji v Johnson Mathey Bank Ltd 1985)*.

Company must not be in administration

Appointment instrument must be received and accepted by AR(s) by end of next business day.

Acceptance can be oral or written (but if oral must be confirmed in writing in 7 days)

Acceptance must state date and time of receipt of appointment and date and time of acceptance. If the appointment is duly accepted it is deemed to take effect at the time the instrument of appointment was received.

Two or more insolvency practitioners may be appointed joint administrative receivers of a company. The acceptance of each must be confirmed in writing and the appointment is effective only when all of them have confirmed acceptance (R3.1(1)). Their appointment is deemed to have been made at the time at which the instrument of appointment was received by or on behalf of all of them (R3.1(1)). The appointment must declare whether any act required or authorised under any enactment to be done by the administrative receiver is to be done by all or any one or more of the persons for the time being holding the office (s231 IA).

2.3 Notification of appointment

If an administrative receiver is appointed the appointor must, under penalty, within seven days give notice in the prescribed form to the Registrar of Companies, and the registrar will note the appointment in the register of charges (s405 CA 1985). On appointment, an administrative receiver of a company must, under penalty, forthwith send to *the company* a notice of his appointment and must also publish an advertisement in the *London Gazette* and in such newspaper as he thinks most appropriate for ensuring that it comes to the notice of the company's creditors (s46(1)(a) and (4) and Sch 10 IA; r3.2(3)).

Unless the court otherwise directs, the administrative receiver must also send a notice to all *creditors* of the company of whose addresses he is aware; the notice to creditors must, under penalty, be sent within 28 days after his appointment (s46(1)(b) and (4) and Sch 10 IA). The contents of the advertisement and the notice to the company and the creditors are specified in r3.2(2) and (4).

The notice must contain the following information (r3.2(2)):

(i)   The registered name of the company as at the date of the appointment, and its registered number;

(ii)   Any other name under which the company has been registered in the twelve months prior to the date of appointment;

(iii)   Any name under which the company has traded at any time within those twelve months, if that name is substantially different from its then registered name;

(iv)   The name and address of the administrative receiver and the date of his appointment;

(v)   The name of the person by whom the appointment was made;

(vi)   The date of the instrument conferring the power under which the appointment was made, together with a brief description of the instrument;

(vii)   A brief description of the assets of the company (if any) in respect of which the person appointed is not made a receiver.

During administrative receivership, if the company, or the administrative receiver, or a liquidator, issues an invoice, order for goods or business letter in which the name of the company appears then the document must include a statement that an administrative receiver has been appointed (s39 IA; penalty in Sch 10).

From 1 October 2008 the duty to disclose their status will also apply to electronic letters and order forms, and any company websites. Disclosure now has to be made whether or not the company's name appears on the electronic or paper document (The Companies (Trading Disclosures) (Insolvency) Regulations 2008 No. 1897.)

3   Effect on directors of the appointment of an AR

Section overview

▶   From the time of his appointment the AR of a company has sole authority to deal with the charged property. The directors of the company no longer have authority to deal with the charged property; they do however retain custody and control of any assets which are not covered by the appointor's charges. To the extent that they seek to trade with these however, they will be trading whilst the company is prima facie insolvent. The AR should warn the directors that they should seek independent professional advice on their position.

3.1   The directors' office

The appointment of an AR does not terminate the director's office.

It follows that the directors retain statutory duties such as the duty to make returns and submit documents to the Registrar of Companies. To facilitate compliance with these residual duties the Administrative Receiver should be prepared to provide necessary information to directors and access to relevant documentation.

It also follows that the directors retain their power to institute proceedings in the company's name, *(Newhart Developments Ltd v Co-operative Commercial Bank Ltd 1978)*. Directors may therefore:

▶   Challenge the validity of the AR's appointment
▶   Oppose a petition to wind-up the company
▶   Or cause the company to sue the AR for breach of duty *(Watts v Midland Bank Plc 1986)*.

3.2   The directors' contract of employment

The appointment of an AR does not automatically terminate contracts of employment. Directors therefore retain their employment unless and until:

- ▸ The AR terminates those contracts or   *P135?*
- ▸ The company is liquidated.

In practice the AR may wish to retain the services of the directors (at least in the short term) to run the day to day operations of the company whilst the AR looks into the viability of trading on and effecting a going concern sale.

In such a situation the AR will at an early meeting with the directors explain:

- ▸ That the co-operation of the directors will assist the AR's attempts to trade on and sell

- ▸ That the directors retain their employment for the time being (although no absolute guarantees for the future can be given)

- ▸ That the AR will, however, make funds available to pay the directors.

3.3 The directors' potential liabilities

One or more directors will be required to submit a statement of affairs.

The administrative receiver is required to report on the conduct of directors to the Secretary of State under the *Company Directors Disqualification Act*. Under the *Insolvent Companies (Reports on Conduct of Directors) Rules 1996*:

- ▸ the AR reports on Form D1 where it appears immediately that the conditions of s6(1) of the CDDA are satisfied (i.e. that there appears to be evidence of unfitted conduct).

- ▸ Interim (i.e. the AR has not to date uncovered evidence of unfitted conduct) or Final returns are made on Form D2.

- ▸ Where there are joint office-holders only one report is required. (see chapter 11 for more details).

3.4 The directors' duties to the AR

Under s235 IA past and present officers of the company have a duty:

- ▸ to give the AR such information as the AR shall require concerning the company and its promotion, formation, business, dealings, affairs or property

- ▸ and to attend on the AR at such times as the AR shall reasonably require.

This also extends to sub-contractors eg consultants (s235(3)(c) IA) and auditors as potential officers of the company. Officers etc. failing to comply (without reasonable excuse) are liable to a fine. A failure by a director to comply is a matter to which the court may pay particular regard when deciding whether to make a disqualification order (CCDA 1986, Sch1, para 10(g)).

Under s234 IA where an administrative receiver has been appointed and any person has in his possession or control any property, books, papers or records to which the company appears entitled the court may require that person to transfer the property etc. to the AR. In other words AR's can obtain court orders to force directors and others to hand over charged property and relevant documentation.

An AR can (under s236 IA) apply to the court for an order that any office holder of the company appear before the court. In addition the court can require such a person to:

- ▸ submit an affidavit containing an account of his dealings with the company

- ▸ or to produce any document relating to the company or to its property, business etc.

If an officer is likely to be uncooperative the court can issue a warrant for

- ▸ arrest and

- ▸ seizure of relevant documentation or goods.

On a practical level the sort of information the AR will require from the directors at an early stage will include whether interest in buying the business has been expressed in the past and the identity of any other parties who may be interested in the future, and any urgent matters which will require the AR's immediate attention.

The directors must submit a statement of affairs within 21 days of the AR's request (s47 IA).

Contracts and correspondence

At an early meeting with the directors, the AR will explain that no orders are to be placed by the directors or employees of the company and no orders are to be accepted without the authority of the AR or the AR's staff.

An underlying reason for this is that in relation to contracts entered into with the company post-commencement of the administrative receivership;

▶ the administrative receiver enters into such contracts as agent of the company (*not* of the appointor)

▶ but is none-the-less said to be personally liable on such contracts subject to a number of caveats.

▶ As the AR is at least potentially liable on post appointment contracts it is clearly important to exert control over contracts entered into by the company.

All incoming mail should be directed unopened to members of the AR's staff. All outgoing mail should likewise be authorised by the AR's staff.

4 Powers of the AR

Section overview

▶ A professionally drafted contract of floating charge will confer on an administrative receiver appointed under the contract a wide range of powers. Now, s42(1) of, and Sch 1 to, IA 1986 confer upon every administrative receiver a standardised list of powers (though a charge contract may exclude any of them). A person dealing with an administrative receiver of a company in good faith and for value is entitled to assume that the receiver is acting within his powers (s42(3) IA). References to the property of the company are to the property of which he is or, but for the appointment of some other person as the receiver of part of the company's property, would be, the receiver or manager.

The AR has the power to:

▶ take possession of, collect and take in the property of the company and, for that purpose, take such proceedings as may seem to him expedient;

▶ sell or otherwise dispose of the property of the company by public auction or private contract; *over which he is the receiver or manager.*

▶ raise or borrow money and thereby grant security over the property of the company;

▶ appoint a solicitor, accountant or other professionally qualified person to assist him in the performance of his functions;

▶ bring or defend any actions or other legal proceedings in the name of and on behalf of the company;

▶ refer to arbitration any question affecting the company;

▶ effect and maintain insurances in respect of the business and property of the company;

▶ use the company's seal;

▶ do all acts and to execute in the name of and on behalf of the company any deed, receipt or other document;

▶ draw, accept, make or endorse any bill of exchange or promissory note in the name of, and on behalf of, the company;

▶ appoint any agent to do any business which he is unable to do himself, or which can more conveniently be done by an agent;

▶ employ and dismiss employees;

- do all such things (including the carrying out of works) as may be necessary for the realisation of the property of the company;

- make any payment which is necessary or incidental to the performance of his functions;

- carry on the business of the company, establish subsidiaries and transfer to subsidiaries the whole or any part of the business and property of the company;

- make any arrangement or compromise on behalf of the company;

- grant or accept a surrender of a lease or tenancy of any property of the company, and take a lease or tenancy of any property required or convenient for the business of the company;

- call up any uncalled share capital of the company;

- rank and claim in the bankruptcy, insolvency, sequestration or liquidation of any person indebted to the company and to receive dividends, or to accede to trust deeds for the creditors of any such person;

- present or defend a petition for the winding up of the company;

- change the situation of the company's registered office;

- lastly, he has the power to do all other things incidental to the exercise of the foregoing powers.

4.1 Application to court for directions

An administrative receiver appointed out of court may apply to the court for directions in relation to any particular matter arising in connection with the carrying out of his functions (s35(1) IA).

The person by whom, or on whose behalf, he was appointed may also apply for such directions.

On any application the court has the option to give directions or make a declaratory order.

4.2 s43 IA power to apply to court for an order sanctioning the disposal of property subject to prior charges

In many situations the most effective way of progressing the administrative receivership will be to dispose of the entire undertaking of the company as a going concern. Clearly the existence of prior charges may impede such a sale.

The AR will seek to negotiate a settlement with the prior chargee.

Where agreement cannot be reached the AR has power to apply to the court.

The court must be satisfied that the disposal (with or without other assets) of the property subject to security would be likely to promote a more advantageous realisation of the company's assets than would otherwise be effected.

It must be a condition of the order that the greater of the proceeds of sale or the open market value of the property as determined by the court is paid to the prior chargeholder. *[handwritten: No see below]*

The AR must give the charge holder notice of the court hearing (r3.31(1) and (2)). If the court makes an order the AR must, under penalty, send an office copy of the order to the Registrar of Companies within 14 days of the making of the order (s43(5) and (6) IA), accompanied by Form 3.8. The AR must also send an office copy to the prior chargee (r3.31(4)).

4.3 Powers the AR does NOT have

- Disclaim a lease
- Pay a dividend to unsecured creditors
- Also act as liquidator of the company

[handwritten: "Shall be applied towards discharging the sums secured by the security."]

*[handwritten: * If deficiency towards discharging security, the deficiency must be made up.]*

- Bring court actions for:
  - director's wrongful/ fraudulent trading
  - preferences
  - transactions at an undervalue
  - s423 IA as AR ie. Only on behalf of appointor as victim of the transaction
  - remove directors from office

5 Agency

Section overview

- By s44(1)(a) IA the AR is deemed to be the company's agent unless and until, the company goes into liquidation. Express provision to this effect is often made in the debenture.

5.1 Implications of s44(1)(a) IA

In the law of agency the principal (the company) is liable on contracts entered into by the agent (the AR). The agent will only be personally liable if acts outside his authority.

This implies that:

- the company will be liable on contracts entered into by the AR.

- The debenture holder will not be (it is NOT the principal), unless it intermeddles in the receivership *(Standard Chartered Bank Ltd v Walker 1982)*.

- No personal liability will attach to the AR. However s44(1)(b) IA modifies this aspect of the general law of agency.

5.2 Personal liability of the AR

By s44(1)(b) IA the AR is personally liable on any contract entered into by him in the carrying out of his functions:

- The rule in s44(1)(b) IA is that the AR is personally liable on contracts *entered into* by him the rule does *not* say that he is liable on pre-appointment contracts.

- Pre-appointment contracts are contracts with the company not with the AR. The AR can either:
  - repudiate such contracts (in which case the 3rd party can sue the company for breach and will be an unsecured creditor)
  - or can allow the contract to continue (sometimes referred to as "adopting" the contract - a misleading term as the AR only "adopts" in the sense of taking some step which confirms that the contract remains one with the company. An AR does *not* become a party to an adopted contract nor is he personally liable on it).

In neither of the above cases is the AR personally liable.

- An AR who re-negotiates a contract does risk that the contract will be treated as a post appointment one and therefore one under which he is personally liable.

This has implications for a trading receivership where AR may be entering into new contracts. IA 86 provides therefore that:

- AR may exclude his liability in the contract (s44(1)(b) IA provides for personal liability 'except in so far as the contract otherwise provides').

> ▸ S44(1)(c) IA the AR 'is entitled in respect of that liability to an indemnity out of the assets of the company'.

> ▸ AR can still demand indemnity from charge holder as term of accepting appointment.

5.3 Nature of agency

Cases such as *Gomba Holdings UK Ltd v Homan (1986)* and *Ratford Northavon District Council (1987)* point out that it is an unusual agency.

> ▸ Company (Principal) cannot dismiss AR (agent)

> ▸ Company cannot instruct AR as to how duties should be performed.

> ▸ AR's prime duty owed to chargeholder not to the company.

5.4 Contracts of employment

Nicoll v Cutts (1985) the appointment of an AR does NOT automatically terminate the company's contracts of employment. AR is free to repudiate or adopt such contracts.

By s44(1)(b) IA the AR is personally liable on any contracts of employment adopted by him.

The AR will be taken to have adopted merely by NOT repudiating such pre-existing contracts.

S44(2) IA, however, provides that the AR shall not be taken to have adopted a contract of employment by reason of anything done or omitted to be done within 14 days after his appointment.

Re Specialised Mouldings Ltd - said that an AR could contract out of personal liability arising out of adoption by sending a letter to all employees within 14 days of appointment, expressly excluding adoption and personal liability.

However *Paramount Airways* (House of Lords) states that such letters are ineffective to exclude adoption and personal liability (see chapter 10 regarding employee claims).

[handwritten margin note: Vary contract of employment? to extent of qualifying liabilities.]

6 Property available to an AR

Section overview

> ▸ When an AR is appointed to a company the property coming into his hands has to be devoted first to paying the company's preferential debts and then to meeting the obligation owed to the charge holder (s40 IA). However, other person's rights to the company's property must be observed if they were acquired before crystallisation (*Re Morrison, Jones & Taylor Ltd 1914*).

If there is *another floating charge* over the same assets and it was created before the charge under which he is appointed then it is still a prior charge on those assets: Re *Household Products Co Ltd* 1981, if and when it crystallises. Also if any property of the company is subject to a *fixed charge* then the administrative receiver cannot utilise that property (except by redeeming the charge) - either to pay the debt secured by the floating charge under which he was appointed (*English & Scottish Mercantile Investment Co Ltd v Brunton* 1892) or to pay preferential debts: Re *Lewis Merthyr Consolidated Collieries Ltd* 1929.

However, the position will be different if the fixed charge ranks after the floating charge under which the administrative receiver is appointed, which will happen:

(i) if there is an express provision in the fixed-charge contract;

(ii) if the fixed and floating chargees agree such priority between themselves;

(iii) if, at the time of making the fixed-charge contract, the fixed chargee had actual notice of a negative-pledge provision in the floating charge.

If the administrative receiver's floating charge has priority then the receiver can utilise the property subject to the fixed charge in order to pay the debt secured by the floating charge but not, in England and Wales, the preferential debts: Re *Woodroffes (Musical Instruments) Ltd* 1986.

An administrative receiver may:

(i)   ignore a charge that should have been registered under s395-s402 CA 1985, but was not registered;

(ii)   not obtain goods that the company has pledged without paying the debt secured by the pledge; or

(iii)   not recover goods held under a possessory lien without paying the fees secured by the lien.

Only the company's property is available to its administrative receiver, not the property of other persons. So property in the possession of the company under leases, conditional sale agreements or hire-purchase agreements is not available. In principle the receiver can exploit the company's rights under these agreements but in practice contracts of this kind usually contain a provision that they will automatically terminate if a creditor of the lessee or hirer appoints an administrative receiver. Similarly, property subject to a retention of title agreement may be repossessed by the seller unless the price is paid by the administrative receiver.

The position with respect to assets acquired under a hire-purchase agreement will invariably be subject to negotiation between the finance company and the receiver. Where the market value of the equipment exceeds the outstanding instalments, the finance company will invariably attempt to repossess the equipment.

The receiver should ensure that the HP agreement has not been breached and that payments are up to date. It may be possible for the receiver to realise the equity in the asset in these circumstances, by selling the asset and settling the outstanding liabilities. Other possibilities include:

▶   Negotiate retention of use on payment of current instalments only.

▶   If the business is being sold as a going concern, it may be possible to negotiate a settlement for less than the outstanding liability or for the purchaser to assume the outstanding liabilities.

If a floating charge is expressed to be a charge on all present and future assets then it will continue to charge assets acquired by the company after it has crystallised Re *Anglo-Austrian Printing & Publishing Union* 1895. Each item of property acquired after crystallisation is subject to a fixed charge immediately on acquisition by the company. So a debt due and payable to the company after crystallisation is charged as from the due date: N W *Robbie & Co Ltd v Witney Warehouse Co Ltd* 1963. In *Ross v Taylor* 1989 a company had returned goods to a creditor in order to reduce the debt; the administrative receiver re-acquired these goods, and it was held that the floating charge under which he was appointed related to these goods, and took precedence over the claims of a subsequently appointed liquidator.

If the debtor delays payment and, during the period of delay, a debt owed to him by the company becomes due and payable, then he cannot set off the new debt against the debt he owes because the whole of the debt he owes is already charged: *Business Computers Ltd v Anglo-African Leasing Ltd* 1977.

7 Duties of the AR

Section overview

The duties of the administrative receiver arise from:

▶   Common law – to take reasonable care to obtain the true market value of assets. This duty is owed primarily to the appointer, but also to preferential creditors, the company and other interested parties such as guarantors.

▶   Equitable fiduciary duties – not to sell assets to himself and to only sell to associated persons if in good faith and for value.

▶   Statutory duties – submit receipts and payments accounts, conduct s48 IA meetings, etc.

The administrative receiver has a general duty to assume control of property comprised in the charge and to safeguard such property.

7.1 Common law duties

Administrative and other receivers have a duty to take care to obtain the best price reasonably obtainable in any sale of charged assets (*Silven Properties v RBS (2003 Court of Appeal)*). The duty is primarily owed to the appointing chargeholder.

An administrative receiver owes a duty to preferential creditors not to dissipate the assets out of which those creditors are paid (*IRC v Goldblatt*).

A receiver owes a duty to the company and to guarantors of the company's debt. However the duty is one which takes effect only in equity. In other words the receiver does not owe a duty of care in the tort of negligence to the company and others who are interested in the 'equity of redemption' (i.e. any surplus left after payment of the appointing debenture holder).

The receiver has no duty:

▶ to postpone exercising the power of sale pending the further pursuit or outcome of an application for planning permission or to take any steps to improve or increase the value of the property.

▶ Generally the AR has no duty to await optimum market conditions before selling (*Cuckmere case*).

▶ Administrative receivers are entitled to choose the time and method of sale of properties under their control (*Bell v Long & Ors 2008*).

However there is a duty to take reasonable precautions to obtain the 'fair' or 'true market value' of the property. In the *Silven Properties case* it was said that neither mortgagees nor receivers were entitled to act in a way which unfairly prejudiced the mortgagor by selling hastily at a knock down price sufficient to pay off the debt. Proper care must be taken to obtain the best price reasonably obtainable at the date of the sale.

NB: The AR has no duty to the company to preserve its goodwill and business (*Re B Johnson & Co (Builders) Ltd*).

Where there is a breach of duty it is no defence that:

▶ the mortgagor/charger consented to the realisation (*Rawlings v Barclays Bank 1990*)
▶ the duty was excluded in the charge instrument (*Bishop v Bonham 1988*)

Examples of lack of care:

▶ Failure to advertise the sale in appropriate publications (*Amex Bank Corp. v Hurley*).

▶ Failure to seek specialist advice (*Amex Bank*).

▶ Failure to inform potential purchasers of factors rendering assets more valuable (e.g. the granting of planning permission - *Cuckmere Brick Company Limited 1971*).

7.2 Equitable fiduciary duties

These derive from the AR's status as agent of the company. The duties are owed to the company which may sue for breach of duty. The company will act through its directors or majority shareholders (*Foss v Harbottle*) so that individual shareholders do not need to bring 'derivative actions' against the AR(*Watts v Midland Bank PLC 1986*) .

The AR should avoid a conflict of interests and should not therefore sell charged assets to himself. This applies even where the price paid is a "fair" one and where the sale is to a person in whom the AR is interested (e.g. the AR's solicitor).

Such a sale is likely to be set aside (*Watts v Midland Bank*) unless the sale is made in good faith and the AR took all reasonable precautions to obtain the best price reasonably obtainable.

The fiduciary duty of an AR is not comparable to that of a director (*Re B Johnson & Co (Builders) Limited 1955*).

The directors have a duty to promote the success of the company (an AR does not). AR's may disclose confidential trading information to competitors in the interests of realising a sale on a going concern basis (*Re Neon Signs (Australasia) Ltd*).

7.3 Statutory duties

I **Statement of Affairs**

An administrative receiver must require some or all of the persons listed below to make out and submit to him a statement of affairs of the company (s47 IA):

▶ Persons who are or have been (at any time) officers of the company;

▶ If the company was formed within one year before the date of appointment of the administrative receiver, persons who took part in its formation;

▶ Persons who are in the company's employment, or who have been in its employment within the year preceding the date of appointment of the administrative receiver, and are, in the administrative receiver's opinion, capable of giving the information required. ('Employment' here includes employment under a contract for services);

▶ If another company is an officer of the company or has been within the year preceding the date of appointment of the administrative receiver, persons who are, or have been within that year, officers of that other company.

A statement of affairs must be in the prescribed form (Form 3.2) (s47(1) IA) and must be verified by affidavit by the persons required to submit it (s47(2) IA). The principal information given by a statement of affairs is (s47(2) IA):

▶ Particulars of the company's assets, debts and liabilities;
▶ The names and addresses of its creditors;
▶ The securities held by creditors;
▶ The dates when securities were given.

The affairs of the company must be shown as at the date of appointment of the administrative receiver.

(For full details of how to draw up a statement of Affairs, see chapter 12).

A sworn copy of the statement of affairs must be retained by the administrative receiver as part of the records of the receivership (r3.4(6)). A copy of the statement of affairs must be sent to the registrar of companies, either with the administrative receiver's report to the creditors (if the statement has been submitted by the time that the report is filed) or later (r3.8(3)).

The administrative receiver's report to creditors must include a summary of the statement of affairs (s48(5) IA).

A person required to 'make out and submit' a statement of affairs has to make an oath saying that it is, to the best of his knowledge and belief, 'a full, true and complete statement as (to) the affairs of (the company)' (s47(2) IA; r.3.4(1) and Sch 4). The administrative receiver may require persons to submit an affidavit of concurrence 'stating that he concurs in the statement of affairs (r3.4(2)) (though an affidavit of concurrence may point out any matter in the statement with which the concurrer disagrees or considers erroneous or misleading, or of which he has no direct knowledge: r3.4(3)). Affidavits of concurrence must be kept with the receivership records (r3.4(6)) and copies must be sent to the registrar of companies when the statement of affairs is filed (r3.8(3) and (4)).

A statement of affairs may be used in evidence against any person who made it or any person who concurred in it (s433 IA). The question whether a statement of affairs is an acknowledgement of a debt for the purposes of deciding whether a limitation period has expired is undecided; it could only acknowledge that the debt existed at the time to which the statement referred, i.e. the date of appointment of the administrative receiver: *Re Overmark Smith Warden Ltd 1982*.

An administrative receiver who wishes to make persons responsible for a statement of affairs must serve notices in the prescribed form on every such person (s47(4); R3.3 IA). Persons served with notice are called 'deponents' (r3.3(2)). Deponents have 21 days in which to prepare the statement (s.47(4) IA), though the notice may specify a longer time or the time may be subsequently extended by the administrator receiver. If the administrator receiver refuses to extend the time limit, the deponent may appeal to the court (s47(6) IA).

Failure by a director to comply with an obligation to make out and submit a statement of affairs is a matter to which the court may pay particular regard when deciding whether to make a disqualification order (CDDA 1986, Sch 1, para 10(b)). The notice must state the names and addresses of all the deponents to whom it has been sent (r3.3(3)(a)). On request, the administrative receiver must furnish each deponent with the forms required for preparing the statement (r3.3(4)).

The expenses of a deponent making a statement of affairs are payable by the administrative receiver from his receipts; the amount payable is what the receiver considers reasonable subject to a right of appeal to the court (r3.7).

The administrative receiver may, at his own discretion or on the request of any deponent, release a deponent from his obligation under a notice requiring him to make out and submit a statement of affairs or extend the time specified in the notice for doing so (s47(5) IA; r3.6(1)). If the administrative receiver rejects a deponent's request for release or extension of time, the deponent may appeal to the court (r3.6(2)).

A statement of affairs must be filed at the companies registry (r3.8(3) and (4)) where it may be inspected by anyone (s1085 CA 2006). If the administrative receiver thinks that it would prejudice the conduct of the receivership for the whole or part of the statement of affairs to be disclosed, he may apply to the court, under r3.5, for an order of limited disclosure in respect of the statement or any part of it. This is an order that the statement, or part of it, is not to be open to inspection otherwise than with leave of court.

When an application for limited disclosure is made the court may order that either the whole statement or a specified part of it should not be open for inspection otherwise than with the court's leave. The court may also include directions as to the delivery of documents to the Registrar and the disclosure of relevant information to any other persons.

When submitting his report to creditors an administrative receiver may omit from his summary of the statement of affairs any information which, if disclosed, would seriously prejudice the carrying out of the receiver's functions (s48(6) IA).

2   S48 IA duty

Within three months of his appointment an administrative receiver of a company must, under penalty, prepare a report for the company's creditors in accordance with s48 IA. The court may extend the time limit. The principal matters on which the receiver must report are:

- the events leading up to his appointment, so far as he is aware of them;

- the disposal or proposed disposal by him of any property of the company and the carrying on or proposed carrying on by him of any business of the company;

- the amounts payable to the chargee by whom he was appointed and the amounts of preferential debts;

- the amount, if any, likely to be available to pay other creditors.

The report must also include a summary of the statement of affairs submitted to the receiver and a summary of the receiver's comments (if any) on the statement (s48(5)). The report may omit any information which, if disclosed, would seriously prejudice the carrying out of the receiver's functions (s48(6) IA).

In the same way he must send copies of the report to the registrar, to any trustees for secured creditors (where a marketable loan is secured by a trust deed) and to all secured creditors of whose addresses he is aware (s48(1) IA). He is also required to send a copy of the report to all unsecured creditors of whose addresses he is aware, unless he publishes a notice in the newspaper in which he advertised his appointment, stating an address to which unsecured creditors may write for copies of the report to be sent to them free of charge (s48(2) IA; r3.8(1)). However, he is relieved of the requirement to inform unsecured creditors if a liquidator of the company is appointed within the three months following his own appointment (s48(4) IA). The court may extend the three-month time-limit for sending copies of the report.

3   **Meeting of unsecured creditors**

(i)   **Convening the meeting:**

An administrative receiver of a company that is not in liquidation must either (s48(2) and (3) IA):

▸   summon a meeting of unsecured creditors, giving not less than 14 days' notice, before which he will lay a copy of the report, or

▸   state in the report that he intends to apply to the court for a direction that no meeting be held.

The report must either be sent to all unsecured creditors whose addresses are known to the administrative receiver or he must advertise in a newspaper that the report is available. If the administrative receiver decides to apply to the court for a direction that no unsecured creditors' meeting need be held, then the application cannot be heard until 14 days have elapsed since the report was published or advertised to the unsecured creditors (s48(3)(b) IA. The venue of the court hearing must be stated in the report or the advertisement (r3.8(2) IA).

If the administrative receiver was appointed to a company already in liquidation, or if the company has gone into liquidation, and the administrative receiver delivers a copy of his report to the liquidator within three months after being appointed, then the report need not be sent to unsecured creditors, no advertisement of it need be published and no meeting of unsecured creditors need by held (s48(4) IA).

The meeting must be held within three months after the date of appointment of the administrative receiver, unless the court allows an extension of time. The administrative receiver is liable to be fined for failing to meet the time limit (s48(2) and (8) and Sch 10 IA).

In deciding the venue for the meeting the administrative receiver must have regard to the convenience of the unsecured creditors (r3.9(1)) and it must in any case start between 10.00 and 16.00 hours on a business day unless the court directs otherwise (r3.9(2)). Not less than 14 days' notice must be given of the meeting (s48(2) IA; r3.9(2)). Notice must be given to all the creditors of the company who are identified in the statement of affairs, or are known to the administrative receiver and have claims against the company at the date of his appointment (r3.9(3)). Proxy forms must be sent with the notice (r3.9(4)).

Notice must also be given by advertisement in the newspaper in which the administrative receiver advertised his appointment (r3.9(6)).

The notice must include a statement of the effect of r3.11(1) (entitlement to vote) and a statement that creditors whose claims are wholly secured are not entitled to attend or be represented at the meeting - it is a meeting of unsecured creditors (r3.9(5) and (7)).

(ii)   **Conduct at the meeting:**

The administrative receiver must chair the meeting or he must nominate someone in writing to chair it (r3.10(1)). A nominated substitute must either be a qualified insolvency practitioner or an employee of the administrative receiver (or the receiver's firm) who is experienced in insolvency matters (r3.10(2)).

The quorum for the unsecured creditors' meeting is one creditor entitled to vote present in person (or by representation under s323 CA 2006) or by proxy (even if the proxy-holder or representative is the chairman) (r12.4A(1), (2) and (3)). If, however, a meeting is at its appointed starting time quorate with only the chairman present, or with only the chairman and one other individual present, and the chairman is aware that any other person would, if attending, be entitled to vote, he must wait 15 minutes before starting the meeting (r12.4A(4)).

If he decides that it is desirable the chairman may adjourn an inquorate meeting to such date, time and place as he thinks fit (r3.14(1)), though he must have regard to the convenience of the persons who are invited to attend and must make the starting time between 10.00 and

16.00 hours on a business day unless the court otherwise directs (rs.3.9(1) and (2) and 3.14(2)).

If there is no quorum and the meeting is not adjourned it is deemed to have been duly summoned and held (r3.14(3)).

Decisions at the meeting of unsecured creditors are taken by a simple majority, *in value*, of the unsecured creditors who are present and vote in person or by proxy (r3.15(1)).

In order to establish an entitlement to vote a creditor must give to the administrative receiver, not later than 12.00 hours on the business day before the day fixed for the meeting, details in writing of the debt claimed to be due (r3.11(1)). A creditor who has failed to comply with this requirement may be allowed by the chairman of the meeting to vote if the chairman is satisfied the failure was due to circumstances beyond the creditor's control (r3.11(2)).

The administrative receiver (or the chairman) may call for documents or other evidence that he thinks necessary for substantiating a claim (r3.11(3)). The following rules apply on valuation of debts:

▶ a debt is valued as at the date of the administrative receiver's appointment but any amount paid in respect of the debt since that date must be deducted (r3.11(4));

▶ a creditor with an unliquidated or unascertained debt is not entitled to vote unless the chairman agrees to assign a value to the debt for the purposes of voting (r3.11(5));

▶ a secured creditor is entitled to vote only in respect of the balance (if any) of his debt after deducting the value of his security as estimated by him (r3.11(6)).

If a debt is on a current bill of exchange or promissory note (or is secured by such a document) and there are parties liable on the document before the company, then the creditor must treat the liability of each such party (unless it is a company that has gone into liquidation against whom a winding up order has been made) as a security; such security must be valued and deducted from the debt and the creditor can vote only in respect of the balance (r3.11(7)).

The chairman of the unsecured creditors' meeting has the power to admit or reject a creditor's claim for the purpose of his entitlement to vote, and may exercise that right over all or part of the claim (r3.12(1)). A decision by the chairman is subject to appeal to the court (r3.12(2)). If the chairman doubts whether a claim should be admitted or rejected he may leave the question for later determination (by himself or the court) and permit the creditor to vote, subject to the vote being disallowed if the claim is subsequently rejected (r3.12(3)).

If on appeal the chairman's decision is reversed or varied, or a creditor's vote is declared invalid, the court may order that another meeting be summoned or make such other order as it thinks just (r3.12(4)).

Neither the administrative receiver nor the chairman is to be personally liable for the costs of an appeal unless the court orders otherwise (r3.12(5)).

The Chair of the meeting shall cause a record to be made of the proceedings and kept as part of the records of the receivership (r3.15(2)). This shall include a list of attendees and if a committee has been established the names and addresses of those elected to be members.

SIP 12 provides best practice in maintaining records of meetings of creditors.

(iii) **Creditors' committee:**

The rules concerning creditors' committees in administrative receivership are virtually identical to those concerning creditors' committees in administrations (r3.17 to r3.30A).

The unsecured creditors' meeting may, if it thinks fit, establish a creditors' committee (s49(1) IA) to assist the administrative receiver in discharging his functions and to act in relation to him in such manner as may be agreed from time to time (r3.18(1)). The committee must consist of three, four or five creditors of the company elected at the meeting (r3.16(1)).

Any creditor may be elected provided his claim has not been rejected for the purpose of his entitlement to vote (r3.16(2)). Thus it is a committee of *unsecured* creditors.

At a meeting of the committee:

▶   Every resolution passed shall be recorded in writing (either separately or as part of the minutes of the meeting) (r3.26(2)).

▶   A record of each resolution shall be signed by the Chair and kept as part of the records of the receivership (r3.26(3)).

▶   A quorum is two members present or represented (r3.20)

Members of the committee have one vote each and a resolution is passed when a majority of the members present or represented have voted in favour.

Rule 3.27 allows resolutions to be taken by post and again a copy of the resolutions passed and a note of the committees' concurrence shall be kept by the IP.

SIP 12 gives advice on best practice on keeping records of meetings of the committee.

(iv)   **Duty to account**

AR has duty to account to the company *(Gomba Holdings UK Ltd v Homan 1986)*,

▶   Directors must be supplied with accounts to enable them to fulfil their statutory duty to prepare annual accounts.

▶   Any liquidator of the company may require AR "to render proper accounts of receipts and payments and to vouch them and pay over to the liquidator the amount properly payable to him" (s41(1)(b) IA).

▶   Further information may be required from the AR by the directors where they demonstrate "a need to know" for the purpose of exercising their duties *(Gomba Holdings)*.

Board has no right to demand current information about the conduct of the business.

Rule 3.32 requires AR to send the requisite accounts of his receipts and payments to:

▶   the appointor

▶   the registrar of companies

▶   the company

▶   each member of the creditors committee

Accounts should be submitted in Form 3.6 within two months after the end of 12 months from the date of appointment and every subsequent 12 month period, and within two months of ceasing to act. (See chapter 12 for details re preparation of the receipts and payments account).

(v)   **IP Regs**

▶   IP Regs 2005 require AR to maintain a record of the appointment. The form is prescribed in Schedule 3 of the Regs. It gives the dates on which each statutory requirement was carried out. (See chapter 11 for more details)

(vi)   **CDDA**

The AR must submit a D return on the conduct of directors (see chapter 11 for more details).

Interactive question 1: Bluegrass Limited

You were appointed administrative receiver of Bluegrass Limited under the terms of a floating charge held by Natby Bank PLC.

What are your duties, as administrative receiver, upon appointment?

See **Answer** at the end of this chapter.

8 SIP 1 An AR's responsibility for the company's records

Section overview

▶ There may be circumstances when an AR is approached by the directors or by liquidators requesting access to or custody of the company's books and records. SIP 1 summarises best practice when such a request occurs both with regard to company records maintained prior to the appointment of the AR and those records prepared after his appointment.

8.1 Company records maintained prior to the appointment of the AR

These records consist of:

(i) Non accounting records which the directors are required to maintain by the Companies Act (the statutory records) ie. Registers of members etc, minute books.

(ii) Accounting records required by statute and all other non-statutory records of the company (statutory accounting and other non statutory records).

Statutory records:

The statutory records should be kept at the company's registered office. The director's responsibility to maintain these records are unaffected by the appointment of the AR and they retain the power to make entries in these records. Accordingly the AR should not maintain them. The AR can either:

(a) Leave the statutory records in the custody of the directors (at the registered office where the AR has a power to inspect them at any time), or

(b) Take possession of them for safe keeping.

If the AR takes possession of them (has statutory power to do so under Schedule 1 IA 86) he should remind the directors of their duties to maintain them and allow them free access for this purpose. He should prepare a detailed receipt of all records taken into his possession which should be signed by a director or other responsible official of the company in receivership. He must also change the location of the company's registered office to his own firm in order to comply with the requirements of the CA for the records to be held at the company's registered office. When the AR vacates office the statutory records should be returned to the directors or the liquidator if applicable.

Statutory accounting and other non statutory records:

▶ A distinction is made between those records which are necessary for the purposes of the receivership and those which are not.

▶ Those which are required should be taken into the AR's possession and/or control. The AR has statutory powers in ss.234-236 IA to enforce co-operation and obtain possession.

▶ Those which are definitely not required may be left with the directors. It is advisable for the AR to list these and note their whereabouts.

▸ The AR is under no statutory duty to bring records up to date although for practical purposes (e.g. where necessary to give potential purchasers an indication of the financial state of the business) the AR may have to do so.

▸ As a separate matter the AR may have to hand over company records to purchasers of company assets (the SIP gives the example of the debtors ledger or plant registers where there are sales of book debts or plant and machinery):

  – Preferably the AR should retain the originals and either provide copies or allow the purchaser to retain the originals long enough to make own copies.

  – If not the asset sale agreement should provide for the purchaser to make original documents available to the AR on demand.

▸ If the AR transfers the business of a company to a third party as a going concern, s49 and para 6 of Schedule 11 to the VAT Act of 1994 place the obligation of preserving records relating to the business on the transferee (i.e. the purchaser):

  – The Transferor (AR) can request the Commissioners of Customs and Excise to direct otherwise.

  – The rule applies even if VAT registration is not transferred and whether or not the transfer itself is treated as one of goods or services.

  – Documents covered by the rule include orders, delivery notes, purchase and sales records, annual accounts, VAT accounts and credit and debit notes.

Entitlement of liquidator to pre-appointment records:

The AR should deliver records relating to the management and business of the company to the liquidator upon request in return for an undertaking that they will be produced to the AR on request (*Lightman & Moss*).

8.2 Post appointment records

These records consist of:

(i) Statutory accounting records relating to the period prior to the appointment of a liquidator:

The AR should establish proper accounting records and render full and proper records to the company so that the directors can comply with their statutory duties under the CA.

The AR also has a duty to make returns of receipts and payments under r3.32 (see Chapter 12).

The AR has no authority to destroy these records and they should be handed over to the directors or the liquidator on the AR's vacation of office.

On appointment a liquidator would become entitled to possession of all books and records relating to the management and business of a company, and this would include the statutory accounting records (*Engel v South Metropolitan Brewing & Bottling Company 1892*).

(ii) Other records:

These consist of company records, chargeholder's records and the AR's personal records.

  (a) Company records:

   – The SIP citing *Gomba Holdings UK Ltd v Minories Finance Ltd (1989)* makes it clear that only documents generated or received pursuant to the AR's duty to manage the company's business or dispose of its assets fall within this category.

   – These records belong to the company.

   – These records should be treated in the same way as the pre-appointment of AR statutory accounting and non-statutory records.

(b) Chargeholder's records:

- These records do *not* belong to the company. They do not therefore need to be handed over to the directors or liquidator on the AR's vacation.

- They include documents containing advice and information to the appointor and notes calculations and memoranda prepared to enable the AR to discharge his professional duty to his appointor.

(c) AR's personal records:

- These are those records prepared by the AR for the purpose of better enabling the AR to discharge his or her professional duties.

- They include records which must be maintained under the IP Regs 1990.

- Disclosure of these records is a matter for the AR's discretion. The SIP points out, however, that in any legal action against the AR these records may have to be disclosed through the process of discovery.

Reference has already been made to the obligation to provide directors with information necessary to them to fulfil their statutory duties.

The SIP states that is best practice to make all the above records available to the company (acting through its directors or liquidator) at their request. There are exceptions;

▸ the chargeholders and AR's personal records.

▸ In any event where disclosure would be contrary to the interests of the appointor (e.g. current negotiations for the sale of assets).

Records an AR is required to keep by the regulations must be preserved for six years from the later of; the AR's resignation or the time when any security or caution maintained in respect of the company ceases to have effect.

9 SIP 14 A receiver's responsibility to preferential creditors

Section overview

▸ Creditors whose debts are preferential may be concerned about the categorisation of assets as between fixed and floating charges and the manner in which costs incurred during a receivership are charged against the different categories of assets. SIP 14 summarises the best practice to be adopted by receivers of the assets of companies where any of those assets are subject to a floating charge. It sets out best practice with regard to the application of the statutory provisions and in particular, the provision of information to creditors.

9.1 The statutory provisions

The rights of preferential creditors derive from s40 IA which states that where a receiver is appointed on behalf of the holders of any debentures of a company secured by a charge which, as created, was a floating charge (and the company is not at the time in the course of being wound up), its preferential debts shall be paid out of the assets coming into the hands of the receiver in priority to any claims in respect of the debentures. Where the receiver is appointed under both fixed and floating charges, this requirement does not extend to assets coming into the receiver's hands pursuant to the fixed charge(s).

Preferential debts are defined in 386 of the Act, are set out in Schedule 6 and are ascertained as at the date of the appointment of the receiver (387(4) IA). Failure by a receiver to pay preferential debts out of available assets is a breach of statutory duty. However the SIP recognises that circumstances may arise when it is administratively convenient or cost-effective to cooperate with a company's liquidator and arrange for him to pay the receivership preferential debts. However, in that situation the receiver is not exonerated from his obligations.

There are no statutory provisions requiring creditors with preferential debts in a receivership to prove those debts in any formal manner and no statutory obligation is imposed on a receiver to advertise for claims.

9.2 Categorisation of assets and allocation of proceeds

Firstly, it is necessary to distinguish, on interpretation of the charging document(s), which assets are subject to a fixed charge and which are subject to a floating charge.

The overriding principle, as laid down by the courts, is that it is not of itself sufficient for the charging document to state that an asset is subject to a fixed charge for it to be subject to such a charge. There have been cases where the courts have struck down charges that purported to be fixed and held that they were floating, for instance a fixed charge over book debts.

It is the duty of a receiver to effect the right categorisation and legal advice should be taken in cases of doubt. In some instances where there is doubt it may be possible to consult preferential creditors and reach agreement with them and the charge holder. It may be necessary to apply to the court for directions.

The SIP reiterates that it is the type of charge at the time of *creation* that defines whether the assets are caught by the fixed or floating charge. Accordingly crystallisation of a floating charge into a fixed charge prior to or upon the appointment of a receiver does not affect the rights of creditors with preferential debts to be paid out of assets subject to a crystallised floating charge.

Further, the conversion, during receivership, of floating charge assets into fixed charge assets e.g. stock subject at the date of appointment into book debts, will not remove them from the pool of assets available to pay the preferential creditors.

The SIP also reminds receivers of their potential tortuous liability to preferential creditors. The SIP gives the example of where assets are sold as part of a going concern and the apportionment of the total consideration suggested by the purchaser, for perhaps for his own financial reasons, may prejudice the preferential creditors. The receiver should ensure that he will be able properly to discharge his obligations to account to holders of fixed charges on the one hand and creditors interested in assets subject to floating charges on the other.

9.3 Apportionment of costs

The amount available to meet preferential debts is also dependent upon the appropriate allocation of costs incurred in effecting, realisations.

The SIP lists the usual three categories of costs:

▶ Liabilities incurred by the company (the receiver being its agent until wind-up) and recoverable by him out of the company's assets under his statutory indemnity

▶ The costs of the receiver in discharging his statutory duties; and

▶ The remuneration and disbursements of the receiver.

▶ Where costs are clearly identifiable as having been incurred in the realisation or collecting in one or other of the two categories they should be recorded as such in the receiver's records and deducted from realisation proceeds in ascertaining the amount available for each class of creditors.

The SIP recognises however, that it is in the nature of receiverships, especially if the receiver is trading on, that it may be difficult to arrive at an appropriate allocation of costs. Many of the activities in a trading receivership will enhance the realisations of fixed and floating charges. They may of necessity be incurred before full categorisation has been completed. In these situations, the SIP advises that the receiver should exercise his professional judgement and make the requisite apportionment with independence of mind and with integrity.

In order to enable a receiver to allocate costs on an appropriate basis, the SIP advises that contemporaneous records of the dominant reasons for incurring costs should be maintained. This is especially important where the receiver is an administrative receiver. These will also assist the receiver in providing explanations as to how he or she arrived at the appropriate allocation. It will further provide evidence should that allocation be the subject of challenge.

The SIP then lists four matters that the receiver should consider when allocating costs:

▶ **the objectives** for which costs were incurred;

▶ **the benefits** actually obtained in terms of protection of assets or augmentation in value;

▶ **any detriment** to the floating charge holder incurred whilst benefiting the fixed charge e.g. where trading losses have been incurred to protect or enhance the value of property or ~~book debts~~ subject to a fixed charge;

▶ **any reduction** in preferential debts where a going concern sale has resulted in the transfer of employment contracts.

A receiver will incur costs in complying with his statutory duties. The extent of those duties depends upon the nature of his appointment and they are more onerous in the case of administrative receivers. The SIP states that there are no decided cases as to how the additional costs incurred by an administrative receiver (as opposed to a receiver not so designated) should be allocated.

The allocation of a receiver's remuneration and disbursements should be undertaken adopting the same principles as those applicable to costs and he should ensure that he maintains contemporaneous records which will enable him to make an appropriate division of his remuneration and disbursements between the different categories of assets.

9.4 Determination of preferential debts

It is a receiver's obligation to pay preferential debts out of assets available for that purpose and no proof of debt or advertisement for creditors is required. The SIP advises that a receiver should:

▶ Notify potential preferential creditors of his appointment;

▶ assess whether there are likely to be sufficient floating charge realisations to pay a distribution; and then

▶ determine the preferential debts.

Where no payment will be made, it is not necessary to agree preferential claims. However, in such circumstances, the SIP advises that the receiver should write to creditors whose claims are preferential explaining why he is unable to make a payment to them.

Assuming that there will be a distribution to preferential creditors, the receiver should assist by providing adequate information to enable them to calculate their claims. Save in the case of employees, the receiver is entitled to assume they have full knowledge of their legal entitlements and should invite them to submit their claims.

Where employees have preferential claims, the receiver should obtain information from either the company's records or from the employee before calculating the claim (other than one which is payable to the Secretary of State by way of subrogation). The employee should be provided with details of the calculation of his claim and any further explanation that he may reasonably require.

The SIP reminds members that paragraph 11 of Schedule 6 IA provides that anyone who has advanced money for the purpose of paying wages etc is a preferential creditor to the extent that the preferential claim of the employee is reduced by such advance.

The SIP also reminds members that where an employee's preferential debt has been paid by the Secretary of State under the Employment Rights Act 1996, the Secretary of State is entitled to the benefit of the employee's preferential debt, in priority to any residual claim of the employee himself. The receiver is not, however, obliged to accept the preferential claim of the Secretary of State without being satisfied that it is correct. In circumstances of doubt, the receiver should contact the Redundancy Payments Service to explain why and attempt to reach agreement on the amount to be admitted.

9.5 Payment of preferential debts

The SIP advises that members take steps to pay preferential debts as soon as possible. Preferential debts do not attract interest and payments to creditors should not be unnecessarily delayed. A receiver who does not comply timeously with his obligations under s40 IA and against whom judgement is obtained may find himself ordered to pay interest by the court. If practicable, the receiver could make payment either in full or on account before all claims have been agreed.

The SIP also mentions that, exceptionally, it may be administratively convenient or cost-effective for a receiver to make arrangements for a liquidator to make payment of the preferential debts arising in the receivership. The SIP warns however that such arrangements are made at the receiver's risk, and should not be on any basis which could result in payment of an amount less than that which would have been available to meet those debts if the receiver had himself paid them, or which would cause delay in paying them. In any event, the receiver should provide preferential creditors with details of any such arrangements and the reason for making them.

9.6 Disclosure to creditors with preferential debts

When the funds realised from assets subject to a floating charge are inadequate to pay the preferential debts in full, the receiver should (unless he has already written to them as suggested by the SIP) send those creditors a statement setting out:

▶ the assets which have, in accordance with the charging document, been categorised as subject to the floating charge; and

▶ the costs charged against the proceeds of the realisation of those assets.

The receiver should also provide any further information that the creditor reasonably requests.

9.7 Other matters

The SIP advises members to seek legal advice if the receiver has been appointed under a second or subsequent charge and he or she has to determine the rights of preferential creditors in priority to a prior floating charge holder. The SIP mentions that it may be necessary to apply to court for directions.

Finally the SIP deals with the situation in which a payment is not encashed and the payee cannot readily be located. The insolvency legislation does not make provision for this eventuality and the SIP advises that where a receiver decides to account to the next person entitled to such monies he should make arrangements to recover the funds from the party whom he has paid so that he will be able to discharge his obligation to any preferential creditor who subsequently asserts his claim to payment.

Interactive question 2: Harris Engineering Limited

You have been approached by North Bank PLC who hold a fixed and floating charge over the assets of Harris Engineering Limited, the floating charge having been created on 23 August 2003.

Harris Engineering Limited have been experiencing cash flow problems and the bank wish to appoint you as administrative receiver under the terms of their debenture.

Requirement

What matters should you consider before accepting appointment as administrative receiver?

See **Answer** at the end of the chapter.

Summary and Self-test

Summary

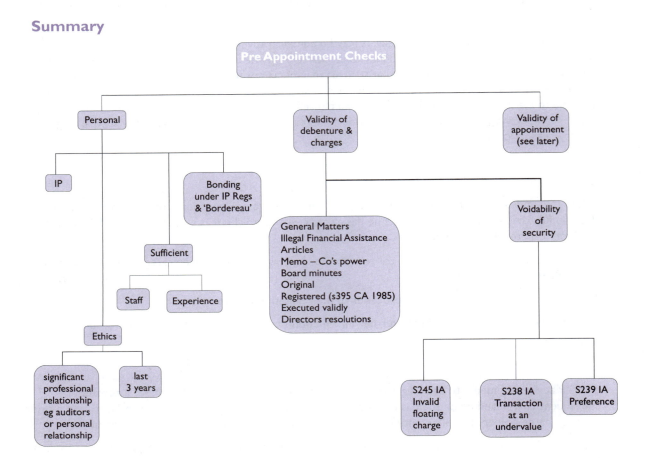

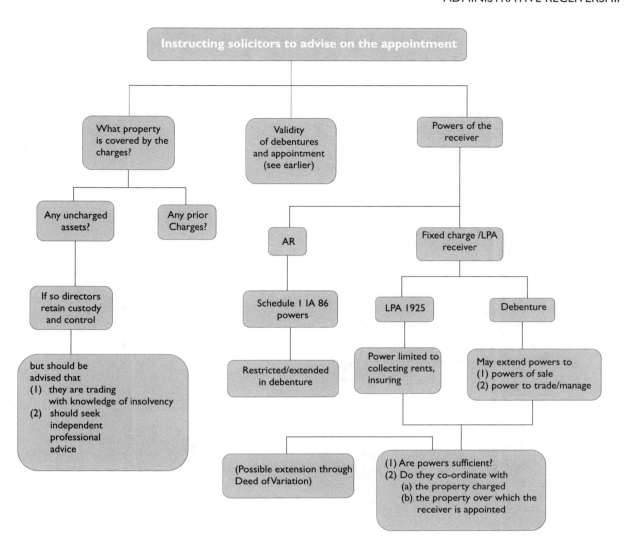

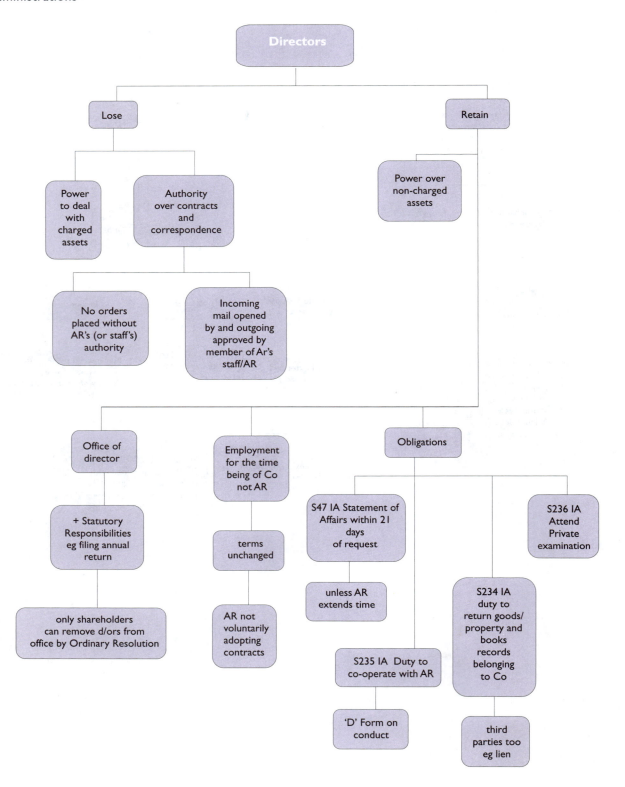

Self-test

Answer the following questions.

1   You have been asked to accept appointment as AR of Sherwood Homes Limited. In order for your appointment to be valid, within what period must you accept the appointment?

2   What are the effects of an AR being appointed?

3   To whom must an AR give notice of his appointment?

4   What is the liability of the AR in respect of employment contracts?

5   Within what period of time from his appointment must an AR prepare a report for the creditors under s48 IA?

6   What matters must be dealt with in the report?

7   What is the quorum for the unsecured creditors meeting held to receive the s48 IA report?

8   How often and to whom, must the AR submit an account of his receipts and payments?

9   What matters should be considered by the AR when allocating costs to fixed and floating charge assets per SIP 14?

Now, go back to the Learning Objectives in the Introduction. If you are satisfied that you have achieved these objectives, please tick them off.

Answers to Self-test

1   Appointment must be received and accepted by the AR by the end of the next business day. Acceptance may be oral or written, but if oral it must be confirmed in writing within 7 days.

2   AR has sole power to deal with charged assets.

   –   Director's have no power to deal with charged assets but do retain custody and control over any assets which are not covered by the appointor's charge.

   –   Director's office is not terminated.

   –   Directors retain statutory duties to maintain statutory records and make returns.

   –   Directors retain the power to institute proceedings in the name of the company.

   –   Contracts of employment are not automatically terminated.

   –   AR will require one or more directors to make and swear a statement of affairs.

   –   Returns under CDDA will be made.

3   –   London Gazette
    –   Newspaper
    –   The company (forthwith)
    –   The creditors (within 28 days)

4   Employment contracts are not automatically terminated on the appointment of an AR.

   The AR will be personally liable on any contracts of employment adopted by him (s44(1)(b) IA).

   AR will not be taken to have adopted a contract of employment by reason of anything done or omitted to be done within 14 days after his appointment.

   AR is not able to exclude adoption or personal liability (*Paramount Airways (House of Lords)*).

   Liability is limited to qualifying liabilities:

   –   Wages, salaries, holiday and sick pay, employer's contributions to occupational pension schemes for post adoption periods.

5   Within three months of his appointment.

6   Events leading up to his appointment.

   Disposal or proposed disposal by him of any property of the company and the carrying on or proposed carrying on by him of any business of the company.

   The amounts payable to the chargee by whom he was appointed and the amounts of the preferential debts.

   The amounts, if any, likely to be available to pay other creditors.

   A summary of the statement of affairs.

7   One creditor entitled to vote in person or by proxy.

8   Within two months after the end of 12 months from the date of appointment and every subsequent 12 months period and within two months of ceasing to act.

   Accounts must be sent to:

   –   the appointor
   –   the Registrar of Companies
   –   the company
   –   each member of the creditors' committee

9   The objectives for which the costs were incurred.

The benefits actually obtained in terms of protection of assets or augmentation in value.

Any detriment to the floating charge holder incurred whilst benefitting the fixed charge holder.

Any reduction in preferential debts where a going concern sale has resulted in the transfer of employment contracts.

Answers to Interactive Questions

Answer to interactive question 1: Bluegrass Limited

1   Ensure appointment is valid. Appoint solicitors to ascertain validity of appointment and charges under which appointed. Ensure appointment was correctly accepted.

2   Give notice of appointment, within seven days, to Registrar of Companies.

3   Send notice of appointment to the company forthwith.

4   Publish notice of appointment in London Gazette and such other newspaper as deemed appropriate.

5   Within 28 days send notice of appointment to all creditors of whose address you are aware.

6   Ensure all invoices, letter heads, e mails, websites all include a statement that an administrative receiver has been appointed.

7   Request one or more directors to submit a statement of affairs.

8   Arrange for a meeting with directors to advise of your appointment and the impact of your appointment on the directors.

9   Assume control of property comprised in the charge and safeguard such property ie. change locks, insure etc.

10 Open IP records.

Answer to Interactive Question 2: Harris Engineering Limited

1   Personal qualification to act as an administrative receiver:

—   Must be qualified IP

2   Ethical considerations:

Should not accept appointment if there has been a significant personal or professional relationship

—   Note: no significant relationship will arise from appointment as investigating accountants

—   Appointment should be declined if the IP or partners or employees of IP's firm have had such a close and distinct business connection with the debenture holder as might impair or appear to impair the IP's objectivity

—   Carry out a company search

—   Check firm's database to ascertain if any partner/ employee has conducted significant professional work with the company/ directors.

—   Check for any potential conflicts of interest.

3   Are there sufficient staff resources to undertake the proposed administrative receivership?

4   Is the IP's experience of insolvency work relevant to the receivership?

5   Does the IP possess the required general penalty sum bond of £250,000?

6   Is the debenture and charge valid?

—   Has the charge instrument been duly executed?

—   Was the giving of the security the provision of financial assistance for the purchase of the company's own shares?

—   Was the giving of the security intra vires the company?

- Was the giving of security intra vires the directors?

- Was the charge registered within 21 days?

- Could the creation of the charge constitute a preference under s239 IA?

- Could the charge be invalidated under s245 IA?

- Could the charge be invalidated as a transaction at an undervalue under s238 IA?

- Was the charge created before 15 September 2003?

7   Has the power to appoint arisen?

- Check that the debenture does authorise appointment of an administrative receiver in the circumstances that have arisen.

- Has a letter of demand been sent?

8   The company must not be in administration.

Closure of administrative receivership

> > > > > > > > > > > > > > >

Introduction

Learning objectives

▶ Effect of liquidation on the administrative receiver

▶ Circumstances in which an administrative receiver can vacate office

▶ Administrative receiver's duties on vacating office

Working context

In a working environment you may be asked to assist with a liquidation of a company in respect of which an administrative receiver has been appointed. It is important to understand the powers and duties of the administrative receiver and the liquidator in such circumstances.

Stop and think

What happens to the administrative receiver if a winding up order is granted? Who has responsibility for assets subject to the appointor's charge? How may an administrative receiver vacate office? Who must be notified of his ceasing to act?

Examination context

The effect of liquidation on administrative receivership has been regularly tested in the JIEB exam.

Past exam questions to look at include:

2005   Question 3(a)

2004   Question 2

1999   Question 1

1997   Question 1

1 Effect of liquidation

Section overview

▸ The appointment of an AR does not prevent a creditor presenting a petition to wind up the company compulsorily.

1.1 Effect of winding up order

The effects of a winding up order being made are summarised below:

(i) **Agency:**

By s44(1)(a) IA the AR's agency relationship with the company is terminated by the winding up order. The significance of this is that:

▸ the AR will now enter post-winding up order contracts as principal.

▸ In relation to such contracts the AR will *not* have any indemnity out of the company's assets in respect of his or her personal liability.

▸ In theory the AR could still seek to exclude liability in the contract itself and

▸ remains entitled to the benefit of the indemnity negotiated with the bank.

The winding up order has no effect on the AR's position in regard to contracts he or she had already entered into prior to the winding up order i.e. the AR retains an indemnity out of the company's assets in relation to these.

The appointor bank will not become the AR's principal as a result of the liquidation (unless the bank 'intermeddles').

The AR retains the right to use the company's name (as in legal proceedings) *Gough's Garages Ltd v Pugsley 1983*.

(ii) **Employees:**

Contracts of employment will be automatically terminated by a compulsory winding up order (*Measures Ltd v Measures*).

The practical problem for the AR is that the employees may be required to trade the business with a view to a going concern sale.

The AR can re-employ the employees as principal but:

▸ will be personally liable on their contracts of employment

▸ that liability not being limited to 'qualifying liabilities'.

▸ Again the AR will not have an indemnity against the company but will retain any indemnity negotiated with the bank.

(iii) **Charges:**

(a) The AR retains custody and control of the charged assets and retains power to realise and sell company property subject to the charges and may continue to carry on the company's business (*Atkins v Merchantile Credits Ltd 1985*) and retains his general powers of management in Schedule 11A.

(b) S245 IA will be triggered by the winding up order, so that:

▸ a floating charge created within 12 months of petition

▸ at a time when the company is insolvent

▸ will be invalid except to the extent that fresh consideration is provided.

In practice the turnover of the company's bank account often provides the new money which validates the appointor's charge.

Note that the effect of s245 IA is not retrospective *(Mace Builders Glasgow Ltd v Lunn)* so that realisations and distributions (e.g. to prefs or appointor) made prior to the winding up order remain valid. The problem which s245 IA creates for the AR therefore is that if the floating charge is invalidated, the AR will be a trespasser if he deals with those assets *after* the date of the winding up order.

(iv) **Statutory effects:**

By s41(1)(b) IA the AR has a duty if the Liquidator so requires to:

▶   render proper accounts of receipts and payments

▶   and pay over any amounts properly payable.

This duty can be enforced by the court.

The AR retains his duty to make returns of receipts and payments to the Registrar of Companies and others under r3.32.

SIP 1 advises members to provide all post appointment company documentation (as opposed to the AR's or appointors papers) to the Liquidator unless disclosure would be contrary to the interests of the appointor.

By s48(4)(a) IA the AR shall provide the Liquidator with a copy of the s48 IA report within 7 days of the later of:

▶   the appointment of the Liquidator or

▶   the AR's compliance with his duty to send the s48 IA report to the Registrar of Companies etc.

▶   In any event if no s48 IA meeting has been held to date none now needs to be held.

A copy of the statement of affairs must be sent to the Liquidator.(s48(5) IA)

The AR has a general duty to co-operate with the Liquidator. (s235(3)(e) IA)

(v) **Potential actions which may be brought by a liquidator against a AR:**

The Liquidator may apply to the court for an order fixing the AR's remuneration (s36(1) IA). This procedure should not however be used as a means of routinely taxing an AR's costs but should only be applied where costs are clearly excessive *(Re Potters Oils Ltd)*.

Misfeasance (s212 IA) – when evidence that the AR is in breach of fiduciary or other duty or has been guilty of a misapplication of company property.

Action against AR for trespass/conversion for benefit of unsecured creditors.

Application to court under s45(1) IA for removal of the AR.

Public examination.

(vi) **The preferential creditors:**

The AR retains his duty to pay preferential creditors under s40 IA (despite the somewhat misleading wording of the section). The relevant date from which the AR calculates preferential creditors remains the date of appointment of the AR and this is not affected by subsequent winding up.

The Liquidator also has a quite separate duty to pay preferential creditors under s175 IA. The Liquidator takes the date of the order as the relevant date. In practise, of course:

▶   the AR may have already discharged the preferential creditors or

▶   the AR may have been appointed so long ago that the relevant periods for calculating preferential creditors all fall within the period of the AR's trading (with new liabilities falling due to employees having been met as they fell due) so that again there is no preferential liability for the Liquidator to discharge or

> ▸ the Liquidator may not have sufficient funds to pay the preferential creditors.

(vii) **Discussions with bank:**

These will focus on the balance between the potential liabilities involved in continuing to trade. In particular the loss of agency status and the need to re-employ the workforce as principal will impact on the banks exposure under the indemnity it provides to the AR, the potential advantages of continuing to trade and effecting a going concern sale.

1.2 Administrative receivership commencing after the date of the winding up order

The notes so far have been concerned with the more common situation where administrative receivership is superseded by winding up.

It is possible however for an Administrative Receiver to be appointed where a company is already in liquidation. The law seems to accept that a chargeholder has a right to protect its interests in this way even though a Liquidator must generally respect the existing property rights of secured creditors and even though two IP's in a company will obviously increase costs.

Here the AR will never have been agent of the company and will act as principal from the outset.

Although the provisions of the Act are far from clear it seems that the AR will acquire a duty to pay prefs in priority to the appointor under the floating charge (see s175 IA). The relevant date used will be the date of the Liquidation not the date of appointment of the AR.

Interactive question: Universal Limited

Your principal, Mr Smith, has been acting as administrative receiver of Universal Limited for the last seven months, having been appointed by Natby Bank PLC under their floating charge.

Universal Limited has just gone into compulsory liquidation and Natby Bank PLC are concerned at how this will affect the receivership.

Your principal has continued to trade the company with a view to achieving a sale as a going concern.

Requirement:

Draft a letter to Natby Bank PLC outlining the consequences for the bank and the administrative receiver of the liquidation of the company.

See **Answer** at the end of the chapter.

2 Debts outstanding at the date of appointment

Section overview

> ▸ The payment of creditors in an administrative receivership is dictated by when the debt arose and whether it is secured or not.

2.1 Unsecured creditors

Unsecured creditors, other than preferential creditors, can continue to pursue their claims against the company though they will not obtain anything by levying execution because all of the company's property will be subject to a prior charge. They can petition for the company to be wound up or for an administration order to be made. They cannot obtain an Administration Order without the agreement of the creditor by whom or on whose behalf the administrative receiver was appointed unless they can satisfy the court that they can get the floating charge discharged or avoided or declared invalid: (s9(3) IA). The unsecured creditors are now entitled to a report by the administrative receiver within three months of his appointment unless a liquidator is appointed before the end of the three months. The report must state how much, if anything, is likely to be available to pay unsecured non-preferential creditors. If the unsecured creditors allow the receivership to continue they can elect a creditors' committee to put their point of view to the receiver. If there is dissatisfaction they always have available the possibility of putting the company into compulsory liquidation.

2.2 Secured creditors with fixed charges

A secured creditor with a fixed charge, ranking before the floating charge under which an administrative receiver is appointed, can ignore the receivership and proceed to enforce the charge. Alternatively the administrative receiver can apply to the court for an order enabling him to dispose of the charged property himself and pay the creditor its market value. The charged property cannot be utilised to pay the preferential creditors.

up to the level of the Security/outstanding debt S.43

If the fixed chargee has yielded priority to the floating charge under which the administrative receiver was appointed, then he must wait, like an unsecured creditor, for the outcome of the administrative receivership, or join with other unsecured creditors in seeking winding up or administration. If the property covered by his charge survives the administrative receivership then he will be able to utilise it in priority to the unsecured creditors. However, it is more likely that the administrative receivership will render his security worthless and he will decide to be treated as an unsecured creditor at creditors' meetings.

2.3 Secured creditors with floating charges

If another floating charge ranks in priority to the floating charge under which the administrative receiver is appointed then it is still a prior charge on the assets (Re *Household Products Co Ltd* 1981) if and when it crystallises.

If a prior floating charge has crystallised then it can be treated in the same way as a prior fixed charge, or the prior chargee can appoint his own administrative receiver to enforce it.

A floating charge ranking after the charge under which the administrative receiver was appointed is in the same position as a subsequent fixed charge.

When an administrative receiver of a company incurs debts in the course of the receivership he does so as agent of the company so that the company is liable for their payment. The person with whom the debt was incurred should have been made aware that an administrative receiver had been appointed.

At the end of a receivership it is necessary to add up all the money received and all the liabilities incurred (whether the liabilities have been settled or not). The liabilities are in principle settled in the following order:

(i)   the cost of selling the company's property and business, collecting its debts and enforcing its claims against other persons;

(ii)   the proper expenses and remuneration of the administrative receiver;

(iii)   the preferential debts;

(iv)   the debt secured by the floating charge.

If the total money received is less than the total of items (i) to (iv) but equal to, or more than, the total of (i) to (iii) then the chargee loses the shortfall. If the amount received is less than the total of items (i) to (iii) but equal to, or more than, the total of (i) and (ii) then the preferential creditors will suffer (all must lose the same proportion of their debts) and so on.

However, an administrative receiver has a duty not to incur liabilities of types (i) and (ii) if to do so would lessen the amount available to pay preferential creditors: *Woods v Winskill* 913, which was concerned with liabilities incurred in carrying on the company's business.

An administrative receiver who has paid debts in the wrong order will have misapplied assets, a misfeasance for which he will be personally liable to any creditor who was deprived of payment.

3 Completion

Section overview

▶ Completion of the administrative receivership will occur if all debts secured by the charge under which the AR was appointed are paid, or if all property covered by the charge is realised by the receiver and the proceeds paid to the persons entitled to them.

3.1 Vacation of office

The AR can vacate office in a number of ways:

An administrative receiver of a company vacates office in the following circumstances:

(1) on death;

(2) on the making of an administration order in relation to the company (para 41(1) of Schedule B1 IA);

(3) on removal from office by order of the court (s45(1) IA) - note that a chargee who appointed a receiver out of court cannot remove him from office;

(4) on giving at least seven day's notice of resignation to the person by whom he was appointed, to the company (or, if it is then in liquidation, to its liquidator) and to the members of the creditors' committee (if any) (s45(1) IA; r.3.33(1)). The notice must state the date from which the resignation is to be effective (r3.33(2));

(5) on ceasing to be qualified to act as an insolvency practitioner (s45(2) IA);

(6) on completion of the receivership, which will occur if all debts secured by the charge under which the receiver was appointed are paid, or if all property covered by the charge is realised by the receiver and the proceeds paid to the persons entitled to them; and

(7) on dissolution of the company.

In circumstances (6) and (7) the office of administrative receiver ceases to exist.

3.2 Notice of vacation of office

S45(4) IA provides that the AR must give notice of his vacation of office to the Registrar of Companies within 14 days (this does not extend to an AR vacating due to death for obvious reasons). R3.35 provides that the AR should also give notice to the company (or liquidator if in liquidation) and the creditors' committee (if any).

Within two months of ceasing to act the AR must send a copy of his final receipts and payments account to:

▶ Registrar of Companies
▶ The company
▶ The appointor
▶ Creditors' committee (if any).

Summary and Self-test

Summary

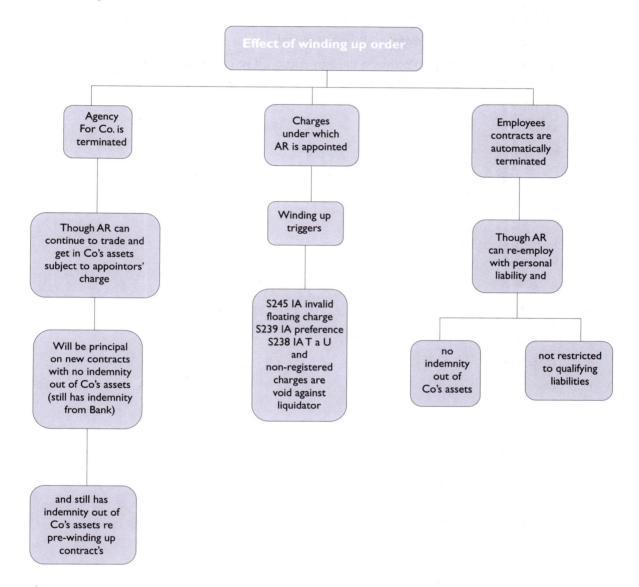

Self-test

Answer the following questions.

1   What actions may be brought by a liquidator against an AR?

2   What duties does an AR owe to a liquidator?

3   How does the liquidation of a company affect the AR's agency?

4   Within how many days of vacating office must the AR give notice to the Registrar of Companies?

5   Who else must be notified of the AR ceasing to act?

Now, go back to the Learning Objectives in the Introduction. If you are satisfied that you have achieved these objectives, please tick them off.

Answers to Self-test

1   Order the fixing of the AR's remuneration – s36(1) IA

Action for misfeasance – s212 IA

Order for trespass/ conversion (if continues to deal with company assets)

Order for removal of the AR – s45(1) IA

Application for the public examination of the AR – s133(3) IA

2   Render proper accounts of receipts and payments.

Pay over amounts properly payable.

Must provide all post appointment company documentation to the liquidator (SIP 1).

Must send a copy of the s48 IA report to the liquidator within seven days of his appointment.

Send the liquidator a copy of the Statement of Affairs – s48(5) IA.

General duty to co-operate with the liquidator – s235(3)(e) IA.

3   AR's agency in relation to the company is terminated (s44(1)(a) IA). He will enter post winding up order contracts as principal and will not have an indemnity out of the company's assets in respect of these contracts. He retains the indemnity in respect of pre winding up order contracts.

4   Within 14 days.

5   The company (or liquidator if applicable) and the creditors' committee (if any).

Answers to Interactive Question

Answer to Interactive Question: Universal Limited

Letter format

1   Impact of liquidation on the bank:

- Bank will not become administrative receiver's principal unless bank intermeddles
- Bank is still liable for the administrative receiver's indemnity
- Administrative receivership continues
- Banks charge over assets remains in force

Liquidation triggers s245 IA – a floating charge created within 12 months of the petition, at a time when the company was insolvent, will be invalid except to the extent that fresh consideration is provided. If the charge is invalidated, the bank will lose the benefit of it. They will become an ordinary unsecured creditor in respect of the debt. The administrative receivership will cease.

The main impact of liquidation is the potential liabilities involved in continuing to trade. In particular, the loss of agency status and the need to re-employ the workforce as principal will impact on the bank's exposure under the indemnity it provides to the administrative receiver.

Problems with employee contracts may mean that the administrative receiver is unable to continue trading. This may lead to lower returns for the bank.

The bank will have to weigh up the potential advantages of continuing to trade and effecting a going concern sale against the increased costs.

Liquidation will also trigger s239 IA preferences and s238 IA transactions at an undervalue.

2   Impact of liquidation on the administrative receiver:

Administrative receiver's agency relationship with the company is terminated by the winding up order (s44(1)(a) IA).

Administrative receiver will now enter post winding up order contracts as principal.

Administrative receiver will be entitled to the benefit of the indemnity negotiated with the bank.

The winding up order has no effect on contracts entered into prior to the winding up order. The administrative receiver will retain the indemnity out of the company's assets in respect of these.

Contracts of employment will be automatically terminated by the winding up order. If employees are still required the administrative receiver will have to employ them as principal. The administrative receiver will be personally liable on their contracts of employment. The liability will not be restricted to qualifying liabilities.

The administrative receiver retains custody and control of the charged assets. He retains the power to realise and sell company property subject to the charge and may continue to carry on the company's business.

If s245 IA applies and the charge is invalidated:

- Realisations and distributions made prior to the winding up order remain valid however, the administrative receiver will be a trespasser if he deals with those assets after the date of the winding up order. If the debenture under which the administrative receiver is appointed proves to be invalid, the liquidator can require the administrative receiver to hand over all of the assets of which he has taken control.

The administrative receiver has a duty, if the liquidator so requires to:

- Render proper accounts of receipts and payments
- Pay over any amounts properly payable

The administrative receiver should provide to the liquidator:

– all post appointment company documentation
– a copy of the s48 IA report
– statement of affairs

The administrative receiver has a general duty to co-operate with the liquidator.

The liquidator can bring the following actions against the administrative receiver:

– order fixing the receiver's remuneration
– order for the removal of the receiver
– action for misfeasance
– action for trespass/conversion
– public examination

The administrative receiver retains the duty to pay the preferential creditors.

10

Trading on and selling the business

> > > > > > > > > > > > > > > > > >

Introduction

Learning objectives

▶ Factors to be considered by the office holder when deciding whether to continue trading ☐

▶ How to deal with ROT and judgment creditors ☐

▶ Understand what hiving down is and when it is appropriate ☐

▶ The responsibility of the office holder for environmental considerations ☐

▶ How to deal with claims by employees ☐

▶ The office holder's responsibility when selling the business ☐

▶ Requirements of SIP 13 ☐

Working context

This is a very practical chapter dealing with matters which office holders have to deal with on a day to day basis when trading and seeking to sell a business. It is likely in a work environment that you will be asked to assist in dealing with claims by ROT creditors or employee claims.

Stop and think

What is the personal liability of the office holder when they continue to trade the business? Why would an administrator and an administrative receiver have different considerations when deciding whether to continue trading? What claims do employees have against an office holder? How does an office holder sell a business?

Examination context

The JIEB exam is a practically based exam and therefore the topics covered in this chapter are examined regularly, in particular the decision to continue trading and selling the business. These topics can be tested either in an administration or an administrative receivership scenario so it is important to understand any differences between how an administrator and an administrative receiver will deal with matters arising.

Past exam questions to look at include:

2007		Question 4
2006		Question 5(b)
2004		Question 3
2003		Question 4
2002		Question 3(b)
2002		Question 4(a), (b), (c)
2001		Question 3(b)
2000		Question 4
2000		Question 5(d)
1999		Question 4(a)
1998		Question 1
1998		Question 5
1997		Question 2
1997		Question 4
1997		Question 5(a)
1996		Question 3(a)
1996		Question 5(b)
1995		Question 1
1995		Question 3(b)
1995		Question 5
1994		Question 1
1994		Question 2
1993		Question 4
1993		Question 5(a), (b)
1992	Paper I	Question 3(c)
1991	Paper II	Question 2

1 Trading on

Section overview

▶   The administrator's primary duty is to rescue the company as a going concern (para 3(1) IA), this will require the administrator to continue trading the company. The administrative receiver's (AR) prime duty is to realise assets to meet the appointing charge holder's claim. The best way of doing this may be to trade on with a view to selling all or part of the business as a going concern. The administrator and administrative receiver both have the statutory power to trade the company under Sch 1 IA. The decision to trade is similar in both scenarios so this chapter deals with matters common to both the administrator and the administrative receiver.

1.1 The decision to trade on

In the short term:

Trade will be completed in the short term in order to:

▶   Complete work in progress thereby increasing its value.

▶   Protect outstanding book debts.

▶   Provide a breathing space during which the office holder can investigate the possibility of a going concern sale, continuing to trade until it is implemented.

▶   Generally low risk, the office holder is completing existing contracts rather than entering into new ones.

(AR only): The AR should, at the initial meeting with the appointing charge holder:

▶   Agree that he will trade on in the short term pending preparation of a report by the AR on the advisability of trading on in the longer term.

▶   Arrange an overdraft facility to finance the trading.

▶   Obtain a suitable indemnity from the charge holder.

▶   Highlight the benefits of continuing to trade.

▶   Agree on the timings of progress reports to the charge holder.

▶   Agree basis of the AR's fees.

The AR will probably have to provide valid security for any further borrowings, particularly where the bankers are not the debenture holders.

The AR should ascertain:

▶   Whether he has the power to raise money on the property charged in priority to the debentures.

▶   Whether the debenture holders consent to a charge being created in priority to the debentures.

▶   Whether the further indebtedness will be repaid from future cash flow.

▶   Whether the bank, being the debenture holder, will grant temporary overdraft facilities.

▶   Where a new charge is created it must be registered in order to prevent it being declared void by any subsequent appointed liquidator.

After his appointment, the office holder should ascertain:

▶   Whether the finished goods would be marketable
▶   The costs of completion
▶   The difference between sale value of the raw materials and the value of the finished goods

And ascertain a cash flow forecast accordingly.

In the longer term:

The administrator owes a duty to all creditors generally and must ensure that the creditors are not prejudiced by the decision to trade. The AR has a duty not to worsen the position of the preferential creditors by continuing to trade (s40 IA).

There are advantages to continuing to trade in the longer term:

▶ Continuing to trade facilitates a going concern sale which should realise more for the assets than a forced sale, achieving a better financial outcome for all creditors.

▶ Minimises bad publicity caused by closures and job losses (this is particularly relevant for administrative receivership where the bank may be seen to be to blame for closing the company).

▶ If the office holder's trading is profitable this will enhance floating charge realisations over and above the increase in asset realisations to be obtained from a going concern sale.

(AR only): However, the AR will be personally liable on any new contracts entered in to (s44(1)(b) IA) and if the company enters liquidation the AR will then enter contracts as principal.

The decision to trade should be based on whether continuing to trade will achieve a better financial outcome. In order to assist in making that decision the office holder should:

▶ Prepare inventories of assets with estimated values on a going concern and break up basis.

▶ Obtain valuations of assets on going concern and break up bases.

▶ Evaluate preferential and prior secured claims as well as claims of own charge holder.

▶ Consider likelihood of achieving a going concern sale of the business and assets.

▶ Consider the level of funding required to support trading evidenced by a detailed cash flow forecast.

▶ Produce estimated outcome statements (see chapter 12 for details) indicating whether there is a financial advantage to continuing to trade.

The AR would also need to consider the likelihood of the company being placed into liquidation which would terminate the receiver's agency (See Chapter 9, section 1).

1.2 Premises

The company may trade from leasehold premises. If rent is in arrears the landlord may have a right of forfeiture or may distrain for unpaid rent.

Under s146 LPA 1925 the court may grant relief against forfeiture on the application of the company or the chargeholder.

If the lease is forfeit the company may be entitled to compensation from the landlord in respect of improvements carried out by the company or its predecessor tenant (s1 Landlord and Tenant Act 1927).

A landlord can distrain for rent before crystallisation of the charge even if the distress is completed by sale only after crystallisation (*Re Roundwood Colliery Co 1897*).

A landlord can serve a notice under s6 of the Law of Distress Amendment Act 1908 requiring the sub-tenants of the company to pay rent directly to the landlord. Rents will be diverted to the landlord and will not be available to the AR *(Rhodes v Allied Dunbar)*.

A landlord can levy distress for rent because he can distrain on goods on the premises regardless of whether they are charged in favour of someone else. More significantly, the lease will probably provide for forfeiture on appointment of an administrative receiver of the tenant: dealing with a landlord may be one of an administrative receiver's most difficult problems.

The landlord will usually levy distress through a person authorised to act as a bailiff certified by the county court. The landlord normally signs a 'distress-warrant' - which is used by the bailiff as his authority.

Force may not be used to enter premises, but it may be used to re-enter premises, and to break open doors internally.

Distress can be levied on any goods that can be removed and subsequently restored in an identical condition.

Business books and records cannot be removed. The goods may be seized either by stating that one article is taken in distress in the name of all, or simply by preventing removal of the goods. Invariably the impounded goods are removed to a place of safety.

Where the tenant believes the threatened distress to be illegal, he may apply for an injunction.

The landlord has a right to levy distress on certain third party goods specified in The Law of Distress Amendments Act 1908. All other third party goods are exempt and the landlord's right to levy distress is restricted. However, the third party must claim the exemption by serving a written declaration to the landlord/bailiff:

▶ the goods are his lawful property/in his lawful possession
▶ the tenant has no beneficial interest/rights in the property
▶ the goods do not fall within the categories defined in the Act as exceptions to the general rule.

With regard to a Local Authority, the case of *ELS Ltd 1995* held that a local authority cannot distrain for rates and council tax post appointment of an administrative receiver. They will be an unsecured claim against the company.

In administration a moratorium will prevent the landlord from being able to enforce his rights without leave of the administrator or the court, however in some circumstances the court will grant leave even when the rent arrears have been settled *(Metro Nominees (Wandsworth) Ltd v Rayment)*.

With the introduction on 1 April 2008 of Reg 4(1) of the Non-Domestic Rating (Unoccupied Property) (England) Regulations 2008, the decision in *Trident* has been reversed and rates in administration are treated the same as in liquidation.

1.3 Customers and suppliers

Generally the office holder will not be liable on existing contracts, he may repudiate such contracts. The 3rd party may claim as an unsecured creditor against the company, but not against the AR *(Airlines Airspace Ltd v Handley Page Ltd (1970))*.

The AR may adopt such contracts, if so, the contract remains with the company and the 3rd party remains bound to perform his part of the agreement. The 3rd party is entitled however, to offset any outstanding liabilities under the contract against any goods or services supplied by the company through the AR *(Rother Iron Works Ltd v Canterbury Precision Engineers Ltd)*. The AR should obtain the agreement of the 3rd party that such liabilities remain unsecured pre receivership liabilities and should not be set off against post appointment transactions.

The office holder should ensure that there will be customers for the finished products and evaluate the effect of a potential lack of after sales services.

Existing contracts should be examined, they may be terminable on receivership or administration. Note should be taken of deposits or stage payments made.

Existing price structures should be examined and competitors identified.

New markets should be identified.

A projected sales forecast should be prepared.

The office holder should confirm that suppliers will be willing to continue supporting the company. This may require the payment of sums due to them as a condition of maintaining supplies.

ROT claims should be identified and the value of stocks subject to ROT should be evaluated. (See later in this chapter for details). Are other suppliers available?

1.4 Production capacity

Will the workforce continue to support the office holder? What arrears are there? These may have to be paid by the office holder to ensure continued employee co-operation. What TUPR liabilities are attached to employee contracts? This may be relevant to achieving a going concern sale. (See later section re calculating employee claims).

Are there any arrears on HP or leasing agreements which may result in the repossession of vital machinery?

Plant age, reliability, safety and quality of existing plant has to be assessed. Any health and safety issues?

Overheads – what are they and can they be reduced?

Are any hauliers claiming liens over the company's property?

1.5 Counter claims and set-off

If the receiver decides to continue trading, he must ensure that the company does not make supplies to anyone who may be a creditor of the company, as payment may not be received for the goods supplied.

Generally, such a right of set-off does not exist and the party to whom a supply is made post receivership cannot set-off their debt against amounts due to them by the company for goods or services provided pre-appointment. Where doubt exists as to the rights of set-off, legal advice should be sought.

1.6 Management

The office holder must depend on existing management as staff are unlikely to be specialists in the company's business. The office holder must assess the capability and motivation of the existing management. Members of the management team should be interviewed by the office holder.

1.7 Product and other liabilities

The office holder should assess the liabilities attaching to any failure of the company's products after sale. If potential liabilities are significant, he should obtain insurance or consider selling the products or services through a separate sales company.

The office holder should also consider the following:

▶ Does the company have all necessary licences?
▶ Is the business of the company lawful?
▶ Potential Environmental Protection Act problems (see later section).
▶ Does the company have all necessary planning permissions?

1.8 Hiving down

It is common for an administrative receiver (as agent of the company in receivership) to sell the assets under his control to a new company, all shares in which are held by his nominees in trust for the company that is in receivership. This procedure is called 'hiving-down' and is usually carried out within days of the receiver's appointment.

It is done so as to create a convenient package of assets to be offered for sale, and payment to the company in receivership is not made until the hive-down company is sold. Power to hive down is given by s42 and Sch 1, paras 15 and 16 IA. An important feature of a hive-down company is that it acquires only the assets and not the liabilities of the company that is in receivership.

Contracts of employment are not taken over by a hive-down company unless and until the hive-down company is sold (*Transfer of Undertakings (Protection of Employment) Regulations* 1981). This means that if the receiver fails to sell the hive-down company then the employee's contracts remain with the company in receivership and are dealt with by that company. However, if the hive-down company is sold, the contracts of employment are instantly transferred from the company in receivership to the buyer of the business.

Under s345 of the *Income and Corporation Taxes Act* 1988, reliefs and allowances from corporation tax which were not used by the company in receivership may be taken over by the hive-down company, which may be an added attraction for potential purchasers.

The receiver's solicitors draft the hiving-down agreement, which must ensure that the following practical aspects have been considered:

- Terms of contracts with other third parties not breached by the hive-down, e.g. leases, licenses, trade marks, secured creditors.

- Convenient accounting reference date.

- Sales of assets agreements should specifically include the term 'exclusive of VAT'.

- Consideration for the sale should be left on a loan account between the two companies.

- No transfer of freehold/leasehold land should be made, as this would give rise to a stamp duty liability.

- Directors of the new company should be the receiver's employees.

- Separate accounting records should be maintained including an inter-company account with the company in receivership.

- The hive-down company should arrange to collect the insolvent company's book debts.

- The purchaser can acquire the shares in the company, or the assets may be sold to him by the hive-down company.

- The consideration received may be utilised to pay off the inter-company loan account.

Advantages of hiving down

- Trading can be conducted through a company which is not insolvent and is not required to state 'In Administration/ administrative receivership' on its letters, invoices etc.

- The hive down procedure creates a package of assets free from historic liabilities which may prove to be a more attractive proposition to a potential purchaser

- A company in administration/ administrative receivership may experience difficulty in completing and disposing of work in progress due to customer reaction to that fact

- It is likely to be easier to obtain funding through a solvent hived down company

Disadvantages of hiving down

- Certain contracts may not be assignable to a wholly owned subsidiary for contractual reasons

- Increases costs

- Employee contracts are likely to vest with the hive down company. TUPR liabilities may make hiving down a less attractive proposition

1.9 Supplies by utilities

Suppliers of essential services, such as electricity and telecommunications, which are usually supplied on credit, have in the past been in a strong position when a customer company has gone into administration or administrative receivership. A receiver or administrator usually wishes the company to continue in business for a week at least in order to continue work on existing contracts and give him a chance to assess the position.

However, suppliers of essential services have been able to refuse to supply them until they have been paid for everything they supplied before the receiver was appointed. This has put them in a preferential position compared to other trade creditors which has been widely resented. s233 IA now curbs this by stating that certain public utilities shall not make it a condition of supplying services to a company in administrative receivership that outstanding charges from before commencement of the receivership be paid.

However, they are entitled to demand that the receiver personally guarantees payment of future charges. In practice, of course, the administrator or administrative receiver will insist on an indemnity from the chargee who appointed him before giving such a guarantee. The services covered by this provision are (s233(3) and (5) IA):

(i)   a supply of gas by the British Gas Corporation or any other public gas supplier;

(ii)   a supply of electricity by an electricity board;

(iii) a supply of water by statutory water undertaking;

(iv)   a supply of telecommunication services (other than cable television) by a public telecommunications operator.

The scope of s235 IA is confined to statutory undertakings and similar bodies which are under a legal obligation to provide a service to the public, a private supplier of, for example, gas or water is not affected.

1.10 Taxation

Administrative receivership: Corporation tax arising on profits made in the period of the receivership are assessable on the company, not the AR. Where the profits are related to a pre winding up period, the tax will rank as an unsecured claim. Where the profits relate to a period post liquidation, the tax will be treated as a liquidation expense.

Administration: Corporation tax arising on profits made will be an expense of the administration.

1.11 ROT claims

Trade suppliers to companies often include in their standard conditions of sale a clause stating that goods supplied to a company will remain the property of the supplier until monies owing to the supplier have been paid. These retention of title clauses are often called 'Romalpa clauses' after the case in which the validity of the clauses was upheld.

A ROT supplier may, following the appointment of the office holder, seek to recover their goods from the company. If the office holder wrongfully prevents the supplier from recovering the goods he may be liable to pay damages to the supplier. However, if the office holder allows the supplier to remove the goods and the ROT claim later turns out to be invalid, he will have dissipated assets which should have been available for the preferential creditors and appointing chargeholder.

In administration the moratorium prevents ROT creditors from enforcing their rights without the leave of the administrator or the court. It is important however that the administrator determines the validity of ROT claims made because the administrator will be unable to deal with assets subject to a valid ROT claim without the agreement of the supplier. If a ROT creditor seeks leave to enforce his claim the administrator should use the guidelines laid down in *Re Atlantic Computers* (see later in this section).

There are two types of ROT clause:

(i)   **Simple clause**: provides that goods supplied under a specific invoice remain the property of the vendor until all goods on the invoice have been paid for.

(ii)   **All monies clause**: this holds that all goods supplied by the vendor remain their property until all sums due to the vendor, on whatever account, are paid.

If the clause is simple the supplier will be required to identify the remaining goods held by the company to an unpaid invoice.

With an all monies clause, the goods do not have to be identified to a particular invoice. All items will remain the property of the supplier until all monies owed are paid. However, when the purchaser has, at some date, cleared all sums due to the vendor, title to all goods supplied prior to that date will pass to the purchaser. It is important therefore for the office holder to check whether the balance on the suppliers account has ever been reduced to zero.

The office holder must ensure that the ROT clause has been accepted and incorporated into the contract. This should be done prior to the supply taking place ie on a separate agreement or order form. If the clause is on the back of an invoice this is a post contractual document and therefore it is not part of the contract. It is possible, where there has been a lengthy course of dealings, that the ROT clause may be accepted as part of the contract because over the course of dealings the purchaser must have become aware of the terms.

ROT clauses which seek to assert title to the proceeds of sale are effectively charges which can only be valid if registered at Companies House (*Re Peachdart 1984*).

The reservation of title will cease to exist over goods once they have become irretrievably incorporated into other goods by manufacture or otherwise (*Re Bond Worth 1979, Re Peachdart 1983*).

It is for the supplier to prove that his reservation of title clause is effective in order to establish a better claim to the goods than the office holder.

When dealing with ROT claims the office holder should:

1   Request copies of all documentation relating to the claim, invoices, delivery notes, ROT clause etc

2   Obtain legal advice re validity of the claim

3   Invite the creditor to attend a stock take and identify goods subject to their ROT claim (simple clause – identify goods to specific invoice). Identification of goods can be difficult when the supplier supplies a product which is indistinguishable from that supplied by other parties or has no identifying marks. If the goods have been incorporated into other goods (ie. During the manufacturing process) and the claimed items cannot be removed from the manufactured product , the ROT claim will fail

4   Place goods identified to one side.

If the ROT claim is valid the creditor should be allowed to recover the goods. The office holder should ensure that any proof of debt submitted by the creditor is amended accordingly.

In practice, whilst the validity of the claim is being established the office holder may agree to pay the supplier for any goods actually used. The office holder is often in a position to negotiate purchasing the goods at a reduced price from the supplier.

(Administration only): When a company enters administration a moratorium comes into force which has the effect of preventing a creditor enforcing a ROT claim without the leave of the administrator or the court. When dealing with a creditor who has sought leave to enforce a ROT claim the administrator should use the guidelines set out in *Re Atlantic Computers*. These guidelines also apply when any creditor with proprietary rights seeks leave to enforce them (ie landlord, HP creditor). The administrator should consider whether the court would be likely to grant leave given the circumstances of the case. The administrator is an officer of the court, therefore when a creditor applies to him for leave he should:

▸   Act speedily (if necessary making an interim decision eg. Retaining the goods/ machinery etc but meeting current payments as an expense of the administration.

▸   Act 'responsibly'.

▸   Not use the moratorium as a bargaining counter.

▸   Give succinct reasons for his decisions.

How the court deals with applications:

▸   The court will not adjudicate on disputes on the existence or validity of security... unless a short issue of law which it is convenient to decide.

▸   The onus is on the applicant for leave to make out their case.

▸   The court will consider all relevant matters including the conduct of the parties.

▸   The court has a broad discretion unfettered by rules of rigid application.

If granting leave is unlikely to impede the achievement of the para 3 Sch B1 IA purpose, the court must carry out a 'balancing exercise'. The court/ administrator must balance the legitimate interests of the applicant against the interests of the creditors generally.

Great importance is attached to the proprietary interests of the applicant:

▸   Administration for the benefit of unsecured creditors should not be conducted at the expense of those who have proprietary rights

▸   The purpose of the power to give leave is to enable the court to relax the moratorium where it would be inequitable for the prohibition to apply.

Therefore if significant loss would be caused by refusal leave will normally be granted. If substantially greater loss would be caused to others by granting leave which is out of all proportion to the loss to the applicant – leave may be refused.

In assessing losses the court will look at the financial position of the company and specifically its capacity to pay on-going interest or rental payments under the agreement.

A likely compromise is for the administrator to retain the goods/ equipment, but subject to the condition that rental and other payments during the period for which the order is in force are paid as a cost of the administration.

1.12 Judgment creditors

Administrative receivership:

If execution is levied on company property at the instance of judgment creditors then the enforcement officer must observe the rights of others to that property if those rights were created before delivery of the writ to the enforcement officer. So any execution levied after crystallisation of a floating charge will yield nothing for the judgment creditor.

Similarly, if a pre-existing floating charge crystallises after the writ is delivered, but before the execution is completed, the judgment creditor gets nothing. This is because the chargee's equitable right to the property was created before the writ bound the property even though it only came into force afterwards: Re *Opera Ltd* 1891. This rule applies even if the execution is put in to enforce a judgment given before the floating charge was created, since the judgment itself creates no rights over property *Ceisse v Taylor & Hartland* 1905. However, if crystallisation does not occur until after the execution is completed then the floating chargee will never have had any rights over the seized property *Royal Bank of Canada v Mohawk Moving & Storage Ltd* 1985.

If a judgment creditor of a company seeks to execute the judgment by garnishee (attachment) proceedings in respect of a debt owed to the company, a floating charge created before the proceedings will take priority if it crystallises at any time before the garnishor actually receives payment: *Robson v Smith* 1895.

Because these are problems of priorities of equitable interests it is irrelevant that a judgment creditor has not had notice of the appointment of an administrative receiver before attempting to obtain payment by execution or garnishment: *MacKay & Hughes (1973) Ltd v Martin Potatoes Inc* 1984.

The court has a power to order delivery to a company's administrative receiver of property to which the company appears to be entitled (s234(1) and (2) IA). The court may also order delivery of property discovered during a private examination under ss236 and 237 IA.

An administrative receiver of a company who seizes or disposes of property that does not belong to the company is not liable for loss or damage arising from the seizure or disposal, provided he was not negligent and provided he believed, and had reasonable grounds for believing, that he was entitled to seize or dispose of the property at the time that he did so (s234(1), (3) and (4) IA).

Administration:

The moratorium will prevent judgment creditors from continuing or taking action against the company.

1.13 Liability for repudiated contracts

Administrative receivership:

If a contract entered into by a company is of a type for which specific performance will be ordered (e.g. a contract for the sale of land) then the appointment of an administrative receiver makes no difference and the court will still order specific performance: *Freevale Ltd v Metrostore Holdings Ltd* 1984. In *Telemetrix plc v Modern Engineers of Bristol (Holdings) plc* 1985 it was said that an administrative receiver cannot ignore the equitable rights of third parties.

Apart from these situations, if a company in administrative receivership fails, at the instance of the receiver, to perform its obligations under a contract formed before the receiver was appointed, the injured party's only remedy is damages in an action against the company for breach of contract, even though the administrative receiver is highly unlikely to leave the company with any money with which to pay damages. An injunction may not be obtained to restrain his repudiation *Airlines Airspares Ltd v Handley Page Ltd* 1970. An administrative receiver is not bound to adopt a contract: *Ardmore Studios (Ireland) Ltd v Lynch* 1965.

Only if an administrative receiver *expressly* assumes liability for a contract will he be liable. Merely performing the contract is not taken to be such assumption of liability *Parsons v Sovereign Bank of Canada* 1913.

As an agent of the company when it breached its contract, the administrative receiver has not committed the tort of inducing another to breach a contract because, as agent, he represented the company when the decision to breach the contract was taken, so he persuaded himself not someone else: *Said v Butt* 1920. This will not apply if the agent is acting outside the scope of his authority, e.g. when acting fraudulently: *Einhorn v Westmount Investments Ltd* 1970.

In Re *B Johnson & Co (Builders) Ltd* 1955, it was said that an administrative receiver of a company does not owe a duty to the company to preserve the goodwill and business of the company, but in *R v Board of Trade (ex parte St Martins Preserving Co Ltd)* 1965, it was said that an administrative receiver does have that duty. Both were *obiter* comments. The problem arises only where the goodwill is of value to the company, for example where the receiver is selling the business as a going concern or where the receiver will have a surplus after meeting the secured debt and will leave the company to continue in business.

1.14 Environmental considerations

The AR and administrator have to be aware of possible environmental problems arising from the manufacturing processes used or the products made by the company or from contaminated land owned by the company:

▶ Prescribed manufacturing and industrial processes require authorisation (reviewed at least every 4 years) and which may be subject to conditions.

▶ Deposit, treatment, storage or movement of waste requires a license. 'Waste' (which may be solid, liquid or gas) includes domestic, industrial and commercial products.

▶ Those dealing with controlled waste have a statutory duty of care to avoid:

– Contravention of the legislation regarding unauthorised or harmful dealings with waste
– Escape of waste
– Transfer of waste other than to other authorised persons

▶ Discharge of poisonous, noxious or polluting waste into 'controlled' waters is only possible if a license and consent is obtained.

The legislation is contained in the:

▶ Environmental Protection Act 1990
▶ Water Resources Act 1991
▶ Environmental Act 1995.

Potential liability of the office holder may be criminal (possible but unlikely) or civil. Generally the office holder acts as the company's agent and therefore it is the company which will be liable, however, the AR's agency will be terminated by the liquidation of the company and agents must act within their authority to avoid personal liability. It could be argued that for an office holder to act criminally in breach of the legislation he will be acting outside his authority.

The main concerns of the office holder will be:

▶ Avoiding personal liability
▶ Costs in rectifying environmental problems may reduce/ eliminate returns to creditors.
▶ Environmental problems may reduce the value of assets to a potential purchaser.

Practical steps for the office holder to take:

▶ Commission an environmental report from a suitably qualified expert.

▸ Discuss with the lender/ charge holder who may have carried out some form of environmental risk assessment at the time of the loan.

▸ If trading on, ensure that all necessary licences and authorisation are in place and any conditions attached to them have been satisfied.

▸ In cases where the environmental risk is high the office holder may wish to refuse the appointment.

▸ Liaise with Environmental Agency in regard to the company's record and the risks of any enforcement action being taken.

Interactive question 1: Home-baked Foods Limited

Seven days ago you were appointed administrator of Home-baked Foods Limited by Wells Bank PLC. The appointment was made out of court in the bank's capacity as a qualifying floating charge holder with the aim of rescuing the company as a going concern under para 3(1)(a) of the schedule.

The company specialises in the provision of hand baked pies on a fast food basis in the South West of England. The company manufactures the majority of its products at a location based in Tiverton employing around 250 staff and sells the food directly to the public through a network of 15 outlets in the high street and shopping malls.

The company's managing director Jane Furner strongly believes that there is a bright future for the provision of a standard menu of home style fast food products but with hindsight regrets starting up in her native South West where local tastes have been relatively slow to respond to the delicacies on offer. Once the company is back on its feet, she hopes to expand the outlets nationally.

During the first few days of administration the following events have occurred:

1 Flurry Flours Limited, a key supplier of the company, has given you notice that it intends to enforce a retention of title claim against Home-baked Foods Limited. A lorry will arrive at the company's Tiverton site on Tuesday to take away large quantities of flour used in the manufacturing process. The flour is delivered in sacks clearly marked with the supplier's name and batch number.

In the first week of administration and in liaison with the company's staff, you performed a stock take which indicated that the majority of the flour supplied was still held as raw materials in their original state. However, you have identified that around 10% are now incorporated within work in progress and finished goods.

Flurry Flours Limited have indicated that if you do not permit them to take back the stock, they intend to apply to court for leave to repossess.

2 This week you received a letter from as trade union representative stating that in the event of any of his members being made redundant, the trade union would be holding you personally liable for all debts due under members' contracts of employment.

3 You have arranged to meet with the company's landlord in three days time to discuss the six months arrears outstanding on the lease for the premises in Plymouth. In the correspondence you have received to date the landlord has stated an intention to exercise his right of forfeiture.

4 The company owns a freehold property in city centre Exeter with considerable potential for redevelopment. In the last few days you have received an informal offer of £275,000 for the property conditional upon a quick sale. This would provide useful working capital in the forthcoming weeks. Your agents advise that the property is worth in the region of £320,000 and that property prices are forecast to rise around 4% in the next 12 months. The property is covered by Wells Bank PLC's floating charge but is also subject to a fixed charge held by Future Finance PLC (you may assume that there is no negative pledge clause in existence).

Requirement

Advise your principal as to how you intend to deal with each of the matters referred to above. Your advice should cover both legal issues and practical commercial considerations in terms of trading on in order to achieve the para 3(a) purpose.

See **Answer** at the end of this chapter.

2 Practical steps to take on appointment

Section overview

▶ There are a number of practical matters which both the administrator and the AR should deal with on their appointment.

The IP should ensure that meetings are arranged with directors and senior management as soon as possible after appointment, in order to:

▶ Advise them of the appointment, and the impact that the appointment has on the business and its officers and employees.

▶ Obtain sufficient information about the company, its operational and administrative procedures and the exact nature of its current position, in order to be able to prepare a schedule of matters requiring urgent attention, and to provide such information as is required in order to assess the validity of continuing the operation of the business in whole or in part. A view of the business and its market should be identified in such interviews with management.

The office holder should assess the strengths and weaknesses of various aspects of the business:

▶ Management team
▶ Management structure
▶ Communication
▶ Internal control
▶ Accounting system
▶ Operational efficiency.

Having discussed such matters with the Directors and senior management, the office holder should be in a position to assess whether or not it will be advantageous to continue to trade.

Identify potential purchasers of the business which may be known by management. The possibility of a management buy-out may also be considered.

Consideration should be given to the nature of the product or services being supplied in order to identify the risk of incoming future liabilities relating to the supply or goods of services.

Obtain an inventory of all assets under his control, a function normally carried out by inventory agents appointed by the receiver. Valuations are required on going concern and break up bases.

A schedule of assets should provide details of ownership of the asset and whether or not any are subject to charges, HP terms, retention of title claims or garnishees.

Review key holders and general security arrangements.

Ensure adequate insurance is available

The movement of goods, assets or stocks from the premises should be stopped as soon as possible after appointment. The office holder will then be in a position to complete a preliminary asset inventory and stock check, in addition to ensuring that an adequate system of control over assets and stock movement is implemented. Goods in transit should be identified.

The company's bankers should be advised of the appointment as soon as possible after the appointment is made. Such notification should be confirmed by letter. A note of the time of notification should be made in order to determine any rights of set-off that may be claimed by the banks.

Open new bank accounts for the company. Following the appointment, all bankings and payments should be made from this account. The receiver should take charge of the company cheque books and credit cards.

Cheques should be banked daily/promptly.

A detailed cash flow should be immediately prepared, in conjunction with management, in order to identify the cash requirements of the business. Cash resources will inevitably have been depleted in the period prior to the appointment. Particularly where the office holder decides to continue to trade, further borrowings from outside sources may be necessary. A list of urgent payments should also be compiled to ensure that efforts to continue to trade are not further prejudiced.

Post appointment trading performance should be reviewed in detail against the forecasts at least weekly and any material variances investigated.

The AR, as the company's agent, has to comply with his statutory duty to keep sufficient accounting records to be able to disclose with reasonable accuracy, at any time, the financial position of the company at that time: CA 2006 ss386-389. As transactions are carried out in the name of the company, the records will remain unchanged. The administrator should ensure a proper cut-off of accounting records.

In order to produce the statement of affairs at the time of the appointment, the accounts should be drawn up to the date of appointment.

It is advisable to open new personal ledgers in the accounts, from the date of appointment. This will facilitate in identifying pre and post appointment liabilities.

A new purchase ordering system should be established to distinguish receivership purchases from pre-appointment purchases.

Unexecuted purchase orders should be reviewed to determine whether goods/services are still required. Existing purchase orders should be cancelled and replaced with receiver's/administrator's purchase orders.

All goods inwards received after appointment should be verified against receiver's/administrator's order prior to being accepted.

All supplier payments should be approved by a senior member of the receiver's/administrator's staff, supported by a purchase order, delivery note and invoice.

The office holder should keep a separate cashbook to run in parallel with the company's cashbook, as a means of control.

Only if the office holder is completely satisfied that the company's own system of internal control provides protection against abuse or error, should the office holder not maintain control of all incoming monies, the receivership chequebook and cash.

New goods outwards records should be set-up to distinguish between goods supplied prior to and during the receivership/administration. No goods should be despatched with external hauliers who are owed money unless written confirmation is received from them that they will not exercise a lien over goods.

All incoming and outgoing mail should be reviewed. Outgoing mail and documents should contain a statement that an administrative receiver or administrator has been appointed, and should preferably be signed by the office holder or his representative.

No commitments should be entered into by the staff without the consent of the receiver or administrator. If a commitment is made without such consent, but within the ostensible authority conferred on the staff, the staff member may become personally liable. The office holder should take charge of the company seal.

The majority of office holders have blanket policies which provides effective insurance cover from the moment the broker is notified. Where such cover is not available, the office holder should review all current insurance policies to assess adequacy of cover, cancel any non-relevant policies and obtain a refund of premiums wherever possible and notify the company's insurers of his appointment. The company's insurance policies should be endorsed accordingly.

Ensure there is adequate site attendance/supervision by the receiver's/administrator's staff.

3 Claims by employees

Section overview

▶ A vital aspect of the conduct of administration or administrative receivership is dealing with claims by employees and limiting the office holder's personal exposure in relation to these claims.

The position of the AR and administrator in respect of employee liabilities is shown in the table below:

	ADMINISTRATIVE RECEIVER	ADMINISTRATOR
Agency	s44(1)(a) IA Deemed to be the co's agent unless and until liquidation	In exercising his powers deemed to act as the co's agent
Contractual Liability	(s44(1)(b) IA)Personally liable on ▶ adopted contracts of employment to extent of qualifying liabilities ▶ contracts entered into in performance of functions AR entitled to: ▶ contract out of liability ▶ an indemnity out of the co's assets ▶ the benefit of any indemnity negotiated with the appointor	Not personally liable. However, ▶ liabilities on adopted contracts of employment for wages and salary and ▶ liabilities on contracts entered into in performance of functions are: – payable out of floating charge assets – in priority to administrators own remuneration and expenses – but ranking equally between each other
Liability Free Period	s44(2) IA Not to be taken to have adopted a contract of employment by reason of anything done/not done within 14 days after his appointment	As for administrative receiver

Definition

Adopt: Defined in Paramount as 'conduct amounting to an election to treat the contract as giving rise to a separate liability in the administrative receivership or administration'.

An office holder accepts the continuance of an employment contract by not repudiating it within 14 days of appointment. Adoption does not mean that the contract becomes one with the AR or administrator, the contract remains with the company.

An office holder cannot adopt some parts of the contract and not others. Adoption is always of the entire contract.

3.1 Qualifying liabilities

An office holder's liability is limited to the extent of 'qualifying liabilities' (s44 IA and s19(7) IA). These are post adoption liabilities for:

▶ Wages and salaries
▶ Contributions to an occupational pension scheme
▶ Holiday pay
▶ Sick pay

Re Leeds United Association Football Club Ltd – damages for wrongful dismissal payable to footballers in the event that administrators of a football club were to adopt their contracts only to subsequently dismiss them did not constitute wages or salary for the purposes of the IA Sch B1 para 99(6).

Liabilities on contracts of employment adopted prior to 15 September 2003are not limited to 'qualifying liabilities'.

Qualifying liabilities do not apply to non-administrative receivers (eg receivers and managers over part only of a company's property). Although debentures may purport to give such a receiver the power to manage the company and to hire and fire staff, the receiver will be reluctant to incur potential personal liability and may prefer to leave employment/ dismissal issues to the company or to cause the company to dismiss employees within 14 days.

Where the company subsequently goes into liquidation the AR will have to re-employ employees as principal. The liability will not then be restricted to qualifying liabilities.

3.2   Claims by employees

Employees may have claims for:

▶   Arrears of pay
▶   Holiday pay
▶   Pay in lieu of notice
▶   Redundancy
▶   Contributions to occupational pension schemes

These will form a claim against the company. The DBERR will agree to pay some monies to employees in respect of their claims subject to certain limits. The amounts claimable by employees are summarised below:

Claim	Preferential	Unsecured	Against DBERR
Arrears of wages/salary	▶ Restricted to four months pre-relevant date ▶ Maximum of £800 per employee	▶ Any excess over the preferential limits	▶ Restricted to the eight weeks accrued pre- 'appropriate' date ▶ Maximum of £330 per week per employee
Holiday Pay	▶ All accrued holiday pay is preferential	▶ Not Applicable	▶ Restricted to six weeks accrued in the 12 months pre-appropriate date ▶ Maximum of £330 per week per employee
Pay in Lieu of Notice	▶ Not Preferential	▶ Valid claim for greater of contractual or statutory period ▶ Employee has duty to mitigate claim	▶ Statutory (but not contractual) notice ▶ Maximum of £330 per week per employee

(handwritten annotation: £350 in 2010 book)

Claim	Preferential	Unsecured	Against DBERR
Redundancy	▶ Not Preferential	▶ Valid claim for greater of contractual or statutory redundancy	▶ Statutory (but not contractual redundancy ▶ Maximum of £~~330~~ *£350 in 2010 book.* per week per employee
Occupational Pension Scheme	▶ Restricted to employer contributions in the 12 months prior to relevant date ▶ and employee contributions in the four months prior to relevant date	▶ Any excess over the preferential limits	▶ Employer contributions - lowest of – 12 mths contribs – 10% of 12 mths pay – amount certified to meet liability to pay employees pension ▶ 12 months employee contributions

Note: The 'appropriate date' in respect of the DBERR claims for arrears of wages and holiday pay is the date of appointment of the AR. However, none of these claims can be brought unless the employees are made redundant.

1 Arrears of pay:

- ▶ Remember that as a practical matter the office holder may have to provide funds for payment of arrears to maintain employee loyalty.

- ▶ Included as employees' remuneration will be statutory sick pay and contractual bonuses and overtime.

- ▶ In respect of the DBERR claim, the weeks need not be the latest weeks of employment, nor need they be consecutive. They should be the eight weeks that are financially most beneficial to the employee.

2 Pay in lieu of notice

- ▶ This claim will be made where the employee has been dismissed without being given proper notice or pay in lieu of notice.

- ▶ 'Proper notice' is the statutory minimum notice period provided for by the *Employment Rights Act 1996* (ERA 1996) (unless the contract of employment provides for a longer period in which case that period applies).

- ▶ Statutory minimum notice periods are as follows:

Period of continuous employment	Min. Notice
Less than one month	–
One month – two years	One week
Two years – less than three years	Two weeks
Three years – less than four years	Three weeks
….and so on up to a maximum of 12 weeks	

3   Redundancy:

  ▸   claim for a statutory redundancy payment may be made where the employee:

  –   is employed under a contract of *service* (as opposed to being a sub-contractor employed under a contract for *services*)

  –   has been continuously employed for a period of two years

  –   has been dismissed (or a fixed term contract has come to an end without renewal)

  –   and redundancy is the reason for the dismissal

  ▸   Redundancy means the dismissal is attributable wholly or mainly to:

  –   employer ceasing or intending to cease carrying on business or

  –   the requirements for employees to carry out work of a particular kind have ceased or diminished

  ▸   The amount of a statutory redundancy payment depends on the length of service and age of the employee and is as follows:

Age of employee	No of weeks pay
18-21 years old	½ week per year of employment
22-40 years old	One week per year of employment
41-65 years old	One ½ weeks per year of employment

  subject to a maximum multiplier of 30 weeks

  ▸   A contract of employment may provide for termination payments exceeding these minimum statutory amounts. This is the "contractual redundancy" referred to earlier.

3.3   Non-preferential claims by employees (Technical release 5)

Technical Release 5 will apply in any situation where an employee of an insolvent employer has been dismissed without proper notice and now has a claim against the employer which the office holder needs to quantify.

The purpose of Technical Release 5 is to harmonise office holder's practice in dealing with non-preferential claims and to ensure that practice is acceptable to the DBERR in processing ERA 96 claims.

The claim is essentially a claim for wrongful dismissal i.e. a breach of contract claim.

The individual will claim for remuneration lost and fringe benefits, for instance a company car, medical insurance and rent free accommodation. In assessing the benefit of the company car an IP should have regard to the Tables published by the AA as the most accurate measure.

An employee may also claim for the lost employer's contribution to an occupational pension scheme during the notice period. In some circumstances a simple computation of payments may not do and an actuarial calculation may be necessary.

The employee must mitigate their claim:

Matters in mitigation	Matters to ignore
Social security payments: non-discretionary benefits e.g. Jobseeker's Allowance, Supplementary Benefit, Invalidity Pay, Maternity Allowance, and Sickness Pay	Social security payments: discretionary

Matters in mitigation	Matters to ignore
Personal Tax: Up to £30,000 – a deduction equivalent to the full amount of tax that would have been payable if the amount in question had been paid as salary Over £30,000 – the calculation is more complex. Three stages – estimate the amount of tax that would have been deducted less an amount for mitigation then take into account the individual's liability to tax on the damages	Pension: all pension payments should be ignored - occupational, state and personal
Unfair Dismissal: ▶ the basic award should be ignored (this is equivalent to the amount payable on redundancy) ▶ only the proportion of the remaining damages that represents loss of earnings should be deducted	Unemployment Benefit: paid by a Trade Union under a Welfare Scheme should be ignored as should any other similar benefits
Remuneration received: which would not have been received but for the termination	Redundancy pay: redundancy is not founded on breach of contract and is therefore irrelevant
Notional earnings: usually only take these off if there's a long notice period or an unreasonable failure to take advantage of an opportunity of employment up to three months the question of mitigation does not need to be pursued 'very far'	National Insurance Contributions: the rationale is that the individual won't get the benefit of the equivalent NIC benefits, so it's not fair to penalise the employee deducting a notional amount representing NIC
	Protective award: this is not certain, but the best answer is probably that it is ignored. The reason being that the ECJ held in *EC Commission v UK 1994* that though a protective award represents remuneration, if it is deducted there would be no incentive on an employer to conform to the relevant labour relations legislation However, there may be a problem of double proof if an employee claims for both If in doubt, the RPS at the DBERR can be approached for guidance

3.4 Claims by directors (Technical Release 6)

Many rights in employment law apply only to employees (i.e. those employed under a *contract of service*) and not to sub-contractors (i.e. those employed under a *contract for services* - often referred to as 'self-employed'). Examples would be the right to statutory redundancy payment or compensation for unfair dismissal, as well as the right to a minimum statutory notice period etc.

It is not always obvious, particularly with directors, whether an individual is an employee or only a sub-contractor. The TR gives guidance to ensure practice is acceptable to the DBERR.

LEARNING MEDIA

Technical Release 6 deals with the treatment of directors' claims as 'employees' in insolvencies

Section 230 of the ERA defines an 'employee' as 'an individual who has entered into or works under a contract of employment.' A contract of employment is defined as "a contract of service ... whether express or implied, and ... oral or in writing'.

Factors to be taken into account in deciding whether to accept a director's claim as employee:

In *SSTI v Bottrill 1999* the Court of Appeal advised that the first question that should be considered is has there been a genuine contract between the company and the director? For instance was the contract signed at a time when insolvency loomed?

Assuming that the contract is not a sham, there a number of factors to decide whether it actually gave rise to an employer/employee relationship.

These are set out in the *Bottrill* case and other cases such as *Eaton v Robert Eaton Ltd 1988, McQuisten v SSE 1996, Buchanan v SSE and Ivey v SSE 1997*.

Remuneration

Firstly, did the director ever forgo salary as this implies that the individual was self employed. Employee factors will be the deduction of PAYE and Class 1 National Insurance Contributions. These do not mean that the director is conclusively an employee however (and vice versa if PAYE was not deducted and self employed NIC contributions were paid this does not mean conclusively that the individual is self employed).

Investment in the company/guarantor

Two other self employed factors are the fact that a director is a controlling shareholder or guarantor of the company's debt.

Is the director an integral part of the company or another business?

The office holder should consider whether the director had other employment. In addition the office holder should consider whether the director was really in business on his own account?

The office holder should also consider whether there is a "mutuality of obligation" between the director and the company.

The degree of control exercised by the company over the employee.

Did the director work under control of the board of directors in respect of the management of his work? Even if a director is a controlling shareholder, this could still apply, for instance there could be directors other than the shareholder director or the Articles of Association could prevent the directors voting in matters in which they are interested (e.g. their dismissal).

Did the director take holidays and was the director entitled to holiday pay and sick pay?

If a director does not take holiday, and therefore seems to be in business on his or her own account, this may be a self employed factor. However, entitlement to holiday pay and sick pay do point towards employee status.

The director's title

For instance, 'Managing Director' gives an impression of a full-time employee.

No single factor is conclusive

Bottrill provides that no single factor is conclusive however and that all the factors must be weighed up to decide whether a director is an employee.

A director has the right to apply to the Employment Tribunal if he or she disagrees with a decision made by the RPS or an IP.

Sole Director employees:

▶   *Salomon v Salomon 1897* - A company is a separate legal entity from its owners (shareholders) and Directors.

> ► In *Lee v Lees Air Farming 1961* it was held that a Director may enter into a valid contract with a company of which he is a Director. This was so even if he was the sole Director and shareholder of the company. Contracts, obviously, include contracts of employment.

> ► In practical terms contracting with a company in these circumstances involves:

>> – assenting to the contract in ones capacity as the employee

>> – assenting on behalf of the company in ones capacity as director and agent of the company.

> ► In *Buchanan v Secretary of State for Employment and Ivey v Secretary of State for Employment 1997* the Employment Appeals Tribunal held that a controlling shareholder could not be an employee for the purposes of the ERA 1996 as it would be inconsistent with the purpose of the act to protect persons who were able to prevent their own dismissal as they had a controlling interest in the shares of a company.

> ► However, in *Secretary of State for Trade and Industry v Bottrill 1999*, it was held that a controlling shareholder of a company could also be an employee of that company.

> ► No single factor is conclusive, however, and each case should be decided on its own facts.

3.5 Transfer of undertakings

Transfer of Undertakings (Protection of Employment) Regulations 1981 came into force on 1 May 1982 and applies whenever a commercial undertaking is being transferred and there is a change of employer. It therefore applies where a business or part of a business is being sold including hiving down. It does not apply where there is purely a sale of assets only or a mere disposal of shares.

TUPER was amended by the Trade Union Reform and Employment Rights Act 1993 (TURERA) and the Transfer of Undertakings (Protection of Employment) Regulations 2006 (TUPER) which came into force on 6 April 2006.

TUPER applies to 'relevant transfers' (Reg 3).

Definition

Relevant transfer: A transfer of an undertaking, business or part of an undertaking or business situated immediately before the transfer in the UK to another person where there is a transfer of an economic entity which retains its identity or a service provision change.

Undertaking: Any trade or business, including non-commercial ventures (s33 TUPERA)

Public sector bodies contracting out and market testing by such bodies, as well as transfers of companies, divisions or subsidiaries of companies and partnerships are now caught by TUPERA.

There is no need for a formal transfer of ownership of the undertaking. The granting of leases, licenses, contracts and franchises may give rise to a transfer of undertakings (ie. A change of employers/ management is sufficient).

The effect of TUPER is that all contracts of employment of those employed in the business at the time of the transfer are automatically transferred to the new owner. No contracting out is permitted. All rights, duties, liabilities and powers under the contracts of employment are transferred to the new owners who are treated as though they have been the employer throughout. There is therefore continuity of employment for the purposes of the employment protection legislation.

By Reg 7, dismissal of any employee (whether before or after the transfer)for any reason connected to the transfer is automatically unfair. It does not matter if:

► The AR dismissed the employee prior to the transfer or
► The purchaser dismisses the employee after the transfer

However the rule does not apply if the dismissal is for "economic, technical or organisational reasons" (ETO) entailing changes in the workforce. If for instance the dismissals are part of a programme of genuine redundancies - there will be no automatic unfair dismissal. The employer will still need to show however that it acted reasonably in selecting the employees for redundancy.

Redundancies will not be genuine where the true purpose of dismissal was:

▶ to break continuity of employment *or*
▶ to ensure a sale takes place *or*
▶ to ensure the business is more attractive to a transferee *or*
▶ to obtain a better price for the business.

The effect of the rules on individuals employed immediately before the transfer is that:

Individual employees retain all their rights (except those under occupational pension schemes) under their "old" contracts. Continuity of employment for e.g. statutory minimum notice, unfair dismissal and redundancy purposes is retained. Rights against the seller of the business e.g. to arrears of pay are now enforceable against the buyer.

The buyer therefore inherits all the liability latent in the employee's contracts of employment.

This has undesirable consequences for an AR or administrator seeking to sell a business as a going concern. The business is less attractive to a buyer as the buyer knows it is acquiring potential contractual and statutory liabilities attaching to the employment contracts.

The office holder cannot avoid these consequences by:

▶ dismissing the employees (so that they are now no longer employed "immediately before the transfer")

▶ hours later transferring the business to the purchaser

▶ who re-engages the freshly sacked workforce now shorn of their accrued employment rights. (*Litster v Forth Dry Dock & Engineering Co Ltd (1989)*). The courts in such a situation interpret 'immediately before' as 'immediately before or would have been if had not been unfairly dismissed'.

▶ The effect of *Litster* is that the transferee becomes liable to the employees sacked by the office holder in an artificial attempt to evade TUPER.

Quite apart from the *Litster* case - the practice would carry the risk that the buyer would pull out at the last moment leaving the office holder to deal with the employee's claims

The office holder:

▶ Should describe the classes of employees whose contracts carry TUPER liabilities in the sales documentation.

▶ Can assist the purchaser in quantifying those liabilities.

▶ May point out that if the buyer is intending to run the business as a going concern employees will not be made redundant and therefore no liabilities will need to be met.

The well informed potential purchaser should take TUPER liabilities into account when deciding how much he is willing to pay for the business.

Under Reg 11 the employers must provide to the transferee the employee liability information of any person employed by him that is the subject of a relevant transfer.

Under Reg 13 the employer must provide affected employees with information concerning the transfer.

'Affected employees' are not just those employed in the undertaking transferred but any employees affected by the proposed transfer or measures taken in relation to it.

Information must be provided 'long enough before a relevant transfer' to enable consultation between employer and employee representatives to take place.

Employee representatives are either a recognised independent trade union or elected representatives of affected employees (added by Collective Redundancies and Transfer of Undertakings (Protection of Employment) (Amendment) Regulations 1995.

The information to be provided is:

▸ Fact, proposed timing, and reasons for transfer

▸ Legal, economic and social implications of the transfer

▸ Measures that employer and transferee envisages will be taken in relation to affected employees in connection with the transfer. Transferee has duty to provide information to employer/transferor to assist in fulfilling this duty.

NOTE: Where 'measures' (e.g. manpower reductions) are proposed "consultation" must take place and any representations made by employee representatives must be considered and reasons given for any rejection to those representations.

There is a defence of 'special circumstances' making it not reasonably practicable for the employer to comply with the above duties. Employer will still need to demonstrate that all such steps were taken as were reasonably practicable to perform the duties.

TUPER expressly states that contractual provisions purporting to contract out of TUPER are VOID.

4 Selling the business

Section overview

▸ There are a number of practical matters to be considered by the office holder when selling the business to avoid claims of breach of duty. The administrator's duty to achieve the para 3 Sch B1 IA purpose is owed to creditors generally. The AR has a duty to maximise realisations which is owed to the appointor, preferential creditors and any guarantors of the company's debt.

1   The office holders have a statutory power to sell under Schedule 1. The debenture should also state that the AR has full power to sell the company's business.

2   The AR should ensure that all assets to be sold are covered by the appointor's charges. He should negotiate or consider a s43 IA application regarding any prior charge holders. The administrator has the power under para 70-71 to sell assets subject to a charge. *on court application.*

3   The office holder should instruct agents to prepare written valuations on alternative bases. In the case of unusual or high value property the office holder may seek a second opinion.

In appropriate circumstances the office holder may consider whether valuation can be enhanced by obtaining planning permission. A failure to inform potential purchasers of the granting of planning permission or other factors likely to enhance asset values has been held to be a breach of duty (*Cuckmere Brick Co Ltd 1979*).

4   The office holder should take advice from agents on the mode of sale. Consider sale by auction or private treaty. If sale by auction ensure that competent, qualified professional auctioneers/ agents are used. The catalogue must fully describe the assets to be sold and should be sufficiently widely circulated. Adequate viewing arrangements must be available.

5   The directors should be asked if there are any known interested parties or if interest is likely from competitors, customers or suppliers. The directors may also be interested in a MBO. Other sources of information include the firm's database, the bank's database and specialist agent's contacts.

6   The business should be advertised in the FT and other appropriate newspapers and specialist press.

7   A sales pack should be prepared containing the following information:

(i)   Description of the company's business:

- ▶ Description of the company's product line and the market in which it operates. Pack can include the company's sales and marketing literature.

- ▶ Premises from which company trades.

- ▶ Turnover/market share.

- ▶ Staff (numbers, staff structure) including key personnel, position regarding pensions and TUPER liabilities.

- ▶ Brief trading history of the company including background to the receivership/ administration.

- ▶ Order book, sales, customers, suppliers etc.

(ii)   Assets and liabilities:

- ▶ Fixed assets such as freehold and leasehold land and buildings. In the case of leasehold:

   - – unexpired term, landlord, rent etc.

   - – if dilapidation liability office holder will have to consider whether to seek to pass on the liability to the purchaser (this will impact on the sale price) or make good dilapidations and sell to purchaser at a higher price.

- ▶ Contracts which will be assigned to purchaser on competition.

- ▶ Plant and Machinery.

- ▶ Intellectual property (valuation can be problematic) such as brands, R&D, patents, trade marks etc.

- ▶ Stock and work-in progress (purchaser will be acquiring stock and WIP as they are on date of purchase <u>not</u> date of sales pack).

- ▶ Debtors. The office holder will either:

   - – include them in the sale (for a value equivalent to anticipated realisations) or

   - – exclude them. The purchaser can agree to collect them holding realisations on trust for the office holder and agreeing not to seek to obtain any rights over realisations by way of set-off or lien.

(iii) Disclaimer:

- ▶ Office holder should disclaim liability for valuations of assets and other figures given in the memo and

- ▶ disclaim personal liability generally.

(iv)   Procedure for interested parties to make their offers:

If sale is to be by tender this will involve:

- ▶ Tenderers to submit their bid and a signed contract (prepared by the office holder's solicitors) together with a cheque for the deposit, by a deadline set out in the sales memo.

- ▶ The sales memo will state that the office holder is not bound to accept the highest offer and that referential bids (i.e. a bid stated to be 'the highest bid received + £1') are not permitted.

- ▶ Tenders remain sealed until the deadline in the tender document.

- ▶ The office holder then selects the appropriate "best" offer, signs the counterpart contract to that submitted by the offeror and returns it to the successful tenderer.

8   All expressions of potential interest need to be followed up. Purchasers will often require more information than that contained in the sales documentation. Care needs to be taken especially re disclosure of information to competitors. The purchaser may be required to sign a confidentiality letter.

The office holder should ensure that all financial information provided is:

▸   relevant to the assets being sold

▸   accompanied by a disclaimer of liability by the office holder

▸   and carries a statement of the source of the information.

The purchaser may wish to visit the premises. Visits should be accompanied by a member of the office holder's staff and management etc. should be briefed re the purpose of the visit.

Interactive question 2: Farmer's Bank PLC

Your principal, Mr Jones, has been appointed administrative receiver of Interior Design Limited by Farmer's Bank PLC who hold fixed and floating charges over the company's assets. The company's only significant asset is its trading premises and its debtor ledger.

Requirement

State what the administrative receiver's general responsibilities are with regards to selling the business and what steps he should take to discharge them.

See **Answer** at the end of this chapter.

4.1   SIP 13 – Acquisition of assets of insolvent companies by directors

The SIP ensures that office holders are familiar with the legal obligations of directors in relation to the acquisition of assets of companies and the statutory provisions relating to such acquisitions. It sets out best practice with regard to the disposal of assets to, and their acquisition by, directors and the disclosure of such transactions.

There are three basic concerns regarding the acquisition of assets by directors:

(i)   Assets are disposed of for less than market value

(ii)   Creditors prejudiced by the insolvency of the disposing company are exposed to further risk by the continued trading of the responsible directors

(iii)   Such transactions are conducted with propriety and are fully disclosed.

The overriding duty of the directors is to promote the success of the company. Failure to do so exposes directors to risks of claims for breach of duty or misfeasance.

They may also be liable for wrongful trading under s214 IA if they failed to take appropriate action when they knew or should have known that insolvent liquidation was unavoidable.

They should also refrain from entering into transactions which may be set aside as transactions at an undervalue or preferences.

Substantial property transactions by the directors and the company will require prior approval in general meeting (s190 CA 2006). This is where the transaction exceeds the lower of:

▸   £100,000 or
▸   10% of the company's net asset value (subject to a minimum of £5,000).

If a company is being wound up (but not a members' voluntary liquidation) or is in administration, approval of the members is not required under s190 CA 2006 (s193 CA 2006).

Note, if the company is in administrative receivership, approval of substantial property transactions is required under s190 CA 2006.

The directors should also be aware of the obligations under s216 IA (phoenix company rules).

The overriding obligation of an office holder when acting as a professional advisor to the directors is to act in accordance with the professional conduct guidance of his licensing body.

When accepting instructions (including when advising re convening s98 IA meeting and GM) the office holder should:

▶ Agree and record the identity of the instructing client (e.g. the company, the board or individual directors).

▶ Act in the best interests of that client (with 'objectivity, integrity and independence').

▶ Ensure directors etc understand their obligations .

▶ Keep under consideration and bring to the clients attention any conflicts of interests of the client which may arise. If the client persists in disregarding material conflicts of interest either:

– cease to act

– or get client to agree to retaining member in regard to one duty or interest only - taking advice on the other elsewhere.

▶ An office holder should not accept instructions to assist a client in conduct which will undermine public confidence in the proper administration of insolvency procedures.

▶ Office holders can incur civil or criminal liability through participation… even in an advisory capacity.

▶ Assisting directors to commit misfeasances is improper and if advice that a proposed action constitutes misfeasance is disregarded the office holder should cease to act. This does not prejudice any duty of a member to give confidential advice in the interests of a client in relation to events which occurred before the member was instructed

▶ Bear in mind requirement for disclosure at s98 IA meeting of transactions between the company and its directors in the year prior to winding up (see SIP 8 generally). Members have a duty to advise directors of need for full disclosure of connected party transactions.

▶ The SIP acknowledges that even when advising re a s98 IA meeting it can be in the creditors best interests for a connected party transaction to be undertaken (e.g. a sale of assets to directors) prior to the winding-up *but*

– thorough appraisal of propriety and benefits expected to accrue to creditors required.

– consider whether appropriate for advising member to seek appointment as liquidator.

Post appointment transactions:

The duty to maximise realisations does not prevent directors and IPs making disposals by way of connected party transactions, …nor does it require disposals to be made in a particular way…. nor that the maximum is obtained from each individual asset providing that the aggregate realisations are maximised.

Generally the office holder should, however, advertise or circularise sales particulars to potentially interested parties.

Generally the office holders have legal control over the assets and should ensure that transactions with directors/connected parties:

▶ at arms length

▶ on the basis of a professional valuation of the assets concerned. Where no such valuation office holder should conduct due enquiries and retain appropriate documents and should consider seeking the views of any committee.

Allocation of consideration between assets can affect creditors rights … so should be made on a basis which can be justified objectively.

Connected party transactions should be disclosed:

1   Administrations – the administrator should include in his proposals reference to any connected party transaction undertaken in the period since the making of the administration order. If a creditors committee is appointed, the members of the committee should be advised of any such transaction undertaken after the meeting of creditors to consider the proposals.

2   Administrative receivership – the AR should include in his report to creditors at the s48 IA meeting information regarding any connected party transaction if this has taken place prior to the meeting and, if it takes place after the meeting, report it to any creditors committee appointed at that meeting.

Any disclosure should include the following information:

▶   The date of the transaction

▶   Details of the assets involved and the nature of the transaction

▶   The consideration for the transaction and when it was paid

▶   The name of the counterparty

▶   The nature of the counterparty's connected party relationship with the vendor

▶   If the transaction took place before the appointment of the member as office holder, the name of any advisor to the vendor

▶   Whether the purchaser and (if the transaction took place before the appointment of the member as office holder) the vendor were independently advised

▶   Where the transaction took place before the commencement of liquidation or administration, the scope of the office holder's investigation and the conclusion reached

▶   Where the disclosure is to a liquidation committee and the committee has not been consulted prior to contract, the reason why such consultation did not take place

▶   Where, in a liquidation, the disclosure is to creditors, whether the liquidation committee (if there is one) has been consulted and the outcome of such consultation.

Summary and self-test

Summary

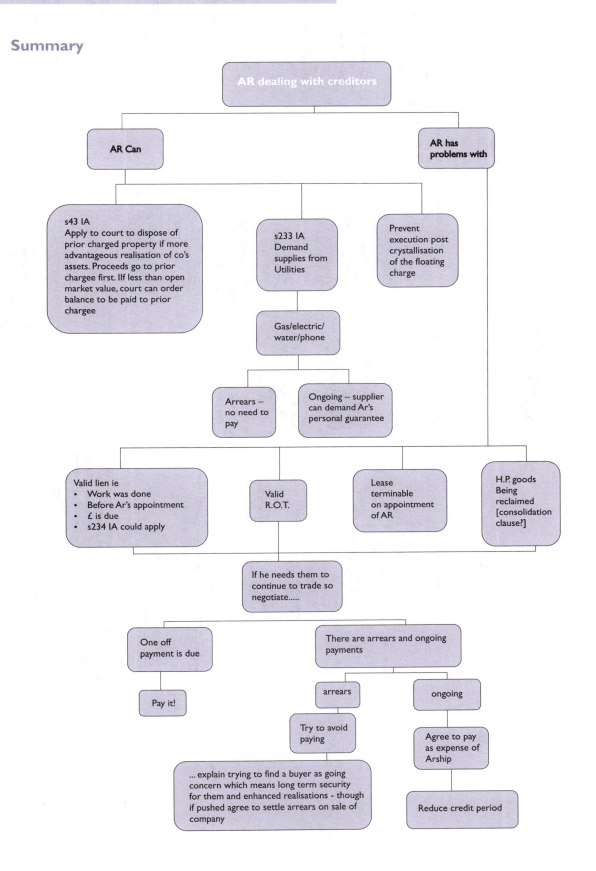

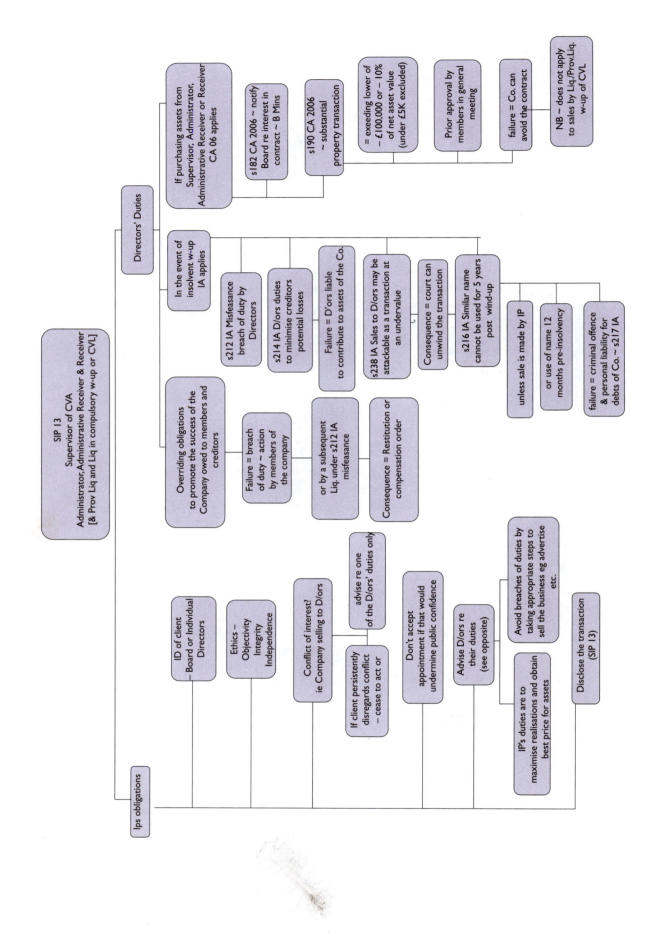

SIP 13
Supervisor of CVA
Administrator, Administrative Receiver & Receiver
[& Prov Liq and Liq in compulsory w-up or CVL]

Directors' Duties

If purchasing assets from Supervisor, Administrator, Administrative Receiver or Receiver CA 06 applies

s182 CA 2006 ~ notify Board re interest in contract ~ B Mins

s190 CA 2006 ~ substantial property transaction

= exeeding lower of – £100,000 or – 10% of net asset value (under £5K excluded)

Prior approval by members in general meeting

failure = Co. can avoid the contract

NB ~ does not apply to sales by Liq./Prov.Liq. w-up of CVL

In the event of insolvent w-up IA applies

s212 IA Misfeasance breach of duty by Directors

s214 IA D/ors duties to minimise creditors potential losses

Failure = D'ors liable to contribute to assets of the Co.

s238 IA Sales to D/ors may be attackable as a transaction at an undervalue

Consequence = court can unwind the transaction

s216 IA Similar name cannot be used for 5 years post wind-up

unless sale is made by IP

or use of name 12 months pre-insolvency

failure = criminal offence & personal liability for debts of Co. ~ s217 IA

Overriding obligations to promote the success of the Company owed to members and creditors

Failure = breach of duty ~ action by members of the company

or by a subsequent Liq. under s212 IA misfeasance

Consequence = Restitution or compensation order

Ips obligations

ID of client – Board or Individual Directors

Ethics – Objectivity Integrity Independence

Conflict of interest? ie Company selling to D/ors

advise re one of the D/ors' duties only

If client persistently disregards conflict – cease to act or

Don't accept appointment if that would undermine public confidence

Advise D/ors re their duties (see opposite)

Avoid breaches of duties by taking appropriate steps to sell the business eg advertise etc.

IP's duties are to maximise realisations and obtain best price for assets

Disclose the transaction (SIP 13)

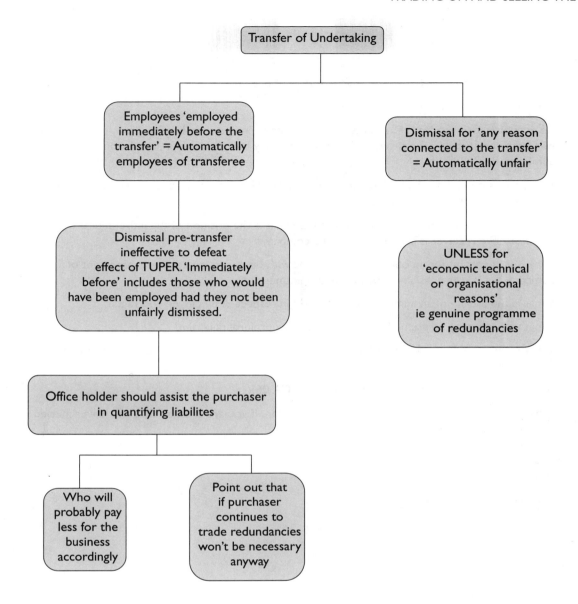

Self-test

Answer the following questions.

1 What are the advantages of continuing to trade in the longer term?

2 What is 'hiving down'?

3 An administrative receiver sells an asset and in doing so incurs a tax liability. How is this liability to be treated and would your answer differ if the company had also been in liquidation or administration?

4 What case set out guidelines which should be followed by an administrator when dealing with a creditor wishing to enforce an ROT claim?

5 A creditor is seeking to execute his judgement. What is the position of the judgement creditor if an administrative receiver is appointed over the company?

6 Why is it important for an office holder to meet with directors and senior management of a company as soon as possible following his appointment?

7 What is the liability of an administrative receiver in respect of employee contracts?

8 What amounts may be claimed by an employee as a preferential claim?

9 What steps should an office holder take to ensure that he has not breached any duties when selling the business?

10 What is a substantial property transaction (s190 CA 06)?

Now, go back to the Learning Objectives in the Introduction. If you are satisfied that you have achieved these objectives, please tick them off.

Answers to self-test

1 ▸ Facilitates a going concern sale which should enhance asset realisations.

   ▸ Minimises bad publicity caused by closure and job losses.

   ▸ If trading is profitable, floating charge realisations will be enhanced over and above the increase in value to be obtained from a going concern sale.

2 Hiving down is where a new company is formed, generally a subsidiary of the insolvent company, consisting of assets, but not liabilities, of the insolvent company. The solvent hived down company can then be sold in a convenient package.

3 Corporation tax is assessable on the company not the AR. If the company was in liquidation and the tax liability related to a post liquidation period, then the liability would be treated as a liquidation expense.

   Corporation tax arising on profits made during administration are an expense of the administration.

4 *Re Atlantic Computers PLC (in Administration)*.

5 Execution must be completed before the appointment of the AR for the creditor to be able to claim the benefit of the execution.

6 (i) To advise them of his appointment and the impact of that on the business, its officers and employees.

   (ii) To obtain information about the company, its business and procedures in order to be able to make a decision on the viability of the company in whole or in part.

   (iii) To identify matters which require urgent attention.

   (iv) Assess the strengths and weaknesses of various parts of the business.

   (v) Identify potential purchasers of the business.

7 The AR will be personally liable on adopted contracts of employment to the extent of qualifying liabilities and contracts entered into by him in the performance of his functions.

   The AR is not taken to have adopted a contract by anything done or not done during the first 14 days after his appointment.

   Qualifying liabilities are post adoption liabilities for wages/ salaries, contributions to occupational pension schemes, holiday and sick pay.

8 Up to four months wage arrears may be claimed preferentially up to a maximum preferential claim of £800 per employee, and

   All holiday pay without limit. *+ Occupational Pension Scheme - 12 mnths employer 4 mnths employee.*

9 ▸ Ensure that all assets to be sold are covered by the appointor's charge.
   ▸ Obtain professional agents written valuations of assets on a going concern and break up basis.
   ▸ Take advice on mode of sale.
   ▸ Identify potential interested parties, enquire if directors interested in a MBO.
   ▸ Advertise business for sale in FT and other appropriate newspapers/ specialist press.
   ▸ Prepare a sales pack.
   ▸ Ensure all expressions of interest are followed up.

10 Where a transaction exceeds the lower of:

   ▸ £100,000 or
   ▸ 10% of the company's net asset value (subject to a minimum of £5,000).

Answers to interactive questions

Interactive question 1: Home-baked Foods Limited

1 On an out of court appointment by a qualifying floating charge holder of an administrator, a moratorium on insolvency proceedings and other legal processes will be effective from when the notice of intention to appoint is filed in court. (Consent of the court or the administrator may be sought to take action).

Other legal process includes repossession by a hire purchase creditor (para 43 Sch B1 IA) which includes retention of title (ROT).

The administrator may apply to court for leave to dispose of goods under a hire purchase agreement.

With regards to the ROT claim, the following matters should be considered:

▶ Has the ROT clause been validly incorporated into the contract? This could be in the terms of the contract itself or through a regular course of dealings. Need to obtain copies of all contractual documentation and seek legal advice as appropriate.

▶ Can the supplier identify goods subject to the ROT clause? If it is an 'all monies' clause it will only be necessary to identify any goods belonging to the supplier (here, raw materials are clearly marked with supplier's name)

▶ Check if account has ever reverted to zero (if so, only stock supplied after that date will be subject to ROT)

▶ If not an all monies clause, can supplier identify goods against specific invoices (here, batch numbers may facilitate this).

▶ Have the goods undergone significant change ie. Have they been used in manufacturing? (here, 10% are now incorporated within WIP and finished goods).

▶ Does the clause purport to extend the supplier's rights into finished goods, debtors and sale proceeds? Court will probably interpret as a floating charge which will be void for non-registration.

Practical considerations:

▶ Do we need the goods? (here, flour is obviously a key ingredient)

▶ Are there alternative sources of supply?

▶ Negotiate with Flurry Flours Limited, agree to pay for goods used, seeking sale as going concern etc.

If Flurry Flours Limited applies to court for leave to repossess the goods under a valid ROT clause the court will apply the *Re Atlantic* guidelines. We should therefore consider the following:

(i) The administrator is an officer of the court and owes a duty of good faith to achieve the para 3(a) Sch B1 IA purpose for creditors generally. On dealing with applications therefore we should:

▶ Deal promptly
▶ Act responsibly
▶ Not use the moratorium as a bargaining tool
▶ Give reasons for decision in writing.

(ii)   Apply the Re Atlantic 'balancing exercise':

▶   Would repossession impede the purpose of the administration? If not, allow repossession. If it would, need to balance interests of creditors generally against the interests of the applicant. If losses to applicant are significant, allow repossession, unless outweighed by substantially greater losses to creditors generally.

2   The administrator is seeking to achieve a para 3(a) Sch B1 IA purpose and rescue the company as a going concern therefore it will be necessary to retain a significant number of staff.

The administration is only seven days old and therefore the administrator is unlikely at this stage to have adopted any contracts of employment (unless he has taken positive steps to do so).

If employment continues after a 14 day period following the appointment of an administrator, he will be deemed to have adopted the contract of appointment.

His liability for adopted contracts of employment will be:

▶   Payable out of company property
▶   In priority to floating charge holders and the administrator's own expenses/ remuneration
▶   Limited to qualifying liabilities (wages, salary, holiday pay etc)

The administrator will not be personally liable as such – the trade union representative is mistaken on this point. He may be confusing the situation with administrative receivership.

Write to the trade union explaining the position and point out that the administrator is looking to retain employees who are willing to co-operate with the purpose of the administration.

3   The moratorium means that the landlord cannot exercise the right of forfeiture by peaceable re-entry in relation to the premises let to the company unless the administrator consents or the court gives permission.

In addition, no other legal process may be instituted or continued by the landlord unless the administrator consents or the court gives permission. This includes:

▶   Legal proceedings
▶   Execution
▶   Diligence
▶   Levying distress

The manufacturing site is clearly key to trading the company and rescuing it as a going concern. A meeting should be arranged with the landlord as soon as possible to explain the purpose of the administration with a view to securing his support. Agree to pay ongoing rent as an expense of the administration – avoid paying any rent arrears.

4   The moratorium states that no steps may be taken to enforce security over the company's property without the consent of the administrator or the permission of the court.

With regard to Wells Bank PLC's floating charge:

▶   The administrator is able to sell assets subject to the floating charge without sanction of the court

▶   The charge holder retains the same priority in respect of the net proceeds of sale or any net property acquired with these proceeds

▶   A sale at an undervalue may however be in breach of the general duty to safeguard creditors' interests

With regard to Future Finance PLC's fixed charge over the property:

▶   Court sanction would ultimately be needed to dispose of the property
▶   Net proceeds would have to be paid to the chargeholder
▶   Any shortfall to market value would have to be made up

Practical/ commercial considerations:

- Seek to negotiate with Future Finance PLC prior to seeking any court sanction
- From the information available, the freehold property may not be essential to the company and disposal may be consistent with pursuing para 3(a) purpose
- Need agents advice re value of property and proposed sale.

Interactive question 2: Farmer's Bank PLC

The administrative receiver (AR) owes a prime duty of care to the bank however he also owes a duty to other interested parties, including guarantors, and to not worsen the position of the preferential creditors.

The AR's specific duty regarding the sale is to achieve the best possible price commensurate with time.

The AR should:

- Obtain specialist agents advice
- Advertise the business in national press and in trade journals
- Consider whether business might appeal to overseas buyers
- Decide on mode of sale – by auction or private treaty
- Obtain list of possible purchasers from directors
- Explain to directors that they could purchase business if they wish
- Prepare sales pack
- Ensure all expressions of interest are followed up
- Prepare listing of all assets
- Obtain agent's valuations on break up and going concern basis.

Practical matters – administration and administrative receivership

> > > > > > > > > > > > > >

Introduction

Learning objectives

Tick off

▶ Understand the statutory requirements re submission of D forms by office holders ☐

▶ State what records office holders are required to maintain by Sch 3 IP Regs 2005 ☐

▶ Understand the function, powers and duties of a creditors' committee ☐

▶ Prepare a closure checklist ☐

Working context

Creditors' committees have an important role to play, it is likely that in a work environment you will have to work with a creditors' committee on an administrative receivership or administration. It is important therefore to understand the functions of the committee and how they work in relation to the office holder. You may be asked to assist in closing insolvency cases so it is important to understand what matters should be checked prior to closing a case.

Stop and think

Why are office holders required to report on the conduct of directors? To whom do they report? What is a creditors' committee? What role does it play? Why is it important to ensure that cases are closed properly?

Examination context

The topics covered in this chapter, whilst not forming an examination question in their own right, nonetheless do appear regularly as parts of a question. In particular the closure checklist can appear in any of the three JIEB exam papers and many of the points contained in the checklist are relevant to all insolvency appointments.

CDDA is also a popular exam topic which could be tested under either JIEB paper 1 or JIEB paper 2.

Past exam questions to look at include:

2007	Question 1(b)
2006	Question 3
2004	Question 1(a)
2004	Question 4(b)
2002	Question 2
1994	Question 4

1 Disqualification of directors

Section overview

▶ IP's who are appointed to a company as administrative receiver (AR) or administrator are required to submit information on the conduct of the directors of the company to the Disqualification Unit of the Insolvency Service. The law relating to the obligations of insolvency office holders in relation to disqualification matters is contained in the Company Directors Disqualification Act 1986 (CDDA) and The Insolvent Companies (Reports on Conduct of Directors) Rules 1996. SIP 4 provides guidance to office holders on their statutory obligations under CDDA and related legislation.

1.1 Statutory requirements

The administrator and AR are required to make the necessary returns within six months of the relevant date.

The relevant dates are:

Administrative receivership - date of appointment of the receiver
Administration – date administration order made by the court

The office holder is required to file a D1 report for those directors with unfit conduct (where it appears to the office holder that the conduct of a director makes him unfit to be concerned in the management of a company) and a D2 return for those directors whose conduct is deemed to be fit. The returns should include all directors and shadow directors who were in office in the three years preceding the relevant date.

The Secretary of State must make an application for a disqualification order within two years of the relevant date.

The court shall make a disqualification order when it is satisfied that:

▶ They are or have been a director of a company which has at any time become insolvent, and

▶ That their conduct as a director of that company or with other companies makes them unfit to be concerned in the management of a company.

The minimum period for a disqualification order is two years with the maximum being 15 years.

1.2 Terms of a disqualification order

A person shall not, without the leave of the court:

▶ Be a director of a company

▶ Act as a receiver of a company's property

▶ In any way, whether directly or indirectly, be concerned or take part in the promotion, formation or management of a company

▶ Act as an Insolvency Practitioner.

1.3 SIP 4 Guidance

SIP 4 – Disqualification of directors:

SIP 4 provides further guidance to IP's on the submission of disqualification reports to the Secretary of State and work that they are required to undertake.

SIP 4 states that if an IP has not found any 'unfitted' conduct within six months or if the information is insufficient to make a decision, they should make an interim return. If they later find any adverse conduct then an adverse report can be submitted.

The SIP states that preferably all reports should be submitted within one year given that the application must be submitted to court within two years.

Office holders do not have to carry out any specific investigations into director's conduct – they can base the return on information coming to light in the ordinary course of their investigations.

The office holder should be aware that the matters of unfitness set out in Schedule 1 to the CDDA are not exhaustive and other matters considered relevant should be included in the return.

IP's shouldn't take a pedantic view of isolated technical failures but should form an overall view of director's conduct.

In the report itself the office holder should:

▶ Avoid defamation
▶ Include copies of accounts and reports to creditors' meetings where relevant
▶ Give specific examples of instances of unfitted conduct where possible
▶ Avoid disclosure of the report to outsiders

The following matters should be dealt with within the body of the report:

▶ The position on any civil recovery actions

▶ The adequacy of the accounting records

▶ Evidence available in support of insolvent trading

▶ Professional advice taken by the directors and specific correspondence which sheds light on director's conduct eg. With solicitors, accountants or creditors.

The Disqualification Unit places particular importance to the following:

(i) Director's misconduct:

▶ Loans to directors to purchase shares in the company

▶ Personal benefits obtained by the directors

▶ Director's criminal convictions

▶ Misfeasance/ breach of duty

▶ Misapplication of funds

▶ Voidable transactions

▶ Attempted concealment of assets or cases where assets have disappeared or a deficiency is unexplained

(ii) Prejudicing creditors:

▶ Dishonoured cheques
▶ Deposits accepted for goods/ services not supplied
▶ Delaying tactics
▶ Retention of crown monies to finance trading
▶ Transactions at an undervalue
▶ Preferences
▶ Phoenix operations

(iii) Miscellaneous:

▶ Overvaluing assets in the accounts to obtain loans etc.

▶ Misconduct in relation to the operation of a factoring account

▶ Breach of CA 2006 provisions regarding the keeping of statutory books and preparation of accounts.

The following items should be submitted with every report where available:

- A copy of the Statement of Affairs
- S 48 IA reports to creditors (receivership)
- Copy accounts as available – last statutory accounts and any other draft, management or interim accounts
- A summary of asset realisations, unrealised assets yet to be dealt with and claims notified
- Dividend prospects
- Aged creditor analysis

1.4 Disqualification undertakings

S5 to s8 of the Insolvency Act 2000 introduced a regime of disqualification undertakings into the CDDA.

A disqualification undertaking is where the Secretary of State accepts an undertaking by any person that for a period of time (specified in the undertaking document) they will not be a director etc of any company and will not act as an insolvency practitioner.

The minimum and maximum periods for undertakings are as per a normal disqualification order (s1 A(2) CDDA 86).

The Secretary of State may accept an undertaking from a person instead of applying for, or proceeding with an application for, a disqualification order.

Following the giving of a disqualification undertaking the court may:

- Reduce the period for which the undertaking is to be in force, or
- Provide for it to cease to be in force.

An application for variation must be made to the court by the person subject to the disqualification undertaking (s8 A(1)).

2 IP Records

Section overview

- Reg 13 IP Regs 2005 provides for office holders to keep minimum records of all insolvency appointments held. Sch 3 IP Regs details the information required to be kept in the case records. Such records must be kept until six years after the office holder has his release.

The following information must be kept:

Name of insolvency practitioner

Insolvency practitioner number

Principal business address of the IP

Authorising body (including competent authority)

Name of the person in relation to whom the IP is acting

Type of insolvency proceeding

Progress of the administration of the case:

- Date of commencement of the proceedings
- Date of appointment of the IP
- Date on which the appointment was notified to the Registrar of Companies

- Bonding arrangements in the case

- Basis on which the IP's remuneration is to be calculated

- Details of creditors' meetings

- Dates on which conduct reports on directors were submitted under CDDA

- Details of final meetings held, vacation of office

- Distributions to creditors and others setting out amounts and dates paid

- Record of filing of statutory returns and accounts

- Time recording – records of amounts of time spent on the case by the IP and any persons assigned to assist in the administration of the case.

3 Creditors' committee

Section overview

- The function of the committee is to assist the office holder in discharging his functions and act in relation to him in such a manner as may be agreed from time to time (r2.52/3.18). The purpose of the committee is to represent the interests of the creditors as a whole, assisting the office holder generally and acting as a sounding board to obtain views on matters pertaining to the administrative receivership/ administration. The rules concerning creditors' committees in administrative receivership and administration are virtually identical, r2.50 – r2.65 for administrations and r 3.16 – r3.30A for administrative receiverships. SIP 15 provides guidance to office holders when reporting and providing information on their functions to creditors' committees.

3.1 Membership of the committee

A creditor's meeting may resolve to establish a creditors' committee consisting of at least 3 and not more than 5 creditors (r2.50(1)/ r3.16(1)).

Any creditor of the company, whose claim has not been rejected for the purpose of his entitlement to vote, is eligible to be a member of the committee (r2.50(2)/ r3.16(2)).

A body corporate may be a member of the committee, but must act through a representative who holds a letter of authority signed on behalf of the company (r2.50(3)/ r3.16(3)). A representative can only act for one member of the committee and cannot be a member of the committee in their own right as well. A representative must not be a body corporate, an undischarged bankrupt, a disqualified director or a person subject to a bankruptcy restriction order or undertaking.

All creditors must agree to act as committee members.

The creditors' committee does not come into being and cannot act until the office holder has issued a certificate of its due constitution (r2.51(1)/ r3.17(1)). The certificate cannot be issued until the minimum number of creditors have agreed to act.

The certificate must be sent to the Registrar of Companies on Form 2.26B (administration) and Form 3.4 (administrative receivership) and to the court (administration only).

Any subsequent changes to the membership of the committee must be notified to the court and the Registrar of Companies, Form 2.27B (administration) and Form 3.5 (administrative receivership).

A member of the committee may resign by giving written notice to the office holder (r2.56/ r3.22).

Membership of the committee is automatically terminated if the member:

- Becomes bankrupt (his trustee in bankruptcy replaces him as a member of the committee)

- At three consecutive meetings of the committee, is neither present nor represented (unless at the 3rd of those meetings it is resolved that this Rule is not to apply)

▸ Ceases to be or is found never to have been, a creditor (r2.57/ r3.23(1)).

A member may be removed by a resolution at a meeting of creditors, at least 14 days notice having been given of the resolution (r2.58/ r3.24). In fact, in administrative receivership no one has authority to summon such a meeting. A meeting of creditors could only be constituted by all of the creditors (not just unsecured) gathering and agreeing that the gathering should be a meeting. An AR should apply to the court for directions if there is a wish to remove a committee member.

A vacancy need not be filled if the administrator/AR and a majority of the remaining members agree, provided that the total number of members does not fall below three (r2.59(2), r3.25(2)).

The administrator/AR may appoint any creditor to fill the vacancy if a majority of the other members of the committee agree to the appointment and the creditor concerned agrees to act.

3.2 Meetings of the committee

Meetings of the committee shall be held when and where determined by the office holder (r2.52(2)/ r3.18(2)).

The first meeting of the committee must be called within six weeks of its establishment – administration (not later than three months after its establishment – administrative receivership) (r2.52(3)/ r3.18(3)).

Subsequent meetings must be held:

▸ Within 14 days of a request being received by the office holder (within 21 days – administrative receivership),or

▸ On a date previously resolved by the committee

The office holder must give seven days' written notice of the venue of the meeting to each committee member (unless notice is waived either at or before the meeting) (r2.52(4)/ r3.18(4)).

The chair of the meeting will be the office holder or a person nominated by him in writing to act.

Note: A nominated person must be either qualified to act as an IP or an employee of the office holder's firm with insolvency experience.

The quorum for a committee meeting is at least two members present or represented.

The acts of a creditors' committee are valid, notwithstanding any defect in the appointment, election or qualifications of any member of the committee or any committee member's representative or in the formalities of its establishment.

3.3 Voting

Each member of the committee has one vote. Resolutions are passed when a majority of the members present or represented have voted in favour of it. (r2.60/ r3.26).

Every resolution passed should be recorded in writing. A record of each resolution should be signed by the chairman and placed in the company's minute book – administration (kept as part of the records of the receivership – administrative receivership). SIP 12 details best practice to be followed when making records of creditor's meetings.

3.4 Postal resolutions

Committee members may pass resolutions by post (r2.61/ r3.27). Members should be sent a copy of the proposed resolution set out in such a way that agreement with or dissent from each separate resolution may be indicated by the recipient on the copy so sent.

Any member of the committee may, within seven days, require the office holder to summon a meeting of the committee to discuss the resolutions.

The resolution is deemed to be passed when the office holder is notified, in writing, by a majority of members that they concur with it.

A copy of every postal resolution should be placed in the company's minute book - administration (with the records of the receivership – administrative receivership).

3.5 Dealings by committee members

Membership of the committee does not prevent a person from dealing with the company whilst the company is in administration or administrative receivership providing that any transactions in the course of such dealings are in good faith and for value.

The court may however, on the application of any interested party, set aside any transaction which isn't in good faith and for value and may give consequential directions as it thinks fit for compensating the company for any loss suffered.

Circumstances may occasionally arise where a legal action or dealing involving a member of the committee or a person connected with him makes it inappropriate for him to attend discussions on the subject in the committee. In such circumstances the member may be asked not to attend the meeting, or part of a meeting, at which the matter is discussed.

3.6 Office holder's duties to the committee

Administrative receiver:

▶ Send an account of his receipts and payments to each member of the committee within two months after the end of 12 months from the date of appointment and every subsequent period of 12 months and within two months of ceasing to act as AR (r3.32).

▶ Give the committee at least seven days notice of his intention to resign (r3.33).

▶ Forthwith, give notice to members of the committee of his vacation of office (r3.35).

Administrator:

▶ Give the committee seven days notice of his intention to resign

No specific obligation to send a receipts and payments account to each committee member (as was the case in pre-15 September 2003 appointments) because there is an obligation to send reports, including receipts and payments accounts, to all creditors.

3.7 Powers/ duties of the committee

Administration:

▶ Fix basis of administrator's remuneration

▶ Approve the drawing of Category 2 disbursements

▶ Request that costs (ie agents/ legal fees) be determined by the court

▶ Review adequacy of the administrator's security (r12.8)

▶ Apply to the court for the administrator to be replaced following the death, resignation or removal of a court appointed administrator – Sch B1 para 91 1A

▶ Determine the release of an administrator appointed by the company, directors or the holder of a floating charge

▶ Receive reasonable travelling costs for attending committee meetings (but not if meeting held within six weeks of a previous meeting unless summoned by the administrator)

▶ Require the attendance of the administrator giving seven days' notice in writing.

Administrative receivership:

- ▶ No power to sanction the actions of the AR

- ▶ Require AR to attend before the committee at any reasonable time giving the AR seven days' written notice

- ▶ Require the AR to furnish the committee with such information relating to the carrying out of his functions as it may reasonably require (s49 IA, r3.18)

- ▶ Review the adequacy of the AR's security (r12.8)

- ▶ Review receipts and payments accounts

- ▶ Receive reasonable travelling expenses (but not if held within three months of a previous meeting unless summoned by the AR)

Interactive question: James Dunt

You have been approached by James Dunt, a creditor of Wooden Toys Limited in administration. He has recently attending a meeting of the company's creditors at which he agreed to sit on the creditors' committee. He is unsure what exactly he has agreed to and has come to you for advice.

Requirement

Write a letter to James Dunt explaining:

(i) The function and powers of the creditors' committee

(ii) How often meetings will be held and whether his attendance is required at each meeting

(iii) Whether he will be able to purchase company assets from the liquidator whilst a member of the committee

(iv) What payments, if any, he may expect to receive as a committee member

See **Answer** at the end of this chapter.

3.8 SIP 15 Reporting and providing information on their functions to committees in insolvencies.

Section overview

- ▶ SIP 15 sets out required practice and guidance to office holders when reporting to creditor committees. It covers compulsory liquidations, CVLs, bankruptcies, administrations, administrative receiverships and voluntary arrangements. A good knowledge of the SIP is required for the JIEB exam.

The SIP gives a brief review of the rules on reporting to committees. These are contained in:

- ▶ Administrations – r2.52, r2,53
- ▶ Administrative receivership – r3.18, r3.19

The SIP then provides guidance notes which should be issued to members of the creditors' committee for each of the formal insolvency procedures. The information may be given in some other suitable format.

All guidance notes have sections dealing with:

- ▶ Introduction – brief explanation of the insolvency procedure and the purpose of the creditor's committee

- The functions of the committee:
  - Control of office holder's powers
  - Acts requiring notice to the committee
  - Office holder's remuneration
  - Expenses and disbursements
  - Taxation of costs
  - Review of office holder's security

- Office holder's obligations to the committee

- Establishment of the committee

- Membership of the committee

- Proceedings of the committee – quorum, chairman, meetings, venue, voting rights, records of meetings etc

- Confidentiality of documents

- Charges for copy documents

- Expenses of committee members

- Dealings by committee members and others

- The security of the office holder

4 Closure checklist

Section overview

- Below is a checklist of matters to be dealt with by the office holder. This list is not exhaustive, if you can think of any other matters please add them to the end of the list.

- Ensure all assets realised

- Ensure all 3rd party assets have been returned or properly dealt with and evidenced

- Review files to ensure all creditors incurred during administration/ administrative receivership period have been paid

- Ensure all undertakings have been withdrawn

- Ensure there is no outstanding correspondence

- Bring accounting records up to date

- Bring returns up to date for PAYE/NIC and VAT

- Obtain clearance from HM Revenue and Customs

- Review insurance cover, cancel if all assets sold

- Ensure all insurance premiums discharged

- Confirm with professional advisors that there are no outstanding matters

- Ensure all solicitors costs/ agents fees have been discharged

- Review own files for outstanding matters

- Ensure CDDA returns submitted

- Obtain creditors' committee approval for the drawing of final expenses and remuneration (administration only)

- Agree remuneration with appointing chargeholder (AR only)

- Separate records of the company and office holder
- Prepare final progress report, distribute in accordance with the rules
- Inform insurers of closure of case for bond purposes
- Ensure secured creditor's debt discharged from the realisation of charged assets
- All ROT claims dealt with
- All employee matters dealt with
- Bring statutory records up to date
- Ensure final meetings held, file requisite notices of ceasing to act
- Ensure bank accounts are reconciled and closed.

Self-test

Answer the following questions.

1   Which SIP gives guidance to office holders on their statutory obligations under CDDA?

2   Within how many months of his appointment must an AR submit a return on the directors of the company?

3   If a person is disqualified under CDDA, what effect does this have on them?

4   What additional items should be submitted with a directors report?

5   For what period after his release must an IP retain the records required under the Reg 13 IP Regs 2005?

6   In what circumstances will membership of a creditors committee be automatically terminated?

7   In an administration when should the first meeting of the committee be held?

8   What is the quorum for a creditors' committee meeting?

9   When is a resolution of the creditors' committee passed?

10 How many days notice of his intention to resign must be given to the committee by the administrator?

Now, go back to the Learning Objectives in the Introduction. If you are satisfied that you have achieved these, please tick them off.

Answers to self-test

1 SIP 4 Disqualification of directors.

2 Within six months.

3 For the period during which the order is in force (minimum two years, maximum 15 years), the person cannot, without the leave of the court:

   ▶   Be a director of a company

   ▶   Act as a receiver of a company's property

   ▶   In any way, whether directly or indirectly, be concerned or take part in the promotion, formation or management of a company

   ▶   Act as an IP

4 Copy of statement of affairs

   S48 IA report to creditors

   Copy accounts as available – last statutory accounts and other draft management or interim accounts

   A summary of asset realisations, unrealised assets yet to be dealt with and claims notified

   Dividend prospects

   Aged creditor analysis

5 Six years.

6 (a) Becomes bankrupt

   (b) At three consecutive meetings of the committee, is neither present nor represented (unless at the third of those it is resolved that this rule is not to apply)

   (c) Ceases to be or is found never to have been, a creditor

7 Within six weeks of its establishment.

8 At least two members present or represented.

9 When a majority of the members present or represented have voted in favour of it.

10 Seven days.

Answers to interactive question

Interactive question: James Dunt

Letter format.

(i)   Functions and powers of the committee:

–   Function of the committee is to assist the administrator in discharging his functions, it represents the interests of the creditors as a whole.

–   The committee is responsible for fixing the administrator's remuneration and approving the drawing of Category 2 disbursements.

–   The administrator is required to have in place security for the proper performance of his functions. It is the duty of the committee to review the adequacy of the administrator's security from time to time.

–   The committee can require the attendance of the administrator on giving seven days notice in writing. One of the committee may act as chairman at the meeting.

–   At meetings of the committee each member has one vote and resolutions are passed when a majority of members vote in favour.

–   When a postal resolution is sent out, the committee may, within seven days of receiving the resolution, require the administrator to convene a meeting of the committee to consider the resolutions.

–   The committee may apply to court for the administrator to be replaced following the death, resignation or removal of a court appointed administrator.

–   The committee will receive an account of the administrator receiver receipts and payments within two months of the end of the first year of administration, and each subsequent year, and within two months of ceasing to act. administrator 1 mth of every 6 months.

(ii)   Meetings:

–   The committee will meet where and when determined by the administrator, however the first meeting of the committee must be called not later than six weeks after its first establishment.

–   Subsequent meetings must be called by the administrator:

(a)   Within 14 days of a request for a meeting being received by the administrator from a committee member

(b)   For a specified date, if the committee has previously resolved that a meeting be held on that date.

–   Quorum at a meeting is at least two members present or represented.

–   James need not attend every meeting therefore, or he could be represented at the meeting by someone else, however, his membership of the committee will be automatically terminated if he does not attend or is not represented at three consecutive meetings of the committee.

(iii)   Purchase of company assets:

–   Membership of the committee does not prevent a person from dealing with the company whilst the company is in administration providing that any transactions in the course of such dealings are in good faith and for value.

–   The court may, however, on the application of any interested party, set aside any transaction which appears to it to be contrary to the above requirement.

(iv) Payments to committee members:

– Committee members do not receive remuneration for being a member of the committee. Any reasonable travelling expenses directly incurred by committee members or their representatives either in attending meetings of the committee or otherwise on the committee's business will be paid by the administrator out of the assets as an expense of the administration.

– Such expenses will not be paid however in respect of any meeting of the committee held within six weeks of a previous meeting, unless the meeting in question was summoned at the instance of the administrator.

12

Numbers questions

➤ ➤ ➤ ➤ ➤ ➤ ➤ ➤ ➤ ➤ ➤ ➤ ➤ ➤ ➤

Contents

Introduction

Learning objectives

▶ Prepare a statement of affairs in the prescribed form ☐

▶ Prepare a deficiency account to reconcile the last set of audited accounts with the statement of affairs ☐

▶ Prepare and present an estimated outcome statement from information available in a format that satisfies the requirements of the entity ☐

▶ Record and account for payments made by the office holder in a suitable format to fulfil the statutory requirements re the submission of annual returns ☐

Working context

It is a statutory requirement for office holders to produce receipts and payments accounts, it is therefore important that you understand how to prepare such returns. In a work environment it is likely that you will be asked to assist your principal in putting together financial information in a format which is easily understood by those receiving the information, for example, preparing estimated outcome statements for a charge holder comparing various options.

Stop and think

Why do office holders prepare financial reports? Who uses them? Why is the statement of affairs an important document? What does it show?

BPP
LEARNING MEDIA

Examination context

The JIEB is a very practical examination with a numbers question appearing in every exam paper to date. It is important to be familiar with the style of questions which often involve a lot of information which must be dealt with in the short period of time available in the exam. It is very important therefore to practice these questions as much as possible. The preparation of receipts and payments accounts and estimated outcome statements are most commonly tested in this exam paper.

Exam questions to look at include:

2007		Question 1(a)
2006		Question 1(a)
2005		Question 3(b)
2004		Question 4(a)
2004		Question 5(b)
2003		Question 3(a)
2002		Question 4(a)
2001		Question 3(a)
2000		Question 4(b)
1999		Question 3(b)
1999		Question 4(a)
1998		Question 4
1997		Question 3
1997		Question 5
1996		Question 1(b)
1996		Question 4
1996		Question 5(a)
1994		Question 2(i)
1994		Question 5(a)
1993		Question 3(a)
1993		Question 4(b)
1991	Paper II	Question 1(a)(i)
1990	Paper II	Question 2(a)

1 Statement of Affairs

Section overview

▶ It is a statutory requirement under the IA 86 to produce a Statement of Affairs in a prescribed format.

Definition

Statement of Affairs: A picture of the company's financial position as at the date of:

▶ Receivership

▶ Administration

▶ Liquidation

▶ Company voluntary arrangement

1.1 Contents

When a Statement of Affairs is produced under any insolvency procedure, it must contain details of the following information:

▶ The company's assets, debts and liabilities
▶ The names and addresses of the company's creditors
▶ What securities are held by any creditors eg a fixed charge over property
▶ Dates upon which the securities were given
▶ The book value and estimated to realise values of assets

Definition

Book value: the value of the assets shown in the accounts at the date of insolvency

Estimated realisable value: what the assets are likely to realise when sold

1.2 Summary of rules re Statement of Affairs:

	Date prepared	Produced by:	Form
Administration	as at date of administration	those who are or have been officers of the company	2.14B
Administrative receivership	as at date of appointment	those who are or have been officers of the company	3.2
		Those in employment deemed able to give information	
Company voluntary arrangement	not more than 14 days before date of notice to nominee under r1.4	Directors	1.6

1.3   The format for a Statement of Affairs

Statement of Affairs

ABC Limited

As at X/X/XX

Assets specifically Pledged [handwritten]

	Notes	Book value £	Estimated to Realise £
~~ASSETS SUBJECT TO FIXED CHARGE~~	1		
Assets		X	X
Less: Amounts due to charge holder			(X)
Assets not specifically pledged [handwritten]			X/(X)
~~ASSETS SUBJECT TO FLOATING CHARGE~~	2		
Assets		X	X
~~UNCHARGED ASSETS~~	3		
Assets		X	X
Total assets available for preferential creditors			X
PREFERENTIAL CREDITORS	4		(X)
Deficiency/ surplus as regards preferential creditors			(X)/X
PRESCRIBED PART (to carry forward)	5		(X)
Total assets available for floating charge holder			X
FLOATING CHARGEHOLDER	6		(X)
Deficiency/surplus of assets after floating charges			(X)/X
PRESCRIBED PART (brought down)	5		~~(X)~~ X
Total assets available to unsecured creditors			X
UNSECURED CREDITORS	2		(X)
(excluding any shortfall to floating charge holders)			
Deficiency/surplus as regards unsecured creditors (excluding any shortfall to floating charge holders)			(X)/X
Shortfall to floating charge holders (brought down)			(X)
Deficiency/surplus as regards creditors			(X)/X
ISSUED AND CALLED UP SHARE CAPITAL			(X)
Total deficiency/surplus as regards members			(X)/X

1.4   Notes to Statement of Affairs:

1   **Assets subject to fixed charge**

This is where the company has given some form of security to a creditor for the advance of funds or purchase of an asset. This will include:

(i)   Assets pledged as fixed charge assets ie freehold property , goodwill

(ii)   Assets subject to HP agreements

(iii)   Debts subject to a factoring agreement

The sums owed to the charge holder should appear under this heading and the net deficiency or surplus carried down.

Definition

Fixed charge: a charge over assets of the company which are ascertained and definite, or capable of being ascertained and defined.

2 **Assets not subject to floating charge**

These are all the assets of the company caught under the company's floating charge. This could include:

- Book debts
- Motor vehicles
- Stock
- Plant and machinery
- Office equipment

3 **Uncharged assets**

These are assets of the company which are free from either fixed or floating charge.

Note: It may be necessary to adjust asset realisable values to take into account bad debt provisions, obsolete assets etc.

4 **Preferential creditors**

These creditors are paid in priority to other creditors. They include:

(i) All holiday pay owed to employees

(ii) Any wages due at the date of insolvency (accruing in four months prior to insolvency) to a maximum claim per employee of £800

5 **Prescribed part**

Where the floating charge is created on or after 15 September 2003 a prescribed part of the net property must be paid to ordinary unsecured creditors.

6 **Floating charge holders**

A bank may hold a floating charge over the assets of the company. The floating charge ranks after the claims of the preferential creditors but before the ordinary unsecured creditors.

Definition

Floating charge: this is a charge over a class of assets both present and future, which change from time to time in the ordinary course of business. The company is free to carry on the business in the usual way in relation to those assets (until crystallisation occurs).

7 **Unsecured creditors**

These are the normal creditors' claims. It will also include employee claims for redundancy and notice pay and any shortfall owed to charge holders. Any claims above preferential limits will also rank as unsecured.

Exam hints

- Always show your workings. Easy marks are always available for showing full workings and assumptions.

- Try to keep to a layout similar to that shown and leave plenty of space. This makes it easier to read and mark . Marks are always available for presentation.

2 The Deficiency account

Section overview

▶ The Deficiency account reconciles the last set of accounts with the position shown in the Statement of Affairs. The Deficiency account explains why a once profitable company now appears insolvent, or why an insolvent company has now become more insolvent.

2.1 Format

A pro forma for a Deficiency account is shown below:

Deficiency account for the period

ABC Limited X/X/00 to X/X/01

	Note	£
Balance on Profit and Loss account as at X/X/00	1	X
Less: Assets written down in Statement of Affairs	2	(X)
Add: Asset gains in Statement of Affairs		X
Less: Items arising on insolvency	3	(X)
~~Less~~ Share capital write off	5	(X)
Balancing figure attributable to (loss)/profit in the period	4	(X)/X
Deficit to creditors per Statement of Affairs		
Deficit to members per Statement of Affairs as at X/X/01	5	(X)

2.2 Notes to Deficiency account:

1 Balance on Profit and Loss account:

- ▶ This is taken from the last audited balance sheet (if available) or management accounts.
- ▶ If a credit (positive) balance, begin with a positive figure.
- ▶ If a debit (negative) balance, begin with a negative figure.
- ▶ If this figure is not available, use net assets instead.

2 Assets written down in Statement of Affairs:

- ▶ This section details the difference between the book values and estimated to realise values of all assets shown in the Statement of Affairs.

- ▶ If assets have increased in value, add this figure instead.

3 Items arising on insolvency:

- ▶ These represent known items which have arisen as a result of the insolvency only and have added to the liabilities of the company.

- ▶ These will include:

  - – Pay in lieu of notice
  - – Redundancy
  - – Damages for breach of contract
  - – Termination payments on a lease

4 Balancing figure attributable to the loss in the period:

- ▶ This will be the balancing figure on the statement.

1–4 add up to creditors deficiency

5 These figures are taken straight from the Statement of Affairs.

Share capital is difference between creditors + members deficiency. (ie creditors deficiency + share capital (neg figures) = members deficiency)

3 Estimated outcome statement

Section overview

▶ The statement quantifies the outcome of a particular course of action for one or more interested parties. It can be used to:

    – Make a comparison of alternative offers for the sale of a business

    – Calculate the return to creditors of pursuing a voluntary arrangement rather than opting for administration (or comparing a company voluntary arrangement with liquidation)

    – Enable a receiver or administrator to decide whether to continue trading by comparing outcomes of ceasing to trade with continuing.

3.1 Format

There is no standard layout for an Estimated Outcome Statement, this will be determined by the information available and the purpose for which it is prepared.

When estimating returns to creditors it is useful to follow the format of the Statement of Affairs as a guide, with comparative Statement of Affairs figures shown wherever possible.

When comparing offers/ comparable outcomes, always try to show the relevant figures side by side. This makes comparisons easier.

Full workings and assumptions made should always be shown clearly. Marks are often awarded to supporting workings.

In order to prepare Estimated Outcome Statements the following knowledge is required:

▶ The order of distribution of funds in insolvency cases
▶ How to calculate the various categories of preferential creditors
▶ Preparation of a simple trading account for the period.

Interactive question: Bailey Swimming Pools

1. You were appointed administrator of Bailey Swimming Pools Limited on 1 September 2008 and over the last four months have made a gross trading profit of £14,000. The following liabilities have been incurred whilst continuing to trade in an attempt to secure a sale as a going concern:

	£
Insurance	500
Wages	16,000
Duress payments – ROT creditors	1,200
HP creditors	800
HP payments	2,500

2. You were appointed under a fixed and floating charge held by Barwest Bank PLC. The bank is owed £573,000 secured by way of a fixed charge over the property and by a floating charge over the company's remaining assets. The floating charge was created on 2 November 2002.

3. Needle Factors Limited have a prior charge over the book debts of the company. At the date of your appointment book debts valued at £98,000 were outstanding. The factoring company were owed £86,000, and 5% of the book debts were considered to be irrecoverable.

4. A review of the company's records indicated that the company had further creditors totalling £418,500 at the date of your appointment. Of this sum, the following ranks preferentially:

	£
Employees – Wage arrears	13,000
Holiday pay	6,000
Barwest Bank PLC – subrogated wages claim	2,500

5   The assets of the company were professionally valued at the date of your appointment. Values attributed are as follows:

	Going concern	Forced sale
Freehold premises	£540,000	£410,000
Stocks	£14,500	nil
Vehicles	£27,000	£20,000
Goodwill	£12,000	nil

6   You have agreed to take remuneration of 10% of realisations made (excluding book debts where you have agreed with the factoring company to receive £5,000 for aiding in the recovery of book debts).

7   Disbursements incurred to date total £1,200.

8   Agent's fees have been agreed at 5% of realisations.

9   Legal fees have been incurred totalling £18,000. Of this sum, £8,000 related to the property, the remainder being legal work in relation to trading on and the receivership generally.

10   Two offers have been received to date for the company, details of which are as follows:

	Mr Smith £	Mr Fields £
Property	577,500	520,000
Stock	14,000	14,500
Vehicles	22,000	27,000
Goodwill	nil	32,000
	613,500	593,500

Requirement

Prepare a statement, in a form suitable to include in a report to the bank, showing the outcome to the bank under the two offers. Include full workings.

See **Answer** at the end of this chapter.

4   Receipts and payments account

Section overview

▶   A receipts and payments account is prepared by office holders to;
 –   provide information to creditors and other interested parties
 –   to fulfil statutory requirements under IA 86 re submission of annual returns.

4.1   Format

Reports to members, creditors, committees and other interested parties should include in the body of the report, or by way of an annex, details of the office holder's receipts and payments.

The receipts and payments account is a summary of all receipts and payments made by the office holder during the relevant period.

The procedure for preparing a receipts and payments account is the same for whatever purpose the account is being prepared.

The layout will be determined to some extent by the requirements on individual cases. SIP 7 provides guidance to office holders when preparing receipts and payments accounts.

4.2 Additional considerations

The following points regarding presentation should be regarded as best practice:

As far as possible, receipts and payments summaries in receivership and administration appointments should show receipts and payments classified under the headings used in the statement of affairs (where this has been prepared by the directors in a sensible form), so as to facilitate comparison.

The Estimated to Realise figures on the statement of affairs should be shown so that comparisons with the actual realisations made to date may be made.

Results of trading should be distinguished from realisations of assets existing at the date of appointment and costs of realisation.

Any payments to pre-insolvency creditors should be stated separately or by category indicating:

▸ amounts paid under duress,
▸ reservation of title or in respect of liens,
▸ payments to preferential creditors
▸ any other pre-insolvency items.

Asset realisations should be shown gross. Costs of realisation should be shown separately as payments.

If assets are sold direct by a mortgagee so that the proceeds do not come into the account, this fact should be stated in a note and a 'nil' realisation included in the account.

Where assets are sold by the office holder which are subject to prior charges, the gross realisation should be shown as receipts and related costs and the amounts accounted for to the charge holder shown as payments.

Where a debenture holder insists on a separate bank account being opened for fixed charge realisations, these transactions should be incorporated into the account without the need to specify that a separate bank account has been operated.

In a receivership or administration the abstract of receipts and payments is prepared in summary form. Accordingly, as an alternative to showing amounts inclusive of VAT it is acceptable to show receipts and payments net of VAT with the total net VAT being shown separately. This method is also acceptable for producing periodic summaries for creditors in any insolvency proceeding.

The practitioner's fees should be stated separately including any additional management fees or fees for other services which should be separately described. The practitioner's fees may be stated net of out of pocket disbursements (which should be shown separately and appropriately described).

The cost of professional services and advice from third party advisers etc. to the practitioner should be shown separately (or by category). The information given in this respect should include not only advisers, but also other hired assistants and such sub-contract labour or self-employment staff as are involved in assisting the practitioner in his function (as opposed to being employed in the ordinary course of the company's business). Any fees to the practitioner's own firm and any firm or person with whom he has a profit or work referral arrangement should be distinguished and shown separately.

If a hive-down has taken place, realisations from assets sold by the hive-down subsidiary should appear in that company's accounts. The proceeds received from the hive-down subsidiary in respect of assets transferred to it and the proceeds from sale of shares in the hive-down subsidiary should be shown in the abstract, so far as possible of hive-down subsidiaries). If separate fees have been charged for the management of the hive-down subsidiary, this fact should be stated and where accounts of the hive-down subsidiary are prepared and filed under the control of the practitioner, such fees should be disclosed separately in its accounts or by way of note.

Amounts received and disbursed under the Employment Protection Act do not form part of the funds of the estate and are normally dealt with through a separate bank account. These items should not be recorded as part of the receipts and payments accounts except where loans to employees are made under the Loan Scheme. The employees representative's fee does not form part of the remuneration from the estate and does not need separate disclosure.

Other amounts received and banked which are not part of the estate and are subsequently paid to the true owner should be shown as a receipt with the payment being shown as a deduction from receipts. Assets collected by the office holder on behalf of a mortgagee should be dealt with similarly and any additional fee charged therefore should be disclosed.

4.3 Summary of statutory of returns

Statutory requirements for the filing of returns are laid down in the IA 86 and rules, a summary of which is provided below.

	Form	Submit to	Timescale re submission	On closure
Administrative Receivership R3.32	3.6	Registrar of Companies The company Appointee Creditors' committee	Within two months after the end of 12 months from the date of appointment; and every subsequent 12 month period	Within two months of ceasing to act
Receivers (other than Administrative Receivers) s38 IA	3.6	Registrar of Companies	Within one month of the expiration of 12 months from the date of appointment; and every subsequent 6 month period	Within one month of ceasing to act
Administrator R2.47	2.24B	Court Registrar of Companies Creditors	Within one month of the expiration of six months from the date of appointment; and every subsequent six month period	Within one month of ceasing to act
Company voluntary Arrangement R1.26	1.3	Court Registrar of Companies The company Bound creditors Bound members Company's auditors	Within two months after the end of 12 months from the date of appointment; and every subsequent 12 month period	Within 28 days of completion of the arrangement

Worked example: Receipts and payments account

If you are asked to prepare a receipts and payments account in the exam the question is likely to consist of a list of information regarding the realisation of company assets to date, assets still to be realised, expenses incurred and outstanding and details of creditors claims.

Question:

Your principal was appointed administrator of Harmans Limited twelve months ago. The following information is available:

1   The company's freehold property was sold for a sum of £285,000. The property was subject to a fixed charge held by Wells Bank PLC in the sum of £115,000. Agents and solicitors fees paid in relation to the sale totalled £21,500. The property was shown in the Statement of Affairs in the sum of £240,000.

2   The company's other assets (machinery, fixtures and stock with a Statement of Affairs value of £55,000) were sold at public auction. The administrator received the sum of £49,000 after the auctioneer deducted the sum of £5,750 in relation to his costs.

3   Book debts with an estimated to realise value of £93,000 have to date been realised in the sum of £72,000. Legal costs of £6,500 have been incurred in realising debtors to date.

4   Administrator's remuneration has been drawn in the sum of £12,500 on a time cost basis.

5   Expenses totalling £2,500 have also been drawn relating to case advertising, copying etc.

6   Insurance costs of £1,800 have been paid.

7   A dividend has been paid to preferential creditors totalling £55,000. No other dividends have been paid.

Requirement

Prepare a Receipts and Payments account for Harmans Limited for the period from your appointment to date.

Solution

Harmans Limited (In Administration)

Receipts and Payments Account for the period X.X.00 TO X.X.01

	Per Sof A	Realised to date
RECEIPTS		
Freehold property	240,000	285,000
Machinery, fixtures, stock	55,000	54,750
Book debts	93,000	72,000
		411,750
PAYMENTS		
Wells Bank PLC		115,000
Agent's and solicitor's fees		21,500
Auctioneer's costs		5,750
Insurance		1,800
Legal fees re debt collection		6,500
Administrator's remuneration		12,500
Administrator's expenses		2,500
Payments to creditors:		
Preferential creditors		55,000
Balance in hand		191,200
		411,750

Self test

Answer the following questions.

1   What information must be shown in the statement of affairs?

2   Who may be required to produce a statement of affairs by an administrative receiver?

3   What does a deficiency account seek to show?

4   Which SIP provides office holders with guidance when preparing a receipts and payments account?

5   How often should an administrator submit a receipts and payments account to the Registrar of Companies?

6   An administrative receiver must submit a final receipts and payments account within how many months of ceasing to act?

7   To whom is an administrative receiver to submit a receipts and payments account?

Now, go back to the Learning Objectives in the Introduction. If you are satisfied that you have achieved these objectives, please tick them off.

Answer to Self test

1   Company's assets, debts and liabilities

   ▸   The names and addresses of the company's creditors

   ▸   What securities are held by any creditor

   ▸   Dates upon which the securities were given

   ▸   The book value and estimated to realise values of assets

2   Those who are or have been officers of the company and those in employment of the company who are deemed able to give information.

3   It reconciles the last set of accounts with the position shown in the statement of affairs. The deficiency account seeks to explain how the deficit to creditors arose. It explains why a once profitable company now appears insolvent or why an insolvent company has now become more insolvent.

4   SIP 7.

5   Within one month of the expiration of six months from the date of appointment and every subsequent six month period.

6   Two months.

7   Registrar of Companies, the company, the appointer and the creditors' committee.

Answers to Interactive Question

Interactive question: Bailey Swimming Pools Limited

Bailey Swimming Pools Limited (in Administration)

Comparative Estimated Outcome Statement.

	Notes	Mr Smith £	Mr Fields £
Freehold property		577,500	520,000
Less: costs	1		
Remuneration		(57,750)	(52,000)
Agents' fees		(28,875)	(26,000)
Legal fees		(8,000)	(8,000)
Available to fixed charge holder		482,875	434,000
Less: Barwest Bank plc		(573,000)	(573,000)
Shortfall under fixed charge		(90,125)	(139,000)
Assets subject to floating charge:			
Stock		14,000	14,500
Vehicles		22,000	27,000
Goodwill		nil	32,000
Book debt surplus	2	2,100	2,100
		38,100	75,600
Less: Remuneration	3	(3,600)	(7,350)
Agent's fees	4	(1,800)	(3,675)
Legal fees		(10,000)	(10,000)
Trading loss	5	(7,000)	(7,000)
Disbursements		(1,200)	(1,200)
Available for preferential creditors		14,500	46,375
Preferential creditors:			
Employees – Wage arrears		(13,000)	(13,000)
Holiday pay		(6,000)	(6,000)
Subrogated wages claim		(2,500)	(2,500)
		(21,500)	(21,500)
Shortfall to Preferential creditors		(7,000)	—
Available to floating charge holder		nil	24,875
Barwest Bank PLC		(90,125)	(139,000)
Shortfall to floating charge holder		(90,125)	(114,125)
Summary of proceedings:			
Shortfall to preferential creditors		7,000	nil
Assets available to unsecured creditors		nil	nil
Shortfall to Barwest Bank PLC		90,125	114,125

Administrations

Workings:

1   Fixed charge costs

		Mr Smith	Mr Fields
Remuneration @ 10% × 577,500 / 520,000		57,750	52,000
Agents' fees @ 5% × 577,500 / 520,000		28,875	26,000

2   Book debts:

	£
Outstanding	98,000
Less: 5 % bad debts	(4,900)
Remuneration	(5,000)
Needle Factors Limited	(86,000)
Surplus available	2,100

3   Remuneration:

10% on realisations excluding book debts:

	Mr Smith	Mr Fields
Floating charge realisations	36,000	73,500
@ 10 %	3,600	7,350

4   Agent's fees:

5% on realisations:

	Mr Smith	Mr Fields
Floating charge realisations	36,000	73,500
@ 5%	1,800	3,675

5   Trading loss:

	£
Gross trading profits	14,000
Less:	
Insurance	(500)
Wages	(16,000)
Duress payments – ROT creditors	(1,200)
HP creditors	(800)
HP payments	(2,500)
Net trading loss	(7,000)

13

Company voluntary arrangements

> > > > > > > > > > > > > > >

Contents

Introduction

Learning objectives

▶ Procedure for obtaining approval for a company voluntary arrangement ☐

▶ Contents of a voluntary arrangement proposal ☐

▶ Advantages and disadvantages of a company voluntary arrangement ☐

▶ S895 CA 2006 scheme, what it is, when it would be used. ☐

Working context

You may be asked to advise directors of an insolvent company on the options available to them. It is important therefore to understand what a voluntary arrangement is and what the benefits would be to the company of entering into a voluntary arrangement. You may also be asked to assist the directors in putting together proposals for a voluntary arrangement.

Stop and think

What is a company voluntary arrangement? How does it differ to an individual voluntary arrangement? Why would a company choose to enter into a voluntary arrangement rather than creditors' voluntary liquidation?

Examination context

Company voluntary arrangements appear regularly as a JIEB examination topic both as an essay style question, for example the nominee's report or the procedure for CVA and also as a numbers style question, for example preparing estimated outcome statements comparing CVA with liquidation.

Past exam questions to look at include:

2007	Question 2
2006	Question 2
2005	Question 2
2004	Question 2
2004	Question 5
2003	Question 5
2001	Question 4
2001	Question 5
1999	Question 2(a)
1999	Question 5
1998	Question 4
1996	Question 4
1994	Question 3

1 Introduction to company voluntary arrangements

Section overview

▶ Company voluntary arrangements (CVA) were introduced by the IA 86 as an alternative to liquidation for companies experiencing difficulties in paying their debts as and when due. There are many similarities with the procedure for individual voluntary arrangement. Legislation regarding CVAs can be found in Part 1 of the Act (s1 – s7B), Schedule A1 and Part 1 of the Rules (r1.1 – r1.54). SIP 3 'Voluntary Arrangements' sets out best practice in relation to the work carried out in connection with voluntary arrangements, both company and individual.

1.1 Advantages of CVA

▶ Possible survival of the company as a going concern

▶ Higher returns to creditors due to:

– sale as a going concern or profitable trading

– lower costs – no Secretary of State fees, possibility of lower costs if directors (rather than IP's staff) remain responsible for managing the business

– Capital gains tax advantages, gains on asset disposals may be set against losses

– Floating charges will not be invalidated under s245 IA

– Binds all creditors who had notice of and were entitled to vote at the creditors' meeting

– Small company moratorium available

– No 'D' return completed by the supervisor

– Supervisor may not bring proceedings for wrongful trading

– No notice on letter head helps to preserve goodwill

– No application to court required

– Directors retain control of the company (albeit under supervision)

1.2 Disadvantages of CVA

Supervisor has no power to clawback under ss238, 239 and 243 IA however:

▶ s423 IA *is* available.

▶ Creditors may demand that directors etc. compromise such claims as a condition of assenting to the arrangement.

If the arrangement fails liquidation is likely to be the only remaining course of action.

Unlike an IVA a CVA does not have an interim order as an intrinsic part of the procedure. Neither is there any asset protection regime such as ss126 to 128 IA in compulsory liquidation.

As there is no interim order creditors may (prior to approval of the arrangement) bring enforcement action against the company in the usual way and the very act of notifying creditors of the meeting may precipitate a run on the assets.

The benefits of protection from duress creditors may, however, be obtained in two ways:

▶ Appointing an administrator and therefore obtaining the benefit of the moratorium. This can have the disadvantage of the costs and potential delays resulting from court proceedings. Note that directors can now appoint an administrator without applying to court.

▶ Obtaining a moratorium under the procedure in Schedule A1 of the *Insolvency Act 1986* introduced by the *Insolvency Act 2000*. The disadvantage is that this procedure is only available for 'small companies'(see later).

1.3 Who may make a proposal for a CVA?

A proposal may be made by:

A liquidator or administrator (if the company is in liquidation or administration)- (s1(3) IA)

The directors – s1(1) IA

1.4 The role of the nominee and supervisor

Nominee: prior to the acceptance of the arrangement by the creditors the IP will act as nominee. He has a duty to balance the interests of the creditors and the company. The nominee is required to report to the court and has a duty to perform an independent objective review and assessment of the proposal.

Supervisor: upon acceptance of the arrangement by the creditors the IP will become the supervisor of the arrangement. His responsibilities will be governed by the terms of the arrangement. His role is to ensure that the arrangement proceeds as anticipated by the terms of the proposal.

The IA 2000 permits other authorised persons to act as nominee and supervisor of a voluntary arrangement. Such a person need not be a qualified IP.

1.5 Initial meeting with directors

The following matters need to be considered by the IP and the directors when considering a CVA:

▶ Can the IP act for the directors in the light of the ethical guide?

▶ Are arrangements in place for the IP to be remunerated for advice given to the directors before the advising IP agrees to become the nominee? The proposal itself can only set out the remuneration of the nominee and the supervisor.

▶ The nominee's advice needs to be confirmed in writing

▶ The IP has a duty to maintain independence i.e. an IP owes duties to creditors generally as well as to the debtor company.

▶ Directors or third parties who are intending to inject funds into the debtor company should be advised to seek their own independent professional advice to avoid any subsequent allegation of conflict of interests.

▶ The nominee is required to report to the court and has a duty to perform an independent objective review and assessment of the proposal. The nominee has a duty to balance the interests of the company and the creditors i.e. the nominee will only report that meetings should be held to consider the proposal if satisfied that a CVA is the best way forward for the creditors.

▶ These duties of the nominee cannot be fettered by the instructions of the directors.

▶ The nominee needs to be satisfied that the proposal is:

   – fit to be put to creditors
   – fair
   – feasible
   – is an acceptable alternative to liquidation or other formal insolvency processes

▶ The nominee should form a view of the general credibility of the directors and whether the proposal appears to satisfy the test in *Greystoke v Hamilton Smith*:

   (i) that the company's true position as to assets and liabilities is not materially different from that represented to the creditors

(ii)   that the proposal has a real prospect of implementation

(iii)   that the proposal is not manifestly unfair.

Valuations of key assets should be obtained.

Antecedent transactions should be identified.

If the IP decides to accept appointment as nominee, notice of the proposal must be returned to the directors endorsed with acceptance (r1.4(3)).

There is no statutory protection from creditors (unlike the interim order in an IVA). The directors therefore need to identify creditors who may be able to take enforcement action against the company. They need to devise a strategy to deal with:

▶   Landlord who may be able to distrain or forfeit the lease

▶   Any secured creditors particularly any bank, entitled to appoint a receiver whose support may be required for ongoing trading.

▶   Judgment creditors who may levy execution

▶   Overseas creditors who may, notwithstanding the CVA, be able to take enforcement action in foreign jurisdictions

▶   HM Revenue and Customs who may be able to levy distress

▶   Creditors with proprietary rights e.g. ROT suppliers or creditors under HP agreements or equipment leases

▶   Any creditors petitioning for winding-up.

Protection from duress creditors could be obtained by:

1   Entering administration
2   Applying for a small company moratorium.
3   Petitioning for a winding up order and applying for the appointment of a provisional liquidator.

A small company moratorium is only possible where the company fulfils the criteria of a 'small company' (s382 CA 2006).ie. Two or more of:

▶   Turnover no greater than £6.5m

▶   Assets on balance sheet no greater than £3.26m

▶   No more than 50 employees in the relevant period (last financial year or the year prior to filing for a moratorium)

The effect of a small company moratorium is that:

▶   petitions for winding-up cannot be presented (and where presented before date of filing s127 IA will NOT apply during the period for which the moratorium is in force) and winding-up orders cannot be made

▶   company meetings can't be called without consent of nominee or court and no resolution to wind-up can be passed

▶   no application for an administration order can be presented

▶   no administrator can be appointed, subject to the leave of the nominee or the court

▶   no administrative receiver can be appointed

▶   landlords cannot exercise a right of forfeiture by peaceful re-entry

▶   no other steps can be taken to enforce any security, or repossess goods under any HP agreement

▶   no other proceeding, execution, or legal process can be commenced or continued and no distress may be levied.

The IP needs to ensure that all creditors have been correctly identified. Addresses of creditors should be accurate to ensure that actual notice of the meeting may be given. Directors should identify future and contingent creditors.

A creditor who was not notified of the creditors' meeting to vote on the proposal is still bound by the CVA providing they would have been entitled to vote at the meeting had they been notified (para 6 Sch 2 IA 2000). None the less, non-notified bound creditors may be able to appeal to the court on the basis of material irregularity or unfair prejudice (s6(2)(aa) IA), so it makes sense to take every precaution to notify all creditors. Non bound creditors also have the right to claim the unpaid portion of their debt on the CVA coming to an end (s5(2)(A) IA).

The directors should be asked whether any creditors have negative control (ie 25% or more by value of total debt). Such creditors or other creditors on whose support the CVA depends should be approached to ascertain their attitude to the proposal.

In relation to members, the register of members should be checked and (where relevant) the voting rights of each class of creditors should be considered.

Who is to be instructed as nominee and the functions of the IP should be considered.

Directors should be warned of the consequences of not making full and accurate disclosure in the Statement of Affairs, the proposal and at the creditors meeting. That is:

▶ Creditors will find out and vote against the proposal or at the very least require adjournments and modification.

▶ Creditors may appeal on the basis of a material irregularity.

▶ The inducing of a CVA through fraud constitutes a criminal offence – now in s6A IA and applies even if the proposal is not approved.

Note that there is no equivalent of the s264(1)(c) IA default petition by a supervisor or any creditor bound on the grounds of false statements/omissions in an IVA. A petition for compulsory winding-up would be presented on the ground of inability to pay debts.

The directors should be made aware of the risks of wrongful trading (trading with actual knowledge of insolvency). They must establish that trading on will be viable:

▶ Ensure that adequate funding is available

▶ Prepare cash flow forecasts, a business plan and projections. Must show that both ongoing trading is viable and that dividends to creditors shown in the proposal are likely to be paid.

Independent confirmation from the bank that it will support the proposal and continue to provide funding

Consider other sources of funds

Do the directors have the support of management, staff, key suppliers and customers?

Are there any major contracts with customers which are voidable on insolvency?

Nominee may give first aid advice on the importance of minimising credit, taking steps to avoid preferring creditors etc.

Interactive question 1: Longdon Nurseries Limited

The directors of Longdon Nurseries Ltd have approached you for some advice. The company has been experiencing cash flow problems for a number of months caused in the main by delays and unforeseen costs incurred during an expansion programme. The directors are confident that when the new garden centre and restaurant facilities opens in four months time that the company will quickly return to profitability. They wish to propose a voluntary arrangement whereby creditors will be paid in full.

Requirement

List the matters that should be discussed with the directors at your first meeting.

See **Answer** at the end of this chapter.

2 The proposal

Section overview

▶ The proposal is a formal legal document which, when approved, becomes legally binding. Many points must be covered as a matter of law or best practice. The required contents of the proposal are set out in r1.3 and are virtually identical to those for an individual voluntary arrangement (IVA). SIP 3 gives additional guidance on matters that should be included. R3 have produced standard terms and conditions for inclusion in the proposal which it hopes the profession will adopt. Reference to these terms in the examination should gain some credit. The director's proposal may be amended at any time, with the written agreement of the nominee, up to delivery of the nominee's report to the court under s2(2) IA.

2.1 Content of proposal

1 Desirability:

A short explanation why, in the director's opinion, a CVA is desirable and reasons why the company's creditors may be expected to concur with it. This should include:

Some background and explanation of the present insolvency

Extracts from trading accounts from previous years

2 Assets:

Details of the company's assets, with an estimate of their respective values.

The extent (if any) to which the assets are charged in favour of creditors.

The extent (if any) to which particular assets are to be excluded from the arrangement.

Particulars of any property, other than assets of the company itself, which it is proposed to be included in the arrangement.

Controls on the disposal of assets (disposal of company assets outside ordinary course of business only with sanction of the supervisor).

3 Liabilities:

The nature and amount of the company's liabilities, the manner in which they are proposed to be met, modified, postponed or otherwise dealt with by means of the arrangement.

How it is proposed to deal with preferential creditors and creditors who are, or claim to be, secured.

How persons connected with the company (being creditors) are proposed to be treated under the arrangement.

How it is proposed to deal with the claim of any person who is bound by the arrangement by virtue of s5(2)(b)(ii) IA.

The rules contain no details on how unliquidated and contingent claims are to be dealt with for dividend purposes.

For unliquidated claims the proposal may provide for:

▶ creditor to submit proof and evidence as to quantum

▶ supervisor to estimate and provide creditor with written notice of estimate

▶ in the event that the creditor does not agree the claim provision can be made for arbitration or appeal to the court under s7(3) IA.

▶ For voting purposes the creditor may vote for £1 unless the chair agrees to allow a higher value (r1.17(3)).

For contingent claims the proposal may provide for:

▶ Retention by the supervisor of funds pending crystallisation of the claim

▶ Perhaps for a limited period after which the sum retained would be paid out to creditors generally.

Importing of voluntary liquidation rules in regard to proofs, set-off, discounts, foreign currency claims and future claims.

Confirmation of when the terms of the CVA have been successfully completed and confirmation that creditors will no longer be entitled to pursue the debtor for any balance of their claim.

How to deal with creditors who have not made claims.

In the event of the arrangement not being successful and the company entering liquidation, clarification of the amounts for which creditors will be entitled to claim.

4   Voidable transactions:

Claims under s238, s239, s244 and s245 IA will need to be detailed and where any such circumstances are present, how it is proposed to indemnify the company in respect of such claims.

Note that as well as the usual transactions at an undervalue, preferences and extortionate credit transactions (of which details must be given in a proposal for an IVA) in a CVA any floating charges which may fall foul of s245 IA must also be detailed.

Remember that s238, s239, s244 and s245 IA are all triggered by liquidation or administration and not by administrative receivership.

5   Prescribed part:

The proposal must set out how much the unsecured creditors would receive if the company went into liquidation under the prescribed part rules. This is so that creditors can make a meaningful comparison between what they are promised in the proposal against what they might receive under creditors' voluntary liquidation.   *or administration.*

6   Guarantees:

Whether any, and if so what, guarantees have been given of the company's debts by other persons, specifying which (if any) of the guarantors are persons connected with the company.

Whether, for the purposes of the arrangement, any guarantees are to be offered by directors, or other persons, and whether (if so) any security is to be given or sought.

7   Duration:

The proposed duration of the arrangement should be given (a certain period of time should be stated – *Re A Debtor (No.222 of 1990)*.

With a CVA, unlike an IVA, the issue of automatic discharge from bankruptcy after one year does not arise so creditors are in a strong position to press for a lengthy duration if that is in their best interests.

8   Distribution and estimates:

The proposed dates of distributions to creditors along with estimates of their amounts should be given.

9   Remuneration and expenses:

The amount proposed to be paid to the nominee by way of remuneration and expenses should be stated.

Also, the manner in which it is proposed that the supervisor of the arrangement should be remunerated and his expenses defrayed.

As a minimum the proposal should provide for:

▶ means of calculating and agreeing supervisor's remuneration ie. By resolution of creditors or a creditors' committee

▶ payment of solicitors, estate agents and other expenses

▶ payment of remuneration and expenses in priority to all other claims.

10 Supervisor:

The functions which are to be undertaken by the supervisor should be set out clearly.

The name, address and qualification of the person proposed as supervisor of the arrangement should be stated and confirmation that he is either qualified to act as an IP in relation to the company or is an authorised person in relation to the company.

Supervisor to have general power to implement the terms of the CVA.

Supervisor to avoid personal liability. Proposal may state that information contained in it derives from directors and supervisor cannot warrant its accuracy.

The proposal should set out the supervisor's powers.

The supervisor should be given a general power to call meetings of creditors.

11 Funds:

The manner in which funds held for the purposes of the arrangement are to be banked, invested or otherwise dealt with pending distribution to creditors.

The manner in which funds held for the purpose of payment to creditors and not so paid on the termination of the arrangement need to be dealt with. For example, if a creditor disappears prior to receiving a final dividend the proposal could provide for this sum to be redistributed amongst the other creditors.

12 Business:

The manner in which the business of the company is proposed to be conducted during the course of the arrangement.

Details of any further credit facilities which it is intended to arrange for the company and how the debts so arising are to be paid.

Supervisor to supervise not manage the business.

Duties of company management to provide supervisor with regular information and accounts.

Provision for which firm of accountants will be responsible for the preparation of accounts and for payment of their costs.

The grounds of the director's belief that the company can return to profitable trading – past trading accounts, realistic forecasts, cash flow statements and projections should be attached.

Can the company rely on the continued support of the bank, major customers and suppliers as well as the workforce?

Availability of working capital.

Company to pay post CVA liabilities as and when they fall due and to be solely responsible for those liabilities.

Supervisor to have powers to demand co-operation from management.

Restrictions on powers of directors (especially in realising assets).

What will happen to surplus funds arising, for instance if the business trades more beneficially than originally envisaged.

13   EC Regulations:

Whether the EC Regulations will apply and, if so, whether the proceedings will be main proceedings, secondary proceedings or territorial proceedings.

14   Creditors' committee:

Whether a committee of creditors will be appointed and what its powers, duties and responsibilities will be.

Interactive question 2: Smith Limited

The directors of Smith Limited have approached you for advice. They are a creditor of Jeyes Engineering Limited and have submitted a claim in the CVA of that company. The claim has been admitted to vote in the sum of £1 however the directors advise you that the company is actually owed £78,000 under a lease agreement covering various items of plant and machinery. In addition it includes a damages claim for £35,000.

Requirement

Explain to the directors why their claim has been admitted in the sum of £1 and what remedies are available to them.

See **Answer** at the end of this chapter.

2.2   Nominee's comments on the proposal

Within 28 days of receiving notice of the proposal the nominee is required to file in court his comments on the proposal (see later). The nominee should normally comment on the following matters:

▶   If the *Greystoke v Hamilton-Smith* conditions (see 1.5) are not met, the basis on which the nominee is nonetheless recommending that meetings should be held to consider the proposal.

▶   The director's attitude – and in particular any instances of failure to co-operate with the nominee

▶   The history of any previous failure in which the directors have been involved in so far as they are known to the nominee.

▶   Basis of asset valuations

▶   The extent to which reliance can be placed on the director's estimate of the company's liabilities

▶   Information on the attitude of any major unsecured creditors

▶   Result of any discussion with secured creditors or other interested parties on whose co-operation the CVA depends

▶   The estimate of the result for creditors if the CVA is approved

▶   Why the CVA is more beneficial for creditors than alternative insolvency proceedings

▶   The likely effect of the proposals being rejected by creditors

▶   Details of claims better pursued in liquidation or administration.

▶   The extent to which the nominee has investigated the company's circumstances, if not already dealt with in the proposals.

▶   The source of any referrals to the nominee or his firm in relation to the proposed voluntary arrangement.

▶   Any payments made or proposed to be made to the source of such referrals.

▶   Any payments made or proposed to be made to the nominee or his firm by the company whether in connection with the proposed VA or otherwise.

- An estimate of the total fee to be paid to the supervisor together with a statement of the assumptions made in producing the estimate.

- If the company has, in the previous 12 months, put forward a proposal that has been rejected, a statement to that effect and why it is considered appropriate for the creditors to consider and vote on the new proposal.

3 Procedure for CVA

Section overview

- Proposals for a CVA can be made by the directors, liquidator or administrator and may or may not include an application for a small company moratorium.

3.1 Directors' proposal, no application for moratorium

S1(1) provides that in situations where the company is not in administration or liquidation it is for the directors to propose a CVA.

The directors provide the intended nominee (who must be an IP or someone else authorised to act as such (s1(2)) with:

(i) A proposal (r1.2). In practice of course the proposal will be prepared by the nominee from information obtained from the directors. (Required contents of the proposal are set out in r1.3).

(ii) Written notice of proposal (r1.4). This is endorsed with acceptance and returned to the directors and acts as the nominees consent to act.

(iii) The directors statement of affairs (required by r1.5, and by r1.6 the nominee can demand further and better particulars and access to the company's accounts and records). The statement of affairs:

- must be delivered within seven days of the proposal (nominee can extend time)

- and must be made up to a date not earlier than two weeks before the date of the notice to the nominee

- and must be certified as correct by two or more directors or one director and the company secretary.

Note: Unlike in an IVA there is no hearing at this stage. Up until the date of delivery of the IP's report to the court the directors may amend their proposals with his written consent (r1.3(3)).

3.2 Application to court to replace nominee

S2(4) IA and r1.8 permits this in three situations:

- On the directors' application where the nominee has died

- On the directors' application where the nominee has failed to submit a report.

- On the directors' or the nominee's application where it is impracticable or inappropriate for the nominee to continue to act.

The directors need to give the nominee seven days notice of their application. Likewise a nominee would need to give seven days notice of his application to the directors (Rule 1.8). Any replacement nominee must provide a statement that he is qualified/authorised and consents to act.

3.3   Calling meetings of creditors and shareholders

Notice

Notice must be given to all creditors in the Statement of Affairs and every other creditor of whom the nominee is aware and to all members to the best of the nominee's belief.

Notice must specify the court to which the nominee's report has been delivered and must explain the rules on majorities.

Notice must be accompanied by:

- Copy proposal
- Statement of Affairs or summary
- Comments on proposals (see section 2.2)
- Proxy form

Meetings must be held between 10.00 and 16.00 hours and in choosing location regard must be had to the convenience of creditors.

14 days notice must be given (r1.9(2)).

Meetings must be held not less than 14 and not more than 28 days from the date of filing the nominee's report (r1.9(1)).

There are two meetings, one of creditors, which must be held first and one of members which can be held up to seven days later than the creditors' meeting and at a different venue.

Chairman

The chair of the meetings should be the convening nominee or an IP or other experienced member of staff from the firm (r1.14(2)).

The chair cannot use any proxy to vote increases in remuneration or expenses unless the proxy specifically directs the chair to vote in that way (r1.15).

Voting requirements

Votes at the creditors meeting are calculated according to the amount of the creditors debt at the date of the meeting. Where a creditor has an unliquidated or unascertained claim r1.17 now provides that the creditor may vote (but) his debt shall be valued at £1 unless the chair agrees to put a higher value on it.

Votes at the members meeting are calculated according to the rights attaching to their shares in accordance with the Articles. (r1.18(1))

Majorities:

- (r1.19(1)) states that in excess of 3/4s of the votes cast at the creditors meeting are required to approve or modify the proposal.

- Any other resolution taken requires a simple majority (r1.19(2)).

- A simple majority of the votes casts at the members meeting is required (r1.20(1)).

- Any resolution is invalid if a simple majority of notified, valid, non-connected creditors vote against it (r19(4)).

Note: The odd rule that members with no voting rights were entitled to vote (r1.18(2)) but their votes were to be left out of account in calculating majorities (r1.20(2)) has been removed.

The decision of the creditors' meeting has effect (ie. Even if the members' meeting reaches a different decision), but subject to the right of any member to apply to court within 28 days (s4A IA).

Appeals:

Appeals may be made by any creditor or member, within 28 days of the filing of the chair's report to the court under s4(6) IA or when the creditor first finds out of the CVA (whichever is the later). The court can reverse, vary or confirm the chairs decision or order another meeting to be held but only if the grounds of appeal reveal unfair prejudice or material irregularity.

Adjournments:

The chair may (and if the meeting resolves) shall adjourn either meeting for up to 14 days.

Multiple adjournments are possible but the final meeting must still be no more than 14 days from the original meeting.

Notice of adjournment must be given to the court

Modifications:

It is not a statutory requirement for directors to consent to modifications, however it is recommended (by SIP 3) that the nominee should find out and report to the meeting their view on any proposed modifications which they may be required to implement if approved.

Reporting the results of the meeting:

The chair prepares a report of the meetings and within four days must file in court. All those notified of the meetings must be sent notice of its result immediately after the filing of the report (r1.24(4)).

If CVA approved a copy of the report must also be sent to the Registrar of Companies (r1.24(5)).

The report should contain (r1.24(2)):

▶ whether the proposal was approved by the creditors or by the creditors and the members (and whether there were any modifications)

▶ sets out resolutions and decision on each

▶ lists creditors and members present/represented (with their values) and how they voted on each resolution

▶ The supervisor's opinion as to applicability of *EC Regulation*

▶ any further information.

3.4 Procedure for directors to obtain a moratorium

Directors are able to apply to court for a moratorium. This is restricted to 'eligible' companies ie. Those falling within the definition of a 'small' company for Companies Act purposes (s382 CA 2006).

The company must not be excluded under Para 4 of Schedule A1 to the IA 86. A company is excluded if at date of filing:

▶ the company is in administration

▶ the company is being wound-up

▶ there is an administrative receiver

▶ there is a CVA

▶ there is a provisional liquidator

▶ there has been a moratorium in force in the previous 12 months and either no CVA had effect or there was a CVA but it came to a premature end.

The company is not one of four types of company mentioned in para 2(2) to the Schedule i.e.

▶ insurance companies
▶ banks
▶ holding companies (unless part of a "small" or "medium" group)
▶ parties to market or money market contracts
▶ participants in settlement systems
▶ parties to capital market arrangements where issued debt = £10m or more
▶ public/private partnerships projects with step in rights.

The directors provide nominee with:

▸ document setting out terms of proposed CVA
▸ statement of affairs
▸ any other information requested by the nominee.

Before obtaining a moratorium the directors need to obtain, from the nominee, a statement to the effect that in the nominee's opinion the:

▸ Proposed CVA has a reasonable prospect of approval/ implementation

▸ The company has sufficient funding to continue trading during the moratorium

▸ Meetings of creditors/ members should be called to consider the proposal.

The directors now file in court:

▸ The document setting out the terms of proposed CVA and the statement of affairs.

▸ A statement that the company is eligible.

▸ The nominee's statement above plus a statement that the nominee consents to act.

The moratorium comes into effect on the date of filing and is initially for 28 days.

The effect of para 8(3) and 29(1) Sch A1 IA is that the nominee should summon both the creditors and members meeting to be held within 28 days of the coming into effect of the moratorium. If this does happen the moratorium will end on the day on which the meetings (or the later of the meetings) are held.

If the meetings are not summonsed or held within 28 days the moratorium will come to an end on day 28.

Members and creditors can agree to extend the moratorium for up to a further two months from the date of the first meeting(s).

A moratorium will come to an end prematurely if:

▸ nominee withdraws consent to act
▸ the meeting or meetings so resolve
▸ there is a successful challenge to the court.

During the moratorium the company's notepaper must state that the moratorium is in force and the company may not obtain credit of £250 or more without disclosing that a moratorium is in force.

Having filed the documents in court the directors give notice to the nominee.

The nominee now:

▸ advertises the moratorium in the gazette and some other newspaper

▸ gives notice to the company

▸ gives notice to Companies House

▸ gives notice to any creditors who have distrained, any creditors petitioning for winding-up and to the court enforcement officer.

Safeguards

The nominee must consider the directors' proposals, and although he can rely on information provided by the directors, is giving his or her opinion when he makes a statement that there is a reasonable prospect of implementation etc, and can be held liable on it.

The nominee must monitor the company during the moratorium and must report to the meetings on this.

The nominee must withdraw his consent to act (and the moratorium will then come to an end) if:

▸ it emerges that the company was not eligible or was excluded

▸ the directors fail to comply with their duties

▸ the nominee no longer believes that there is a reasonable prospect of implementation or that the CVA can be funded.

Credit of £250 or more may not be obtained without disclosing that the company is subject to a moratorium. As with bankruptcy there is a broad definition of credit including the receipt or deposits for goods/services to be delivered/provided later.

Asset disposals outside the ordinary course of business require nominee approval. The meetings can vote to extend the moratorium and if they do so a committee can be formed which can also sanction such disposals.

There is an equivalent for s15 IA in administrations whereby floating charge assets can be disposed of but assets subject to a fixed charge require agreement of the charge holder or court sanction.

3.5 Procedure where proposal made by liquidator or administrator.

The procedure is the same as for the directors but:

▶ The proposal must give names, addresses and values of preferential creditors if company is in administration.

▶ The Statement of Affairs in the CVA is that already obtained in the existing insolvency proceedings.

▶ A report to the court and comments on the proposals are not required if the liquidator or administrator is to act as nominee.

▶ The company's assets are immediately protected whereas where CVA is a stand alone procedure no such protection is available (at least until the CVA is approved).

▶ Votes are calculated as at the amount of the creditor's debt as at the date the company went into administration.

4 Post approval matters

Section overview

▶ There are a number of matters which the supervisor will have to deal with after approval of the arrangement.

4.1 Effect of approval of the arrangement

A voluntary arrangement comes into effect under s5 IA when the proposal has been approved by both a meeting of the company and a meeting of its creditors.

The approved voluntary arrangement:

▶ Takes effect as if made by the company at the creditors' meeting, and

▶ Binds every person who in accordance with the rules had notice of and was entitled to vote at, that meeting (whether or not he was present or represented at the meeting) as if he were a party to the voluntary arrangement, and

▶ If members vote against a proposal approved by the creditors the CVA takes effect subject to a right of appeal of the members.

4.2 Challenge of decision of the meeting S.6.

An application to court may be made on the grounds that:

▶ A voluntary arrangement approved at the meetings summoned under s3 IA unfairly prejudices the interests of a creditor, member or contributory of the company and/or

▶ There has been some material irregularity at or in relation to either of the meetings.

A claim of unfair prejudice will only succeed where the prejudice arises from the unfairness of the proposal itself, for instance, treating different types of unsecured creditors differently in regard to the payment of dividends.

Material irregularity involves procedural matters, for example, a complaint that the chair has rejected a valid claim for voting purposes.

The persons who may apply are:

▶ A person entitled, in accordance with the rules, to vote at either of the meetings

▶ The nominee or any person who has replaced him, and

▶ If the company is being wound up or an administration order is in force, the liquidator or the administrator

The application must be made within 28 days of the chairs report to the court (see later).

4.3 IP's duties post meetings

Recording the meetings:

SIP 12 ('Records of Meetings in Formal Insolvency Proceedings') provides that it is best practice that records should be kept of all meetings of creditors and members.

This includes all such meetings in CVAs, administrative receiverships and administrations as well as meetings of any creditors committees, which are set up within these procedures.

The record should include as a minimum the following information:

▶ Title of the proceedings.

▶ Date, time and venue of meeting.

▶ Name and description of chair and any others involved in conduct of meeting.

▶ A list of attendees (either in the report or appended to it). This should include creditors, members, officers and former officers of the company.

▶ The exercise of any discretion by the Chair in relation to the admissibility or value of any claim for voting purposes.

▶ The resolutions taken and the decision on each one and in the event of a poll being taken the value or number of votes for and against each resolution.

▶ Where a committee is established the names and addresses of the members.

▶ Such other matters as are required by statute or the proposal.

The record should be signed by the Chair and be either:

▶ retained with the record or

▶ entered in the company's minute book with a copy retained with the record of the proceedings, whichever is appropriate.

If the meeting has approved the setting up of a committee then copy records of committee meetings should be sent to attendees of those committee meetings.

Forms of proxy and poll cards should also be retained. This is in any event a requirement of Rule 8.4. It will be particularly important in CVAs if any appeal on the basis of a material irregularity is later made.

Information provided at a meeting in support of a request that the meeting approve the IP's remuneration should also be retained.

If the nominee/supervisor has not chaired the meeting he or she should ensure that the record complies with the above principles.

Reporting the meetings:

R1.24 requires that the chair of the meetings prepares a report containing the following details:

▶ Whether the proposal was accepted or rejected

▶ And if approved, any modifications

▶ The resolutions taken at each meeting and the decision on each one

▶ A list of the creditors and members of the company (with their respective values) who were present or represented at the meetings and how they voted on each resolution, and

▶ Any further information the chair thinks appropriate.

A copy of the chair's report must be filed in court within four days of the meeting (s4(6) and r1.24(3)).

If the CVA was approved the supervisor sends a copy of the report to the Registrar of Companies forthwith (r1.24(5)).

SIP 12 reminds members of the reporting requirements above.

S4(6) IA requires the chair of the meeting to give notice of the result of the meeting immediately after reporting to the court to such persons as may be prescribed. The 'prescribed persons' are all those notified of the members and creditors meetings (r1.24(4)).

4.4 Monies outstanding to a liquidator, administrator or OR

(r1.23(2)). Where the company is in liquidation or administration the supervisor of the CVA on taking possession of the company's assets shall discharge any balance due to the IP by way of:

▶ remuneration or

▶ on account of fees, costs, charges and expenses or

▶ on account of any advances made in respect of the company at the date it went into liquidation or became subject to an administration order (plus interest at the Judgements Act Rate).

As an alternative the supervisor can give a written undertaking to the IP to discharge sums due out of first realisations.

In any event the liquidator, administrator or OR has a charge on the CVA assets for the sums due until they have been discharged. The supervisor is entitled to deduct first the cost etc. of realisation.

4.5 Annual reports

The supervisor must, at least once every 12 months prepare an abstract of receipts and payments and send it (within two months) to the court, Registrar of Companies, the company, all creditors and members bound by the CVA and the company's auditors. This must be accompanied by his comments on the progress and efficacy of the arrangement.

4.6 Completion of the arrangement

Following completion of the arrangement the supervisor must send notice to all creditors and members that the CVA has been fully implemented together with his report summarising his receipts and payments within 28 days.

The supervisor must also send a copy of the notice and the report to the Registrar of Companies and the court within 28 days.

4.7 Failure

In circumstances of failure or default it will be necessary to consider how matters should proceed. It is essential that the proposal should set out in specific terms the circumstances in which it shall be deemed to have failed and state what action the supervisor is required to take in the event of failure.

When failure has occurred the supervisor should notify the creditors accordingly and advise them what action he has taken or proposes to take.

The supervisor has the power to present a winding up petition.

4.8 Resignation and release

There are no statutory provisions dealing with the resignation and release of a supervisor. The terms of the arrangement would have to be checked to ascertain the mechanism by which the supervisor may resign and be released from office.

The agreement of 100% of the creditors may be required unless a specific majority is stated in the proposal.

In the absence of a specific clause, the supervisor would need to obtain a court order to deal with his release.

5 s895 CA 2006 Scheme of Arrangement

Section overview

▸ A s895 CA 2006 scheme is a compromise or arrangement between the company and its creditors (or any class of them) and/or its members (or any class of them). Strictly speaking a s895 CA 2006 scheme of arrangement is not an insolvency procedure therefore the administrator of a s895 CA 2006 scheme does not need to be an IP. The procedure is rarely used in practice with insolvent companies.

▸ s895 CA 2006 replaces s425 CA 1985 and sets out the procedure for a court sanctioned scheme of arrangement or reconstruction between a company and a majority of its members or creditors. There are no changes of substance from s425 of the 1985 CA.

Definition

Compromise: In *Re NFU Development Trust Ltd 1973* compromise was defined as an agreement between two parties resolving a dispute where genuine difficulties faced the claimant and the result of the claim was therefore in doubt.

Arrangement: In *Re Savoy Hotel Ltd 1981* arrangement was given a wider definition and will include the same types of agreements that can be made with creditors in a CVA.

5.1 Advantages of s895 CA 2006 scheme

▸ Flexibility
▸ Wide range of potential applicants
▸ Useful where large company and complex arrangement
▸ Binds all members and creditors whether or not they had notice

5.2 Disadvantages of s895 CA 2006 scheme

- ▶ Two applications to court are necessary, therefore costs disadvantages and scope for delays
- ▶ Approval of every class of creditor and shareholder generally required (plus sanction of the court)
- ▶ Not appropriate where s110 IA can be used (see Liquidation study manual for details)
- ▶ Cannot be used to sanction a scheme beyond the company's capacity (*Re Savoy Hotel Ltd*)
- ▶ Absence of an interim order

5.3 Who may apply

The following persons may apply to court for a s895 CA 2006 scheme by originating summons (Order 102 Rules of the Supreme Court):

- ▶ Liquidator or administrator
- ▶ The company
- ▶ Any creditor
- ▶ Any member

The court will order the calling of meetings and may give directions re the number, timing and calling of the meetings.

5.4 The meetings

1 Calling the meetings:

This must be done in accordance with the courts directions.

What constitutes?

Separate meetings of each class of creditor and each class of member must generally be called. However:

- ▶ If company solvent only one meeting of all creditors need be called as all creditors will be paid.

- ▶ If company insolvent court may dispense with need for consent of shareholders as they have no "interest" in outcome of arrangement (*Re Tea Corporation*). Compare with a CVA where meeting of members cannot be dispensed with.

Notice calling meeting must be accompanied by explanatory circular stating:

- ▶ effect of scheme
- ▶ any material interests of directors (whether as members or creditors)

The circular:

- ▶ must give all reasonably necessary information and be "perfectly fair" (*Re Dorman Long and Co*).

- ▶ There is a continuing duty of disclosure (*Re Jessel Trust Ltd (1985)*)

2 Holding the meetings

Requisite majorities:

- ▶ 75% by value of those attending and voting in person or by proxy
- ▶ plus a simple majority in number.
- ▶ Each and every meeting must vote in favour for the scheme to be approved.

Creditors and members must vote in the best interests of the class (*Re MB Group plc 1989*).

If scheme approved and court sanction obtained all creditors and members will be bound.

3 Court is petitioned for sanction

Any dissentients may appear at the hearing.

Role of court is to ensure:

▶ proper procedure followed

▶ fairness observed in

   – disclosures made in circular

   – members of class voting in best interests of the class

5.5 Contrasting CVA with s895 CA 2006 scheme of arrangement

	s895 CA 2006 Scheme of Arrangement	Company Voluntary Arrangement
Potential Applicants	As for CVA plus members and creditors.	Liquidator, administrator, directors.
Court Sanction to Initiate	Required.	Not required
Status	Administrator of scheme not required to be an IP.	Nominee/supervisor must be an IP.
Documentation	Scheme is circularised to creditors/ members in an explanatory circular.	Arrangement embodied in the Proposal.
Notice of meeting(s) to approve scheme/ arrangement	Actual notice NOT required.	Actual notice is required (*Bradford & Bingley Building Society*). Non notified creditors now bound.
Meeting(s) of Shareholders	Can be dispensed with if company insolvent.	Cannot be dispensed with.
Meetings	Separate meetings of each class of member/creditor generally required.	Only one meeting of members and one meeting of creditors required.
Meeting(s) of Members	If held 75% by voting rights must approve scheme.	Simple majority of voting rights must approve CVA.
Meeting(s) of Creditors	75% by value and a simple majority in number must approve.	In excess of 75% by value must approve. No need for simple majority in number.
Court sanction to implement scheme	Required.	Not required.

6 Partnership voluntary arrangements

Section overview

▶ Before IA 86 all insolvent partnerships were dealt with under bankruptcy law. The IA 86 did not make specific provision for insolvent partnerships; however the Insolvent Partnerships Order 1994 (IPO 94) introduced (amongst other things) a partnership voluntary arrangement (PVA). The legislation for partnership voluntary arrangements is contained in the IPO 94 as amended by the Insolvent Partnership (Amendment) Order 2002 and IA 86. Partnership voluntary arrangements are modelled on company voluntary arrangements and the following sections of the IA 86 apply:

▶ S233 IA
▶ Part VII (but not s250 IA)
▶ Parts XII and XIII
▶ S411, 413, 414, 419 Part XV IA
▶ Parts XVI – XIX

6.1 Advantages of PVAs

- One proposal – one creditors' meeting
- Limited disclosure – deals with partnership assets and liabilities only, not personal ones
- Partners' claims may be deferred
- Simple and cheap
- No court involvement necessary (but can apply for interim order)
- Interim order provides protection from pressing creditors

6.2 Disadvantages of PVAs

- Unanimity is required

- Doesn't deal with personal liabilities, IVA may be required to protect individual's assets

- Joint and several liability

- Need to be careful when considering voting rights of partners, conflicts may arise

- May well be unfair prejudice in relation to junior/ salaried/ retired or newly admitted partners

- Proposal must also deal with effect of subsequent liquidation of the partnership or bankruptcy of individual partners

6.3 Who may propose a PVA?

A PVA may be proposed by:

- The members (but not if partnership is in administration, or being wound up as an unregistered company, or if an order has been made under Article 11 IPO 94)

- The administrator (if partnership is in administration)

- The liquidator (if partnership being wound up as unregistered company)

- Trustee of the partnership (where an order has been made by virtue of Article 11 IPO 94)

6.4 Role of nominee/ supervisor

Nominee acts in relation to the VA either as trustee or otherwise for the purpose of supervising its implementation.

Upon acceptance of the arrangement by the creditors the IP will become supervisor of the arrangement.

6.5 PVA checklist for IP instructed by partners

Many of these items would be important in any case where an IP is instructed by partners of an insolvent firm and not only where they wish to propose a PVA.

1   Who are the partners?

The IP should obtain a full list of the names and addresses of all the partners in the firm. Identifying partners is important because:

- The decision to propose a PVA must probably be taken unanimously

- All partners must be notified of the meeting to approve the PVA

- If any partner is bankrupted this will dissolve the partnership in the absence of contrary intention

Sources of information include the partners, firm's notepaper, list of partners at principal place of business, the partnership agreement etc.

The IP needs to consider the status of salaried, junior and associate partners. Prior to 1 January 2003 partners who had no right to vote within the partnership were nevertheless entitled to vote on any proposal. Although the vote would not be counted towards the majority required to approve a PVA it did mean that such partners were entitled to challenge the meeting's decision. Since 1 January 2003 a partner with no right to vote at the meeting is unable to challenge a PVA. (Note: if a person participates in profits and management he will generally be a partner in the true sense).

2   Valid resolution of partners is required authorising:

▶   Proposing a PVA
▶   The agreement of the firm to pay the nominee's fees in relation to the PVA

3   Information concerning the firm:

▶   Description of the partnership business including:

–   last accounts and trading history
–   background to the insolvency
–   major assets and liabilities of the partnership
–   details of all creditors and their status

▶   Intentions regarding the conduct of the partnership business. If this is to continue, the partners should be advised of the need to obtain business plans, cash flow forecasts, budgets and arrangements for the provision of trading information to the supervisor

▶   Information regarding the partners:

–   solvency of each individual

–   to what extent the personal assets of each partner will be brought into the PVA

–   whether partners are prepared to defer their claims against the firm to all other creditors

4   The proposal for a PVA must demonstrate that a PVA offers creditors a better commercial outcome than any other available option.

5   The proposal must comply with r1.3 (as modified) and SIP 3.

6.6   Moratorium

Members of the partnership are able to apply for a moratorium under Schedule 1 Part 1 1A(1) IPO 94 if certain criteria are met. To be eligible the partnership must satisfy two of the following conditions:

▶   Turnover not more than £6.5m
▶   Assets of not more than £3.26m
▶   No more than 50 employees

The partners cannot apply for a moratorium if:

▶   Partnership is in administration

▶   Partnership is being wound up as an unregistered company

▶   There is appointed an agricultural receiver

▶   A voluntary arrangement has effect in relation to the insolvent partnership

▶   A provisional liquidator has been appointed

▶   An order has been made by virtue of Article 11 of IPO 94.

▶   A moratorium has been in force for the insolvent partnership at any time during the period of 12 months ending with the date of filing and no VA came into effect

The effect of the moratorium is that:

▸ No petition may be presented for the winding up of the partnership as an unregistered company

▸ No meeting of the members of the partnership may be called or requisitioned except with the consent of the nominee or leave of the court

▸ No order may be made for the winding up of the insolvent partnership as an unregistered company

▸ No administration application may be made in respect of the partnership

▸ No administrator of the partnership may be appointed under para 14 or 22 of Schedule B1

▸ No agricultural receiver of the partnership may be appointed except with the leave of the court and subject to such terms as the court may impose

▸ No landlord or other person to whom rent is payable may exercise any rights of forfeiture by peaceable re-entry in relation to premises, forming part of the partnership property or let to one or more officers of the partnership in their capacity as such except with leave of the court

▸ No other steps may be taken to enforce any security over the partnership property or to repossess goods in the possession, under any HP agreement, of one or more officers of the partnership, except with leave of the court.

▸ No other proceedings and no execution or other legal process may be commenced or continued, and no distress may be levied, against the insolvent partnership or the partnership property except with leave of the court

▸ No petition may be presented and no order may be made, by virtue of Article 11 IPO 94

▸ No application or order may be made under s35 Partnership Act 1890

6.7 Procedure – members' proposal, no application for moratorium

The procedure to be followed by members is as follows:

1 The members give notice of the proposal to the nominee to include:

▸ Document setting out terms of the proposed VA

▸ Statement of the partnership affairs (particulars of partnership creditors, debts and other liabilities, details of partnership property and such other information as may be prescribed)

2 Within 28 days of receiving notice, the nominee must submit a report to court (Schedule 1 part 1 2(2) IPO 94) stating:

▸ Whether, in his opinion, the proposed voluntary arrangement has a reasonable prospect of being approved and implemented

▸ Whether, in his opinion, meetings of the members of the partnership and of the partnership's creditors should be summoned to consider the proposal

▸ If in his opinion such meetings should be summoned, the date on which, and time and place at which, he proposes such meetings should be held

▸ Whether there are in existence any insolvency proceedings in respect of the insolvent partnership or any of its members

3 Convening meetings of members and creditors:

Nominee must summon creditors' meeting for the time, date and place stated in his report to court.

All creditors of the partnership of whose claim and address the nominee is aware must be given notice.

4   Creditors' meeting:

The purpose of the meeting is to decide whether or not to approve the PVA (with or without modifications).

Any modifications cannot affect the rights of secured or preferential creditors without their consent.

A modification may be agreed which nominates another person to act as nominee/ supervisor.

5   After meeting:

The chair must report the result to the court and give notice of the result of the meeting to all creditors who were sent notice of the meeting.

If the decision taking by the creditors' meeting differs from that taken by the meeting of the members of the partnership, a member may, within 28 days of the meeting, apply to the court.

The court may order the decision of the meeting of the members of the partnership to have effect instead of the decision of the creditors' meeting, or make such other order as it sees fit.

6   Appeals:

Under Schedule 1 part 1 s6(1) IPO 94 an appeal may be made by:

▸   A person entitled to vote at either of the meetings

▸   A person who would have been entitled to vote at the creditors' meeting if he had had notice of it

▸   The nominee

Any appeal must be made within 28 days of the reports being made to court.

An appeal may be made on the grounds:

▸   That the interests of a creditor, member or contributory of the partnership are unfairly prejudiced

▸   That there was some material irregularity at or in relation to either of the meetings

7   Effect of approval:

The approved VA takes effect as if made by the members of the partnership at the creditors' meeting and binds every person who was entitled to vote at the meeting (whether or not he was present or represented at it) or would have been so entitled if he had had notice of it.

6.8   Powers of supervisor

The supervisor has few statutory powers, his powers will be derived from the proposal which must be detailed enough to include any powers he may need.

The following statutory powers are available:

▸   May apply to court for directions Schedule 1 part 1 (s7(4) IPO 94)

▸   May apply to court for the winding up of the partnership as an unregistered company or for an administration order to be made in relation to the partnership

▸   Power to obtain supplies from utilities (s233 IA)

▸   Power to take action in respect of transactions defrauding creditors (s423 IA)

6.9   Duties of supervisor

If it appears to the nominee/ supervisor that any past or present officer of the insolvent partnership has been guilty of any offence in connection with the moratorium or voluntary arrangement, for which the officer is criminally liable, the nominee/ supervisor must (Schedule 1 part 1 s7A(2) IPO 94):

- ▸ Report the matter to the Secretary of State
- ▸ Provide the Secretary of State with such information and give him access to and facilities for inspecting and taking copies of, documents

The supervisor is not required to report on the conduct of the partners under CDDA.

Records should be kept of all meetings of members and creditors.

6.10 Resignation and release

There are no statutory provisions dealing with the resignation and release of a supervisor of a PVA. The terms of the arrangement would have to be checked to ascertain the mechanism by which the supervisor may resign or be released from office. In the absence of a specific clause the supervisor would need to obtain a court order to deal with his release.

6.11 Procedure when made by liquidator or administrator

The procedure is the same as for the members however, the statement of affairs will be that already obtained in the existing proceedings and a report to court and nominee's comments are not required.

Summary and self-test

Summary

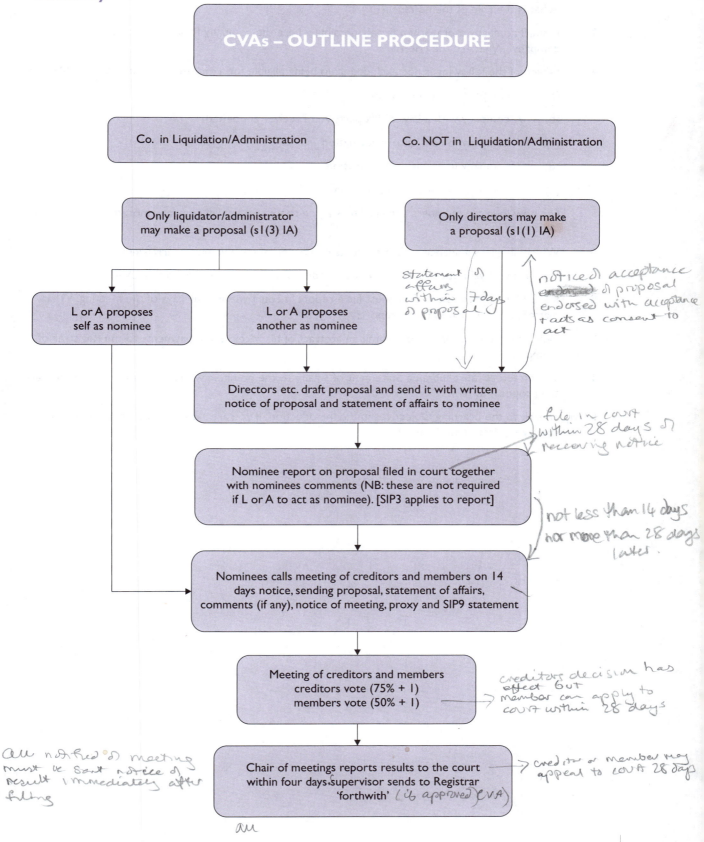

CVAs – OUTLINE PROCEDURE

Co. in Liquidation/Administration

Co. NOT in Liquidation/Administration

Only liquidator/administrator may make a proposal (s1(3) IA)

Only directors may make a proposal (s1(1) IA)

L or A proposes self as nominee

L or A proposes another as nominee

Statement of affairs within 7 days of proposal

noticed acceptance ~~endorsed~~ of proposal endorsed with acceptance + acts as consent to act

Directors etc. draft proposal and send it with written notice of proposal and statement of affairs to nominee

file in court within 28 days of receiving notice

Nominee report on proposal filed in court together with nominees comments (NB: these are not required if L or A to act as nominee). [SIP3 applies to report]

not less than 14 days nor more than 28 days later.

Nominees calls meeting of creditors and members on 14 days notice, sending proposal, statement of affairs, comments (if any), notice of meeting, proxy and SIP9 statement

Meeting of creditors and members creditors vote (75% + 1) members vote (50% + 1)

creditors decision has effect but member can apply to court within 28 days

all notified of meeting must be sent notice of result immediately after filing

Chair of meetings reports results to the court within four days supervisor sends to Registrar 'forthwith' *(if approved CVA)*

creditor or member may appeal to court 28 days

au

Self-test

Answer the following questions.

1   Who may make a proposal for a CVA?

2   What is the role of the nominee?

3   A small company moratorium is only possible where the company fulfils the criteria of a small company. What are the criteria?

4   Which of the following is not excluded from being eligible for a moratorium under Sch A1 IA?

   (a)   A company in administration

   (b)   A company with a Law of Property Act receiver appointed

   (c)   A company in compulsory liquidation

   (d)   A company in provisional liquidation

   (e)   A company in voluntary liquidation

5   For how long can members and creditors agree to extend a small company moratorium under the IA?

6   Which SIP gives guidance on the contents of a proposal for a voluntary arrangement?

7   How many days' notice must be given to creditors of a meeting to approve a CVA?

8   If a CVA is approved the chair must file a report in court within four days of the meeting. What matters must be stated in the report?

9   How often must a supervisor submit an abstract of his receipts and payments to the Registrar of Companies?

10   The directors must submit a Statement of Affairs to the nominee within how many days of delivering the proposal to him?

Now, go back to the Learning Objectives in the Introduction. If you are satisfied that you have achieved these objectives, please tick them off.

Answers to self-test

1
- liquidator (if company in liquidation)
- administrator (if company in administration)
- the directors

2 To carry out an independent objective review and assessment of the proposal and to report to court as to whether the proposal is achievable and whether meetings of members and creditors should be called to consider the proposal.

3 Two or more of:
- turnover no greater than £6.5m
- assets on balance sheet no greater than £3.26m
- no more than 50 employees in the relevant period.

4 b

5 Up to two months from the date of the first meetings.

6 SIP 3

7 14 days notice r1.9(2)

8
- whether proposal was accepted or rejected

- if approved, any modifications

- the resolutions taken at each meeting and the decision on each one

- a list of creditors and members of the company who were present or represented at the meetings and how they voted on each resolution

- any other information chair thinks appropriate

9 At least once every 12 months and within 28 days of completion of the arrangement.

10 Within seven days or such longer period as the nominee allows.

Answers to interactive questions

Interactive question 1: Longdon Nurseries Limited

Identify rational behind the directors wishing to enter into a CVA

Explain to the directors the different roles of nominee and supervisor, their different duties and responsibilities.

Explain role of nominee in relation to director's proposals and duty to perform an independent, objective review and assessment of the proposal for the purposes of reporting to the court, and requirement to balance the interests of the company and the creditors.

Nominee's duties cannot be fettered by any instructions of the directors or any third party.

Member should send out a letter of engagement to the directors setting out their respective duties and responsibilities in relation to the proposal.

Consideration should be given to the most appropriate entry route into CVA, having regard to the level of protection which may be required given the circumstances of the case.

Where consideration is given to a moratorium under Sch A1 IA the member should explain to the directors the additional duties that fall on the nominee and the responsibilities that fall on the directors during the moratorium.

The need for separate representation of any third parties who intend to inject funds should be considered.

Explain consequences of making false representations.

Explain importance of identifying all creditors – will largest creditor support the CVA

Will members support CVA?

Explain implications of wrongful trading.

Have directors been involved in any previous business failures?

Enquire into possible antecedent transactions.

Obtain basis of realisations of assets.

Explain what will happen if CVA fails.

Interactive question 2: Smith Limited

Proposal will state how claims will be agreed (usually incorporate rules re creditors' claims in liquidations).

The terms of the lease should be looked at to determine the claim – this should be calculated by reference to the outstanding instalments. The claim should be admitted in this sum.

With reference to the damages claim – has this been quantified or is it estimated by the directors? The creditor should submit any evidence available to substantiate his claim.

Chairman has the right to value unliquidated claims in the sum of £1, however he should make every effort to ascertain the value of the claim.

If the meeting has not yet been held, the creditor should object to the chairs' estimate. The chair should mark the proof as objected to and allow the creditor to vote subject to the appeal being upheld.

Will an additional claim result in a change to the voting?

If the meeting has been held the creditor may, within 28 days of the filing of the chair's report to the court, appeal to the court under s4(6) IA on the grounds of unfair prejudice or material irregularity. The court may reverse, vary or confirm the chair's decision.

Under s7(3) IA any creditor who is dissatisfied by any act, omission or decision of the supervisor may apply to court to have the decision confirmed, reversed or modified.

14

Options

> > > > > > > > > > > > > >

Introduction

Learning objectives

▶ To summarise and contrast the main insolvency options available to the directors and change holders ☐

▶ To identify antecedent transactions such as preferences, transactions at an undervalue, extortionate credit transactions, avoidance of floating charges, transactions defrauding creditors and wrongful trading ☐

Working context

It is very likely in a work environment that you will be asked to assist the directors of a company who have approached your firm for advice. It is important therefore to be familiar with the main insolvency options available and the main features, advantages and disadvantages of each.

Stop and think

What are the consequences of choosing one insolvency option as opposed to another? What is likely to happen if the directors choose to do nothing? What is an antecedent transaction?

Examination context

The JIEB Administrations paper is a very practical exam. There are many questions where you will be provided with information and asked to provide advice on the appropriate action to be taken.

Past exam questions to look at include:

2007   Question 3(a)

2005   Question 1(a)

2003   Question 1

2002   Question 2

2002   Question 5

2000   Question 2

2000   Question 3

2000   Question 5

1999   Question 3(a)

1999   Question 5(a)

1996   Question 4

1995   Question 3(a)

1995   Question 4

1993   Question 1

1991   Paper II Question 2(b)

1990   Paper II Question 2(a)

1 Options

Section overview

▶ A major role of an IP is in offering advice with regards to insolvency matters. An IP may be approached by a creditor or charge holder looking to recover their debt, or by the directors of a company who wish to enter into some formal or informal arrangement with creditors to avoid the risk of enforcement action or liquidation.

1.1 Options for directors

In the exam the options to consider as available to the directors are:

1 Trading on outside formal insolvency
2 S895 CA 2006 scheme of arrangement
3 CVA
4 Administration
5 CVL or petition for compulsory liquidation

1 **Trading on outside formal insolvency**

Insolvency does not require cessation of trading, however the directors should be made aware of the consequences of continuing to trade and not taking steps to address the financial situation of the company, such as wrongful trading (see later in the chapter).

Advantages of trading on:

▶ Directors retain control of the company.
▶ No legal/IP costs beyond costs of any preliminary advice obtained.

Disadvantages of trading on:

Although the inability of the company to pay its debts is not a bar to continued trading, the directors are trading with knowledge of insolvency and may become liable for wrongful trading should the company subsequently go into liquidation. It follows that the directors will need to:

▶ avoid taking new credit; paying suppliers as debts fall due
▶ avoid preferring creditors in respect of existing debts.

Any informal arrangement or agreement entered into with a creditor or creditors will not be binding. Duress creditors will be able to bring enforcement action against the directors/company in the usual way.

The directors will want the co-operation of the bank. This is more likely to be forthcoming if the bank is satisfied that its exposure is covered by its security over the company's assets and/or any personal guarantees given by the directors. The bank will be concerned to ensure:

▶ that the value of its security does not fall

▶ in which case the bank may make a hostile receivership or administration appointment to protect its position.

Where directors are proposing to sell the business, prospective purchasers will become aware that the company is in difficulties and may prefer to delay entering into any agreement to buy pending the appointment of a receiver or liquidator with a view to obtaining a lower price of the assets whilst avoiding any risk of a later transaction at undervalue action.

2 **S895 CA 2006 scheme of arrangement**

S895 CA 2006 schemes of arrangement have been dealt with in more detail in Chapter 13. The main points to note are as follows.

Advantages of s895 CA 2006 scheme:

- Flexibility
- Wide range of potential applicants
- Useful where large company and complex arrangement
- Administrator of the scheme does not have to be an IP

Disadvantages of s895 CA 2006 scheme:

- Two applications to court are necessary, therefore costs disadvantages and scope for delays

- Approval of every class of creditor and shareholder generally required (plus sanction of the court)

- Not appropriate where s110 IA can be used (see Liquidation study manual for details)

- Cannot be used to sanction a scheme beyond the company's capacity (*Re Savoy Hotel Ltd*)

Absence of an interim order

3   CVA

Company voluntary arrangements were dealt with in more detail in Chapter 13. The main points to consider when advising directors are as follows.

Advantages of CVA:

- Possible survival of the company as a going concern

- Higher returns to creditors due to:

    - sale as a going concern or profitable trading or fraudulent trading

    - lower costs – no Secretary of State fees, possibility of lower costs if directors (rather than IP's staff) remain responsible for managing the business

- Capital gains tax advantages, gains on asset disposals may be set against losses

- Floating charges will not be invalidated under s245 IA

- Binds all creditors who had notice of and were entitled to vote at the creditors' meeting

- Small company moratorium available

- No 'D' return completed by the supervisor

- Supervisor may not bring proceedings for wrongful trading or fraudulent trading

- No notice on letter head helps to preserve goodwill

- No application to court required

- Directors retain control of the company (albeit under supervision)

Disadvantages of CVA:

- Supervisor has no power to claw back under ss 238, 239 and 243 IA (Possible advantage for directors however such transactions have to be disclosed in the proposal)

- If the arrangement fails, liquidation is likely to be the only remaining course of action.

- No protection from duress creditors unless eligible for a small company moratorium

4   Administration

Administration was dealt with in more detail in Chapter 3. The main points to consider here are as follows.

Advantages of administration:

- Quick and easy for directors to appoint an administrator
- Recognised under EU Regulations
- Benefit of moratorium
- Administrator has powers to trade, manage and sell the business as a going concern

–   One year time limit
–   Flexible exit routes

Disadvantages of administration:

–   Corporation tax on a capital gain is an expense of the administration

–   New tax period will commence which will prevent the bringing forward of tax losses to reduce any tax liabilities on capital gains

–   Administrator's duty is to achieve one of the three para 3 Sch B1 IA purposes

–   12 month time limit

–   Administrator's duty owed to the court and the creditors generally

–   Directors lose control of the company

–   Administrator obliged to file a D return on directors.

5   Liquidation

Liquidation is not considered as an option here for the directors, as it does not lead to the survival of the company.

1.2   Options for the bank

There are many options for a bank that has lent a company money, depending on whether the debt is secured by a fixed or floating charge. The bank can sue, foreclose, sell, take possession or appoint some form of receiver. In terms of the JIEB exam, the options to explore are:

1   Appoint LPA receiver
2   Appoint a receiver under the fixed charge
3   Appoint an administrative receiver
4   Appoint an administrator

1   LPA receivership

A receiver may be appointed under LPA 1925 - this was dealt with in more detail in Chapter 7. The main points to note are as follows:

Advantages:

–   Cheaper option
–   LPA receiver need not be a qualified IP

Disadvantages:

–   Receiver has limited powers, ie collect rents and income
–   Must have been some default under the terms of the agreement

2   Fixed charge receiver

A receiver may be appointed by the holder of a fixed charge (see Chapter 7 for more details). The important points to note are as follows.

Advantages:

–   Cheaper option
–   Receiver need not be a qualified IP
–   Receiver has limited statutory duties

Disadvantages:

–   Can deal with assets subject to fixed charge only
–   Unlikely to be able to continue trading
–   Subject to indemnity from the bank

3 **Administrative receivership**

If the floating charge was created prior to 15 September 2003 the charge holder has the power to appoint an administrative receiver. (See Chapter 7 for more details). The main points to note are as follows.

Advantages:

- Quick and easy to appoint
- Can be appointed whether or not the company is in liquidation
- Appointment of an AR will block an administration appointment
- Primary duty owed to charge holder to realise assets subject to floating charge
- Bank will control receivership strategy
- No statutory time limit
- Any corporation tax will be an unsecured claim

Disadvantages:

- AR has duty to pay preferential creditors out of floating charge assets
- AR has extensive statutory duties which leads to extra costs
- Bank will have to indemnify receiver
- Perception that bank is pulling the plug – adverse publicity
- Lack of recognition under EC Regs
- No moratorium

4 **Administration**

The bank, as holders of a qualifying floating charge, may appoint an administrator. (See Chapter 3 for more details). The main points to note are as follows.

Advantages:

- Easy to appoint
- Charge holder can choose who is to be IP
- Seen as a rescue procedure so less adverse publicity for the bank than appointing an AR
- Recognised under EU Regs
- Benefit of moratorium
- Powers to trade, manage and sell the business
- Charge holder has no potential liability to indemnify the administrator
- Flexible exit routes

Disadvantages:

- Administrator's duty owed to creditors generally
- Prime duty is to achieve para 3 Sch B1 IA purpose
- 12 month time limit
- Corporation tax is an expense of the administration
- Bank will have no control over administration strategy

Interactive question 1: Myers Bank plc

You have been contacted by Myers Bank PLC who hold a debenture over the assets of Webbs Limited executed in May 2003, which includes a fixed charge over the company's property and goodwill and a floating charge over all other assets. The company's property is its most significant asset. The directors have advised the bank that the company is experiencing cash flow problems and will be unable to service its loans for the foreseeable future. Though the bank is a clearing bank, its officers are not familiar with insolvency proceedings.

Requirement

Draft a letter to the bank setting out the alternative insolvency options available to it and the consequences for the directors and the bank of each alternative. (Note: do not consider liquidation as an option).

See **Answer** at the end of this chapter.

2 Antecedent transactions

2.1 Transaction at an undervalue s238 IA

S238 IA applies when a company has entered into liquidation or administration.

A transaction at an undervalue is where there has been a gift (or other transaction with no consideration) or the value received by the company is significantly less in money or money's worth than that given.

The company must have been insolvent at the time of, or become insolvent as a result of, the transaction taking place.

The transaction must have taken place at a relevant time:

–   Unconnected person – within two years of onset of insolvency and company insolvent at time of transaction

–   Connected person – within two years of onset of insolvency and company presumed insolvent.

There is a defence that the company entered into the transaction in good faith, for value and there were reasonable grounds for believing that it would benefit the company.

Either the liquidator or administrator can apply to court for the position of the company to be restored to what it was prior to the transaction.

2.2 Preference s239 IA

S239 IA applies when a company has entered into liquidation or administration.

A preference is a transaction where:

–   The person preferred must be a creditor, guarantor or surety

–   The company must 'do anything' or 'suffer anything to be done' which puts that creditor, guarantor or surety in a better position in the event of insolvent liquidation or administration, than they would otherwise have been in.

–   The company must have been influenced by a desire to prefer (ie the company must actually wish to improve the position of the creditor). Desire is presumed the parties are connected.

The company must have been insolvent at the time of, or become insolvent as a result of, the preference taking place.

The preference must have taken place at a relevant time:

–   Unconnected person – within six months of the onset of insolvency.

–   Connected person - within two years of the onset of insolvency

Either a liquidator or administrator can apply to court for the position of the company to be restored to what it was prior to the transaction.

2.3 Extortionate credit transaction s244 IA

An extortionate credit transaction is where:

- The company is or has been a party to a transaction involving the provision of credit to the company, and

- Having regard to the risk undertaken by the giver of the credit the terms of the agreement:

  - require grossly exorbitant payments to be made, or
  - otherwise grossly contravenes the ordinary principles of fair dealing

It is assumed by the court that transactions are extortionate and it is therefore left to the defence to prove that this is not the case.

The provision of credit must have taken place within the relevant time:

- Within three years of the onset of insolvency for both connected and unconnected persons.

The liquidator or administrator can apply to the court to have the whole or part of the obligation set aside or for the variation of the agreement.

2.4 Avoidance of floating charges s245 IA

A floating charge on the company's undertaking or property is invalid except to the extent of the aggregate of any fresh consideration given for it.

The creation of the floating charge must have been within the relevant time period: *(to be invalid)*

- Unconnected person – within 12 months of the onset of insolvency and the company must be insolvent at the time of the transaction

- Connected person – within two years of the onset of insolvency

If a liquidator or administrator is able to prove that a floating charge is invalid, the assets covered by the charge can be claimed, security free, for the benefit of the estate.

S245 IA does not have retrospective effect (*Mace Builders (Glasgow v Lunn)*). The acts of an administrative receiver prior to winding up remain valid where the AR was appointed under a floating charge which has now been invalidated under s245 IA.

2.5 Transactions defrauding creditors s423 IA

This is where the company has transacted and caused a 'gift' to be made (ie no consideration received), or received 'significantly less' consideration under the transaction than it ought to have done.

There has to be an intention to either prejudice the interests of the victim (ie the persons taking the action under s423 IA) or to put the assets beyond the reach of the claimants or potential claimants.

There is no relevant time in respect of transactions under s423 IA. It will also apply where the company was solvent at the time it transacted as there is no reference to insolvency in the definition.

The court can order restoration as under s238 IA or under s212 IA an action can be taken for misfeasance against the directors of the company.

2.6 Wrongful trading s214 IA

Wrongful trading is where a director of a company in insolvent liquidation, knew, or ought to have known, that the company was unable to pay its debts and did not take steps to minimise losses to creditors.

Wrongful trading is a civil matter and the court can make an order that the director contributes to the company's assets, as it thinks proper.

The onus is on the director to prove that he took every step to minimise the loss to creditors. The position of creditors whose debts have already been incurred should not be prejudiced in any way. This would include:

– Consulting with bankers early

– Preparing up to date management accounts and ensuring prompt filing of statutory accounts

– Consulting professional advisors

– Preserving the value of the company's assets

– Any disposals of assets outside the ordinary course of business should be on the basis of professional advice

– Trading losses should be stemmed

– No payments should be made to existing creditors

– Customer deposits should be paid into a separate bank account

– Customer receipts should not be paid into an overdrawn bank account

– Hauliers owed money should not be used unless they confirm that they will not exercise a lien

– Making cash payments to avoid dissipation of assets

– Avoiding last ditch hazardous action to save the business

– Avoiding making supplies to creditors who may exercise a right of set off

– Refine the company's overheads. Deal only in cash.

– Document any decision to continue to trade, supporting the decision with reference to ongoing trading

– Avoid taking new credit

– Resignation is not an appropriate step

Interactive question 2: WJ Manufacturing Limited

Fred and Jo are directors of WJ Manufacturing Limited (hereafter WJ). They have come to you for advice regarding the financial position of WJ and their own position as directors of the company. The company has traded profitably for many years supplying a local car manufacturer with components. Due to general economic factors and an increase in the costs of raw materials the company has been experiencing cash flow problems in recent months. Trade creditor arrears are beginning to build up and PAYE and VAT payments are now only made when the local offices chase payment.

There is a total of five directors on the board and there is disagreement as to how the current problems should be dealt with.

Fred and Jo are very keen to obtain professional advice and put the company into some form of formal insolvency procedure. The other directors however feel that the current problems are only temporary and that the company will be able to trade out of its current difficulties. They have decided to sell one of the company's surplus machines to a company owned by Simon, a fellow director of WJ, for the sum of £50,000. This would provide some much needed cash, however Jo believes that the machine could fetch up to £70,000 if marketed properly.

Trade creditors have not been paid for the last two months, however payment of a debt owed to Flemming Limited has been made in the last two weeks in the sum of £43,000. Fred states that Sandra, the wife of Simon, is a director of Flemming Limited.

The company granted a floating charge to Satby Bank PLC four months ago to secure a further trading overdraft. The company is now operating at the limit of the new agreed overdraft limit.

Fred and Jo have requested that full management accounts be prepared however the other directors feel that this would be an unnecessary expense at this time.

Requirement

Write a letter to Fred and Jo setting out the issues they should have regard to in the light of relevant legislation.

See **Answer** at the end of this chapter.

Summary

Summary

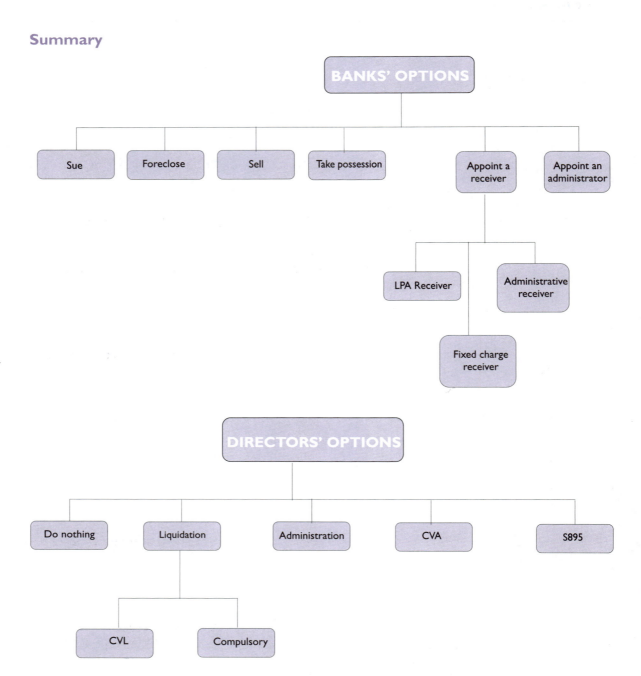

BPP
LEARNING MEDIA

Answers to interactive questions

Interactive question 1: Myers Bank plc

Letter format.

The alternatives available to the bank are:

- Appoint a receiver under fixed charge over property
- Appoint administrative receiver under floating charge
- Appoint administrator under qualifying floating charge

Fixed charge receivership:

- The receiver can only deal with assets over which specifically appointed
- Receiver's powers are restricted
- Can only exercise powers included in LPA 1925 or as extended by the charging document
- Cannot continue to trade
- Directors remain responsible for all other assets
- Directors may decide to petition for administration order or place company into liquidation
- Receiver's costs will only relate to dealing with charged assets

Administrative receivership:

- Bank can appoint AR since floating charge created prior to 15 September 2003

- All powers of directors over charged assets cease although they remain responsible for any non charged assets

- Statutory duties of directors remain

- Receiver responsible for all charged assets

- Owes prime duty to charge holder

- AR has a number of statutory duties which increases costs:

    - deal with EPA matters
    - CDDA requirements
    - call creditors meeting under s48 IA

- AR has power to continue trading which might benefit debtor realisations or realise some value for goodwill

- if AR appointed, administrator cannot be appointed unless bank consents

Administration:

- Bank is entitled to appoint administrator out of court as qualifying charge holder
- Administrator's duties owed to creditors generally to achieve para 3 Sch B1 IA purpose
- Directors' powers cease to the extent that they conflict with powers of the administrator
- Bank's security remains, but rights of enforcement are lost
- Administrator may only realise fixed charge assets with agreement of bank or order of the court
- Net proceeds must be paid to charge holder
- Administrator may deal with floating charge assets as if they were not subject to a charge

Interactive question 2: WJ Manufacturing Limited

Letter format.

Explanation of company's current position:

- Trade creditor arrears beginning to build up
- Non payment of crown debts
- Increased raw material costs
- Company profitable in the past

Company may be, or will become, insolvent since debts cannot be paid as and when they fall due.

Discussion of directors' duties (to creditors, guarantors, shareholders) and explanation of consequences of breaches of these duties (disqualification as director, personal liability).

Possible breaches to be aware of:

(i) **Wrongful trading**

- Explanation of wrongful trading

- Advice to avoid claims of wrongful trading (preparation of profit and loss accounts, cash flow forecasts, management accounts, avoid incurring new credit, do not dissipate assets)

- Document all decisions made

- Only arises on liquidation of the company

(ii) **Payment of debt to Flemming Limited**

Payments to creditors could lead to claims of preference.

- Explanation of what a preference is
- Relevant time scales
- Identify Sandra as a connected person

Consequence – restoration of position, CDDA implications

Payments to creditors should only be made where absolutely necessary to allow trading to continue. The aim of this is to preserve the position of assets available to creditors and the position as between such creditors.

(iii) **Sale of asset to Simon**

The directors must ensure that company assets are not sold for less than their true value. If it is, could be liable for a claim of a transaction at an undervalue.

- Explanation of what a transaction at an undervalue is
- Relevant time scales
- Identify Simon as a connected person

Explain consequence of such a transaction: CDDA implications, directors may be sued for breach of duty.

Directors must ensure that any sales are on the basis of professional advice and that all steps have been taken to receive the best price for the assets.

(iv) **Creation of floating charge**

If company enters insolvent liquidation, may be challenged under s245 IA.

- If created within 12 months of liquidation
- Valid to extent of new monies

Any other relevant points

Style.

BPP))))
LEARNING MEDIA

Index

> > > > > > > > > > > > > >